Microsoft Works 2000 explained

Books Available

By both authors:

BP327 DOS one step at a time
BP337 A Concise User's Guide to Lotus 1-2-3 for Windows
BP341 MS-DOS explained
BP346 Programming in Visual Basic for Windows
BP352 Excel 5 explained
BP362 Access one step at a time
BP387 Windows one step at a time
BP388 Why not personalise your PC
BP400 Windows 95 explained
BP406 MS Word 95 explained
BP407 Excel 95 explained
BP408 Access 95 one step at a time
BP409 MS Office 95 one step at a time
BP415 Using Netscape on the Internet*
BP420 E-mail on the Internet*
BP426 MS-Office 97 explained
BP428 MS-Word 97 explained
BP429 MS-Excel 97 explained
BP430 MS-Access 97 one step at a time
BP433 Your own Web site on the Internet
BP448 Lotus SmartSuite 97 explained
BP456 Windows 98 explained*
BP460 Using Microsoft Explorer 4 on the Internet*
BP464 E-mail and News with Outlook Express*
BP465 Lotus SmartSuite Millennium explained
BP471 Microsoft Office 2000 explained
BP472 Microsoft Word 2000 explained
BP473 Microsoft Excel 2000 explained
BP474 Microsoft Access 2000 explained
BP478 Microsoft Works 2000 explained

By Noel Kantaris:

BP258 Learning to Program in C
BP259 A Concise Introduction to UNIX*
BP284 Programming in QuickBASIC
BP325 A Concise User's Guide to Windows 3.1

Microsoft Works 2000 explained

by

P.R.M. Oliver
and
N. Kantaris

Bernard Babani (publishing) Ltd
The Grampians
Shepherds Bush Road
London W6 7NF
England

Please Note

Although every care has been taken with the production of this book to ensure that any projects, designs, modifications and/or programs, etc., contained herewith, operate in a correct and safe manner and also that any components specified are normally available in Great Britain, the Publishers and Author(s) do not accept responsibility in any way for the failure (including fault in design) of any project, design, modification or program to work correctly or to cause damage to any equipment that it may be connected to or used in conjunction with, or in respect of any other damage or injury that may be so caused, nor do the Publishers accept responsibility in any way for the failure to obtain specified components.

Notice is also given that if equipment that is still under warranty is modified in any way or used or connected with home-built equipment then that warranty may be void.

First Published - February 2000

British Library Cataloguing in Publication Data:

A catalogue record for this book is available from the British Library

ISBN 0 85934 478 9

Cover Design by Gregor Arthur
Printed and Bound in Great Britain by Bath Press

About this Book

This book *Microsoft Works 2000 explained* was written to help both the beginner and those transferring from another version of Microsoft Works. The material in the book is presented on the 'what you need to know first, appears first' basis, but you don't have to start at the beginning and go right through to the end. The more experienced user can start from any section, as they have been designed to be self-contained. The book does not, however, describe the workings of Microsoft Windows, or how to set up your computer hardware. If you need to know more about these, then may we suggest that you refer to our other books, also published by BERNARD BABANI (publishing) Ltd, and listed earlier in this book.

Microsoft Works 2000 is actually version 5 of Works and is a powerful integrated package containing several major types of applications; word processing with drawing, spreadsheets with graphing, database management with reporting, a calendar, an address book and electronic communications using Outlook Express. It has a new Task Launcher as a front end and has been designed for 'home users', but it contains all the power that most of us will ever need.

Works 2000 also forms the core of Microsoft's WorksSuite 2000 and this book has been written for users of both packages. The main differences being that WorksSuite has Word 2000 as its word processor, and comes bundled with other Microsoft goodies. If you have WorksSuite, you should ignore the section on the new Works 2000 word processor, and concentrate on the Word 2000 section as well as the sections on the Works 2000 spreadsheet, database, calendar, address book and on Outlook Express.

The power and versatility of Works 2000 is evident in its integration which allows data from any module to be quickly and easily transferred into any of the other modules. The package is a powerful one, offering many commands, and functions. We found the new Works 2000 word processor to be almost as powerful as many of the 'stand alone' packages available today. Any missing features are the least used anyway, and probably not used at all by most people. As is usual now, Microsoft have gone to town regarding the number and quality of Tasks and Wizards supplied with the Works 2000 package. As with previous books, we have not, however, spent much time describing these for two good reasons:

1. They are very user friendly and almost anyone should be able to work through them without too many problems.
2. We feel strongly that you will become more proficient with the Works 2000 program, as a whole, if you build your own applications.

If you want to start off using these 'tailor made' files and documents, have a look through Chapter 15, before getting too much further in the book.

This book is intended as a supplement to the on-line Help material, and to the very limited documentation that now seems to come with Microsoft's packages. It will provide the new user with a set of examples that will help with the learning of the most commonly used features of the package, and also help provide the confidence needed to tackle some of the more advanced features later.

If you would like to purchase a Companion Disc for any of the listed books by the same author(s), apart from the ones marked with an asterisk, containing the file/program listings which appear in them, then fill in the form at the back of the book and send it to Phil Oliver at the stipulated address.

About the Authors

Phil Oliver graduated in Mining Engineering at Camborne School of Mines in 1967 and since then has specialised in most aspects of surface mining technology, with a particular emphasis on computer related techniques. He has worked in Guyana, Canada, several Middle Eastern and Central Asian countries, South Africa and the United Kingdom, on such diverse projects as: the planning and management of bauxite, iron, gold and coal mines; rock excavation contracting in the UK; international mining equipment sales and international mine consulting. In 1988 he took up a lecturing position at Camborne School of Mines (part of Exeter University) in Surface Mining and Management. He retired from full-time lecturing in 1998, to spend more time consulting, writing, and developing Web sites.

Noel Kantaris graduated in Electrical Engineering at Bristol University and after spending three years in the Electronics Industry in London, took up a Tutorship in Physics at the University of Queensland. Research interests in Ionospheric Physics, led to the degrees of M.E. in Electronics and Ph.D. in Physics. On return to the UK, he took up a Post-Doctoral Research Fellowship in Radio Physics at the University of Leicester, and then in 1973 a lecturing position in Engineering at the Camborne School of Mines, Cornwall, (part of Exeter University), where between 1978 and 1997 he was also the CSM Computing Manager. At present he is IT Director of FFC Ltd.

Acknowledgements

We would like to thank the staff of Microsoft UK and August.one Communications Ltd, for providing the software programs on which this work was based.

Trademarks

Arial and **Times New Roman** are registered trademarks of The Monotype Corporation plc.

HP and LaserJet are registered trademarks of Hewlett Packard Corporation.

IBM is a registered trademark of International Business Machines, Inc.

Intel is a registered trademark of Intel Corporation.

Lotus, 1-2-3 are registered trademarks of Lotus Development Corporation, a subsidiary of IBM.

Microsoft, **Encarta**, **IntelliMouse**, **MS-DOS**, **Windows**, are either registered trademarks or trademarks of Microsoft Corporation.

PostScript is a registered trademark of Adobe Systems Incorporated.

TrueType is a registered trademark of Apple Corporation.

All other brand and product names used in the book are recognised as trademarks, or registered trademarks, of their respective companies.

Contents

1

Package Overview

Microsoft Works 2000 is a collection of powerful, featured, programs with a similar look and feel and with a new Task Launcher that can help them work together as if they were a single program. The package was specifically designed for 'home use' to let you work with your information and data in an easily understood, but powerful, environment which enables you to quickly and efficiently obtain the results you want.

Microsoft Works 2000 also forms the core of Microsoft's WorksSuite 2000 package and this book has been written for users of both versions. The main differences being:

- WorksSuite 2000 has Microsoft Word 2000 as its word processor, not the newly developed, but slightly cut-down word processor that is included with the standard Works 2000 package.
- WorksSuite 2000 comes bundled with other Microsoft goodies, such as Money 2000, Encarta Interactive World Atlas 2000, Home Publishing 2000 and AutoRoute Express 2000.

We include an introduction to Word 2000 in Chapters 5, 6 and 7, but have not covered the other bundled programs in WorksSuite. They are fairly intuitive anyway.

If you have WorksSuite 2000, you should ignore the section on the new Works 2000 word processor in Chapters 2 and 3. If you have the standard Works 2000 package, you should ignore the section on Word 2000 in Chapters 5, 6 and 7. It's not really as complicated as it sounds!

All the other sections of the book, on the spreadsheet, database, calendar, address book and Outlook Express 5 are common to both versions.

If you are new to computing, the various Works 2000 applications have the following main functions:

Word Processor
Use this to write and enhance text, such as letters and reports and to make simple lists and create mail merge documents.

Spreadsheet
Use this to make a complex list, or to calculate numbers. From a spreadsheet, you can display your information, such as financial projections, in easily viewed charts.

Database
Use this to organise and track collections or other items in detail. A phone directory is a good example of a simple, but usually large, database. You can print reports showing all or part of the items in your database.

Calendar
Use this to keep track of appointments and special events, like an electronic diary.

Address Book
Use this to create and manage a list of addresses, especially for sending e-mails or doing a mail merge.

Outlook Express
Use this to get full e-mail and Internet News features, as long as you have the required access to the Internet.

All of these program functions can be very easily accessed from the Task Launcher, or from the Windows **Start** cascade menu system. The Task Launcher is new to Works 2000, and gives you three choices:

- You can tell Works what task you want to carry out, and let it select the program and template to use.
- You can select the program you want to work with.
- You can select to open a file or document you have previously worked on.

All the Works applications have a built-in consistency and style which makes them easier to use.

Hardware and Software Requirements

If Microsoft Works is already installed on your computer, you can safely skip this and the next section of this chapter.

Works 2000

To install and use the standard Microsoft Works 2000, you need an IBM-compatible PC equipped with a Pentium 90 MHz or higher processor. As is usual these days though, the more powerful the processor the better. In addition, you need the following:

- Windows 95/98 (or higher) operating system.
- 32 MB of random access memory (RAM) is recommended, but you may get away with 16 MB.
- 120 - 155 MB of hard disc space required, but different sources seem to vary on this!
- Quad-speed or faster CD-ROM drive.
- Super VGA, 256-colour or higher resolution monitor.
- A Microsoft Mouse, or compatible pointing device.
- Microsoft Internet Explorer 5 browser software, which is included on the CD-ROM.
- For some features you will need a 14,400 baud, or higher, modem and Internet access, which may require payment of a separate fee to an Internet service provider (ISP). To run Works 2000 from a network, you must also have a network compatible with your Windows operating environment, such as Microsoft's Windows 95/98 or higher, Windows NT, LAN Manager, etc.

WorksSuite 2000

Some of the standard requirements for WorksSuite 2000 are a little higher. For this to work properly you will need:

- A multimedia PC with a Pentium 166 MHz or higher processor.

- At least 24 MB of RAM; 32 MB of RAM recommended.
- 785 MB to 1.4 GB of available hard-disc space if you install all the applications, or 820 MB for a typical installation.
- A super VGA, 256-colour monitor supporting 640 x 480 or higher resolution; 800 x 600 recommended.
- Local bus video with 1 MB or more of video memory.

This may all sound a little daunting if you have an older PC, but entry level PCs come far better equipped than this these days. And they are still coming down in price all the time.

Installing Works 2000

Installing Works on your computer's hard disc is made very easy using the SETUP program, which also configures Works automatically to take advantage of the computer's hardware. **Note:** If you are using a virus detection utility, disable it before running SETUP, or you might get conflicts. Also make sure you have no other programs active.

To install Works, place the distribution CD, or Disc 1, in your CD drive and close it. The auto-start program on the CD should start the SETUP program automatically. If not, click the Windows **Start** button, and select the **Run** command which opens the Run dialogue box, as shown below.

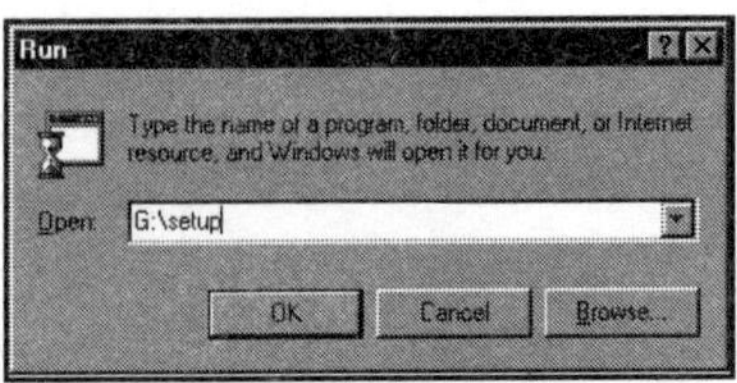

Next, type in the **Open** text box:

```
g:\setup
```

In our case we used the CD-ROM in the G: drive; yours will probably be different. Clicking the **OK** button, starts the installation of Microsoft Works 2000. Our version of Works displayed the following Setup screen. Your version may be different, but the basic procedures should be very similar.

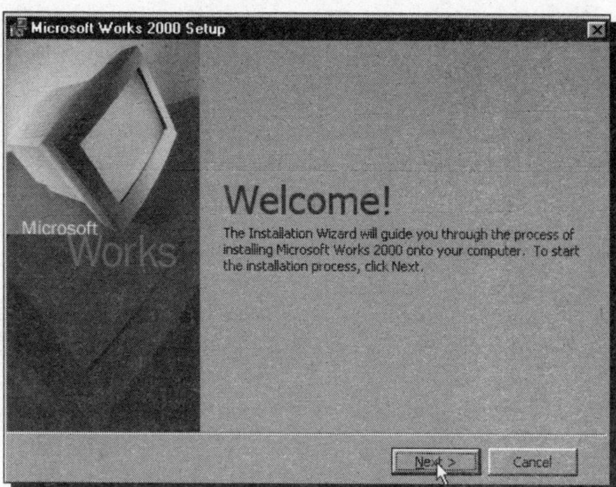

We suggest that you follow the instructions displayed on the screen. Clicking the **Next** button in each window causes Setup to go through the following procedure:

- Prompts you to accept a default location folder to install the Works program in. We suggest you accept this. If not, click the **Change** button and select an alternative location.
- You then get the choice of a **Complete**, or a **Minimum** installation. We will assume you use the **Complete Installation** option, but if there is not enough space on your hard disc drive, you should use the other option.
- You are then informed that Internet Explorer 5 will be installed if you do not already have it. Microsoft seems to insist that we all use this instead of Netscape. Luckily it is an excellent browser, and Outlook Express 5 is really part of it.
- Clicking the **Install** button starts the file copying process, and gives you some message windows to help pass the time.
- When the fairly painless operation is complete you should see the window shown next. Finally, in the last Wizard window select **Yes** to restart your computer.

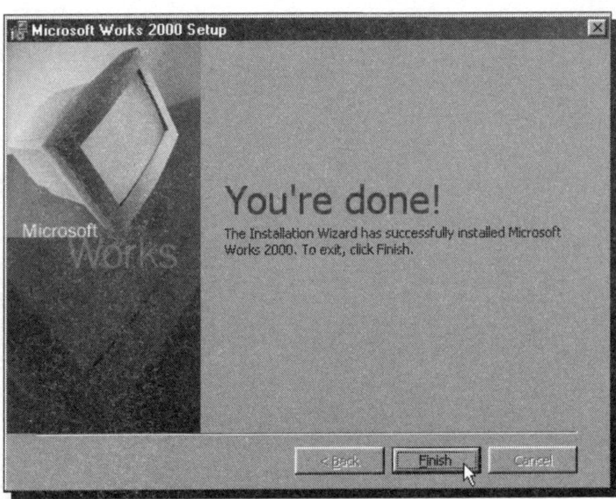

Hopefully you should have a successful installation and when you return to the Windows desktop there should be a new Shortcut icon, as shown below. Also, when you open the cascading **Start** menus there should be several Works options, similar to those shown. What actually displays will depend on your version of Works.

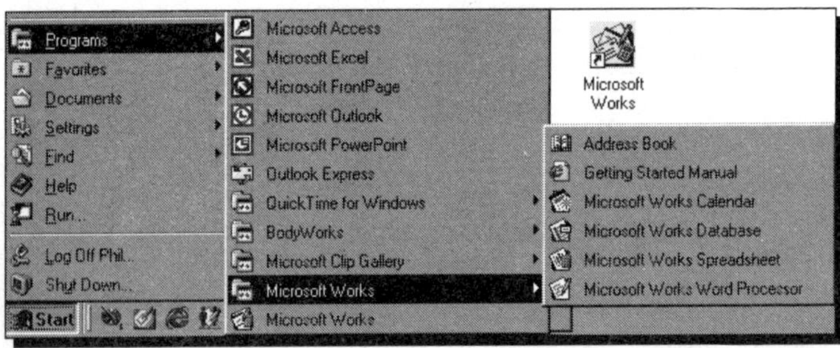

The **Getting Started Manual** option opens an Adobe Acrobat file version of the short booklet that comes with the Works 2000 package. If you do not have the Acrobat reader, you are given the option to install it, from your hard disc. It was downloaded during the Works insallation process. Perhaps this would be a good time to take this tour, either on-line, or with the paper version. The choice is yours.

Starting Works

There are two main ways to start the Works program for the first time, either by double-clicking the Shortcut to Microsoft Works icon shown on the left, or selecting Microsoft Works from the opened cascade menu, as shown on the right.

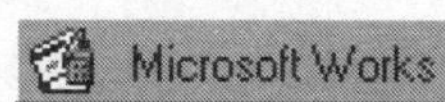

When the program is opened by these methods the following Task Launcher window is displayed.

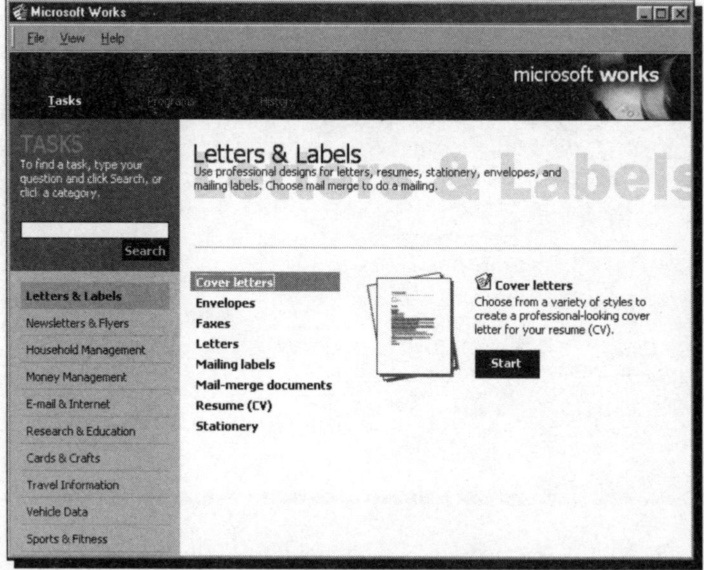

Alternatively, if you know which Works application you want to open you can by-pass the Task Launcher by selecting it from the Start cascade menu, as shown on the facing page. We must admit that this is the method we tend to use, unless we want to use one of the standard templates that are built into the Works 2000 package.

The Task Launcher

The new Task Launcher has three tabbed sections, the default one **Tasks**, shown open on the previous page, gives rapid access to all the **Tasks** that come with the package. If you want to use these, fine, but we will first spend some time getting used to the different tools that make up the Works program. For a brief description of using the **Tasks** you could look at Chapter 15, otherwise click the **Programs** tab to change the Launcher to that shown here.

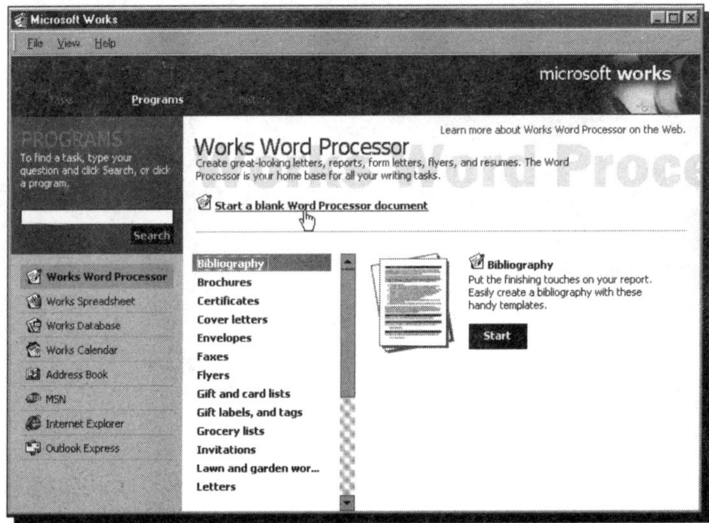

This window gives you access to all the programs included in the Works 2000 packages. With WorksSuite 2000, Word is listed as the word processor. Clicking a button in the list on the left opens a list of the Tasks with prepared templates that are available for that application. Those seen above are for the Works Word Processor. When you select a Task and click its **Start** button, you are usually given a selection of styles to choose from in the Wizard that opens.

To simply start an empty Works application, select it in the above list, and then click the **Start a blank.....** link as shown above with the 'hand' pointer shown.

The **History** tab option is used to open files or documents already created in the Works 2000 applications. A list of previous files (if any!) is displayed and double-clicking on one of them will rapidly open it in the relevant Works tool.

We suggest you experiment with these options and Tasks later, but at the moment simply press the **Start a blank Word Processor document** option in the **Programs** tab Launcher window. This should open the word processor, as shown below.

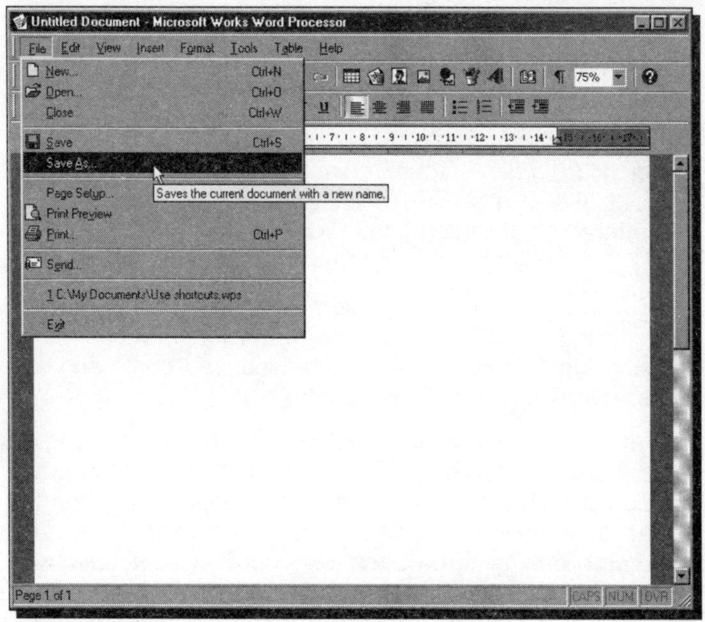

Works Menus

The menu bar, as shown above, has the item 'File' in the menu highlighted, with its pull-down sub-menu displayed underneath. The pull-down sub-menus associated with the other menu items can be seen by pressing the right arrow key, or by clicking on them with the mouse. Pressing the <Esc> key clears the sub-menus.

To activate the main menu of any Works application either use the mouse to point to an item, or press the <Alt> key, which causes the first item of the menu (in this case **File**) to be highlighted, then use the right and left arrow keys to highlight any of the items in the menu. Pressing either the <Enter> key, or the left mouse button, reveals the pull-down sub-menu of the highlighted menu item.

Menu options can also be activated directly by pressing the <Alt> key followed by the underlined letter of the required option. Thus pressing <Alt+O>, causes the pull-down sub-menu of **Format** to be displayed. You can use the up and down arrow keys to move the highlighted bar up and down a sub-menu, or the right and left arrow keys to move along the options of the main menu. As each option is highlighted, a short description of the function of the relevant option or command appears in a yellow banner below it. Pressing the <Enter> key selects the highlighted option, or executes the highlighted command. Pressing the <Esc> key closes the menu system and returns you to the main menu.

Selection of a sub-menu item can also be achieved by either typing the underlined letter of the required command, or using the mouse to point to the required command and pressing the left mouse button.

If you use a mouse, there is a quick way of selecting an item from the main menu by pointing to it and pressing the left mouse button; then, with the button depressed, drag the mouse down the revealed sub-menu which highlights each sub-menu item in turn. Once the required item has been highlighted, release the mouse button to select it.

Some sub-menu options have quick keys attached to them, for example pressing the <Ctrl+S> keys together will at any time save the current word processor file, without the menu system even being opened. Throughout this book we use the above convention to indicate these quick key combinations. Getting to know them will speed up your work considerably.

Dialogue Boxes

Three periods after a sub-menu option or command, means that a dialogue box will open when the option is selected. A dialogue box lets you enter additional information, such as the name of a file, or lets you change settings.

To illustrate how they work, select the **File**, **Page Setup**, command which will display a tabbed dialogue box, part of which is shown below.

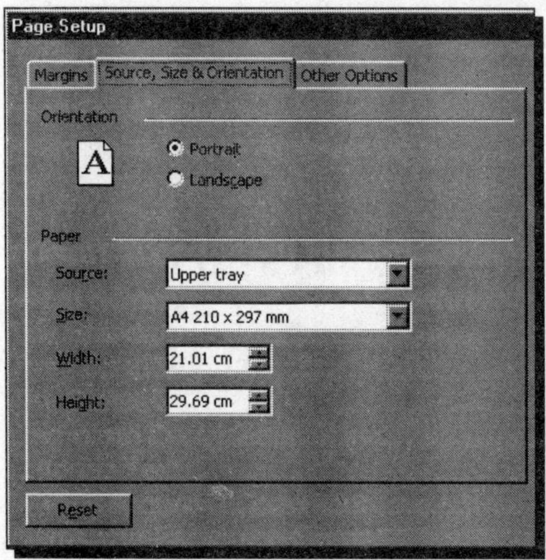

You usually move round a dialogue box with the mouse, but the <Tab> key can be used to move the highlight, or focus to be technical, from one field to the next, (<Shift+Tab> moves the cursor backwards) or alternatively you can move directly to a desired field by holding the <Alt> key down and pressing the underlined letter in the field name. Within a group of options you can use the arrow keys to move from one option to another. Having selected an option or typed in information, you must press a command button such as the **OK** or **Cancel** button, (not shown above) or choose from additional options. To select the **OK** button with the mouse, simply point and click, while with the keyboard, you must first press the <Tab> key until the dotted rectangle, or focus, moves to the required button, and then press the <Enter> key.

Some dialogue boxes contain Combo boxes which show a column of available choices when their right arrow is clicked. If there are more choices than can be seen in the area provided, you use the scroll bars to reveal them. To select a single item from a Combo, or List box, either double-click the item, or use the arrow keys to highlight the item and press <Enter>.

Dialogue boxes may contain Option, or radio, boxes with a list of mutually exclusive items, as shown here. The default choice is marked with a black dot against its name.

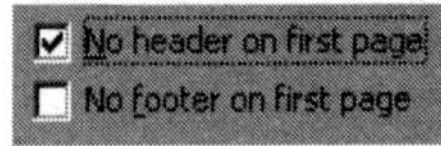

Another type of dialogue box option is the Check box, which can be seen on the **Other Options** tab, this offers a list of features you can switch on or off. Selected options show a tick in the box against the option.

If you can't work out the function of something in a dialogue box there is a quick way of getting context sensitive help. Clicking the **?** button, next to the Close button in the top right corner of the box, will add a question mark to the pointer. Click this on the unknown item and an explanation window will open up.

To cancel a dialogue box, either press the **Cancel** button, or press the <Esc> key enough times, to close the dialogue box and then the menu system.

The Works Screen

It is perhaps worth spending some time looking at the various parts that make up the Works 2000 screen. To illustrate our discussion, click the **Programs** tab in the Task Launcher window and select **Works Spreadsheet**, and click **Start a blank Spreadsheet**. Note that the screen window produced now displays a new list of menu names at the top, a Toolbar, a window title (Unsaved Spreadsheet, in this case), an empty worksheet with numbered rows and lettered columns, and the reduced Help window down the right side of the screen with its own control buttons.

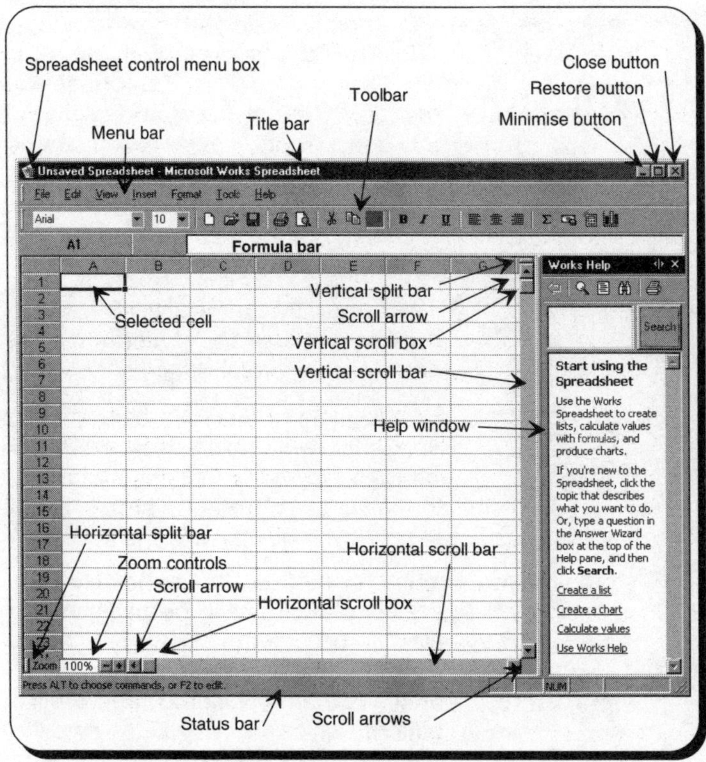

The spreadsheet window, as shown above, opens in a separate window to the Task Launcher and here takes up the full screen area available. If you click on the restore button, you can make it show in a smaller window. This can be useful when you are working with several sheets, or documents, at the same time and you want to transfer between them with the mouse. Although multiple worksheet, database and document files can be displayed simultaneously in their own windows, you can only enter data into the active window (highlighted at the top). Title bars of non active windows appear in a lighter shade.

The Works 2000 screen is divided into several areas which have the following functions. These are described from the top of the screen down, working from left to right.

Area	*Function*
Control box  	Clicking on the control menu box, which is located in the upper left corner of the window, displays the pull-down Control menu which can be used to control the program window. It includes commands for restoring, re-sizing, moving, maximising, minimising and closing the window.
Title bar	The bar at the top of a window which displays the application name and the name of the current document.
Minimise button 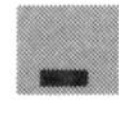	Clicking this reduces the Works application window to an icon on the Taskbar. You click this icon to restore the Works window and even maintain the cursor position.
Restore button 	When clicked on, this button restores the active window to the position and size occupied before being maximised or minimised. The restore button is then replaced by a Maximise button, which is used to set the window to its former size.
Close button	The Windows X button that you click to close an application, or document window.
Menu bar	The bar below the title bar which allows you to choose from several menu options. The names of the main menu commands might be different when using different Works tools.
Toolbar	Displays a set of icons for each tool, which can be clicked to quickly carry out menu commands or functions.
Scroll bars	The areas on the screen (right and bottom of each window) that contain

	scroll boxes in vertical and horizontal bars. Clicking on these bars allows you to control the part of a document which is visible on the screen.
Scroll arrows	The arrowheads at each end of each scroll bar which you can click to scroll the screen up and down one line, or left and right one cell, at a time.
Help window	The window that you can open (by clicking the Help icon) to display help text alongside your document.
Status bar	The bottom line of the window that displays the current program status and information regarding the present process.

Manipulating Windows

Like all standard Windows programs, Works allows the display of multiple sets of data within a given application tool, or several windows encompassing files from different tools, each within its own window. Unlike previous versions of Works these all open as completely separate application windows, not as windows within a main Works window.

You will need to manipulate these windows, by selecting which is the active one, moving them so that you can see all the relevant parts of an application, re-sizing them, or indeed closing unwanted windows once you have finished with them. A short discussion follows on how to manipulate windows so that you can get the best of what Works 2000 can provide.

In order to illustrate our discussion, use the **File, New** menu command several times and open some more spreadsheet or word processor documents, from the Task Launcher (which opens each time). As each selection is made, a new window is displayed placed on top of any existing ones.

Changing the Active Window

You can select the active window, from amongst those displayed on the screen, by pointing to any part of it, and clicking the left mouse button.

Closing a Window

Any window (provided it is the active window), can be closed at any time, maybe to save screen space and memory. There are several ways to close the active window; the easiest is to click on its Close button (the X button in the top right hand corner), also you can double click on the File Control Menu Box (the icon in the upper-left corner of the window), or press the <Ctrl+F4> keys, or use the **File, Close** command.

If you have made any changes to a file in a window since the last time you saved it, Works will warn you with the appearance of a dialogue box giving you the option to save the file before closing it.

Moving Windows and Dialogue Boxes

When you have multiple windows or dialogue boxes on the screen, you might want to move a particular one to a different part of the screen. This can be achieved with either the mouse or the keyboard, but not if the window occupies the full screen, for obvious reasons.

To move a window, or a dialogue box, with the mouse, point to the title bar and drag it (press the left button and keep it pressed while moving the mouse) until it is where you want it to be. Then release the mouse button to fix it into its new position.

To move with the keyboard, press <Alt+Spacebar> to reveal the Application Control Menu. Then, press 'M', to select **Move,** which causes a four-headed arrow to appear in the title bar and use the arrow keys to move the shadow border of the window to the required place. Press <Enter> to fix the window to its new position, or <Esc> to cancel the relocation.

Sizing a Window

You can change the size of a window with either the mouse or the keyboard. To size an active window with the mouse, move the window so that the side you want to change is visible, then move the mouse pointer to the edge of the window or corner, so that it changes to a two-headed arrow (see page 21), then drag the two-headed arrow in the direction you want that side or corner to move. Continue dragging until the window is the size you require, then release the mouse button.

To size with the keyboard, press the <Alt+Spacebar> keys to open the Application Control menu, then press 'S' to select **Size**, which causes the four-headed arrow to appear. Now press the arrow key that corresponds to the edge you want to move, or if a corner, press the two arrow keys (one after the other) corresponding to the particular corner, which causes the pointer to change to a two-headed arrow. Press an appropriate arrow key in the direction you want that side or corner to move and continue to do so until the window is the size you require, then press <Enter> to fix the new window size.

Splitting a Window

The windows of the Works spreadsheet application tool can be split both horizontally and vertically, so that you can see different parts of your work side by side in the same window.

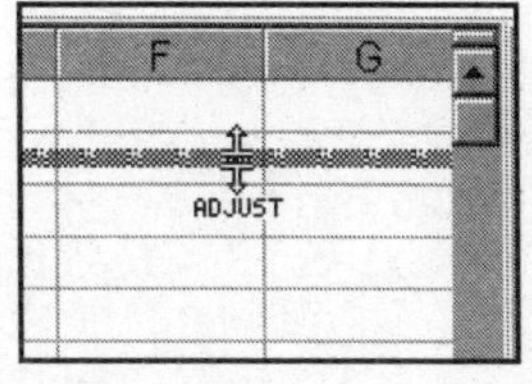

To split a window, move the mouse pointer onto a split bar (the bar either above the top scroll arrow, or to the left of the zoom controls), drag the new pointer shape to the required position as shown in our example, and release the mouse button.

Managing Files

With Works applications you can create, save, open, or generally operate on files, by using the **File** command from the menu bar, the toolbar icons, or by using controls in the Open, Save and Save As dialogue boxes.

Saving a File

Once a document has been prepared, under any of the tool applications, you can save it by using the **File, Save** command, or by clicking the Save toolbar icon. The first time you use this command with, say, the word processor, Works opens the Save As dialogue box, shown here. You type a new name without any extension in

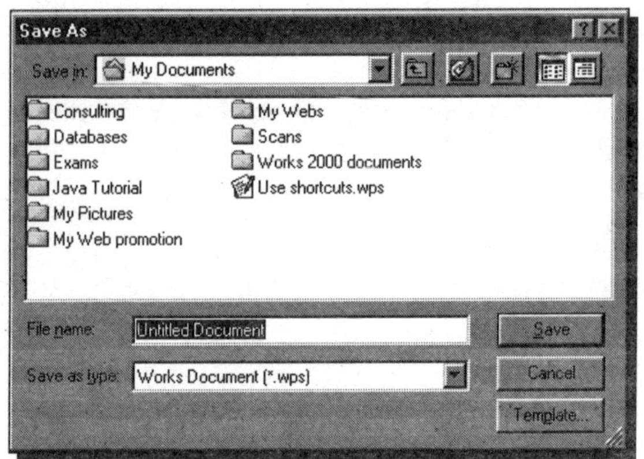

the **File name** text box. By default all Microsoft applications use the **My Documents** folder created by Windows itself, so unless you want to store your work somewhere else just accept this destination in the **Save in** text box. Pressing **Save**, or the <Enter> key, causes your typed filename to become the new document title. Once a file has been saved, subsequent use of the **File, Save** command, saves the file automatically under that filename, and in the same folder as you first saved your work.

If you want to save an already saved file under a different name, then use the **File, Save As** command and type a different name, without an extension (the moment you start typing the new name, the default name vanishes from the display). When you press <Enter>, the program automatically adds the appropriate extension for you and saves the file.

The **Save as type** list box allows you to save the file in any of the formats listed. For example, you would select 'WordPerfect 5.1 for DOS (*.doc)', if you wanted to use the file later in that package. As usual Microsoft's list of supported file conversion filters is anything but complete, but they do seem to be getting better.

Retrieving a File

To retrieve an already saved document from disc, use the **File, Open** menu command, or click the Open toolbar button, from whatever application you are in. This will bring up the standard Windows Open dialogue box, as shown below.

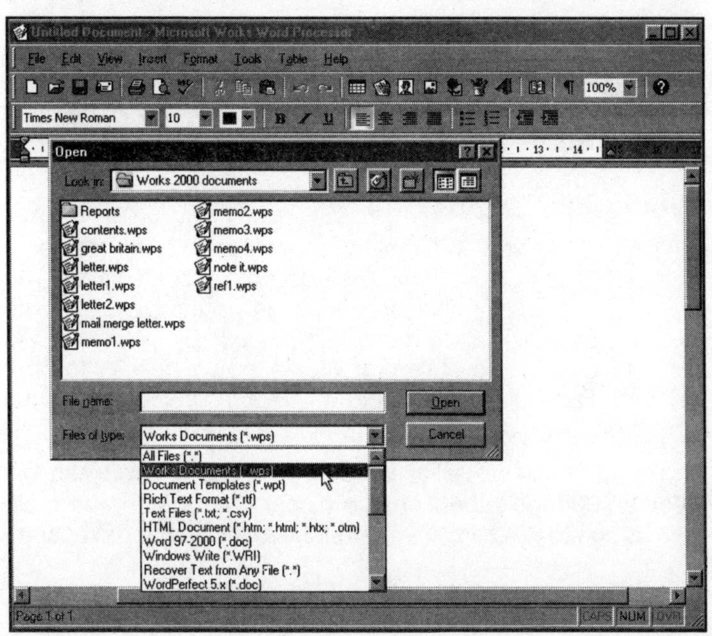

In this case the default 'Works Documents (*.wps)' has been selected in the **Files of type** box, so all the Works word processor files in the selected folder are shown. To select a file, you would either click at its name with the mouse pointer, or press <Alt+n> to move into the **File name** box, press <Tab> enough times to move the highlight down into the file list, highlight the required file with the arrow keys and press <Enter>. The mouse method is definitely preferable!

Using the Right-Click Menu

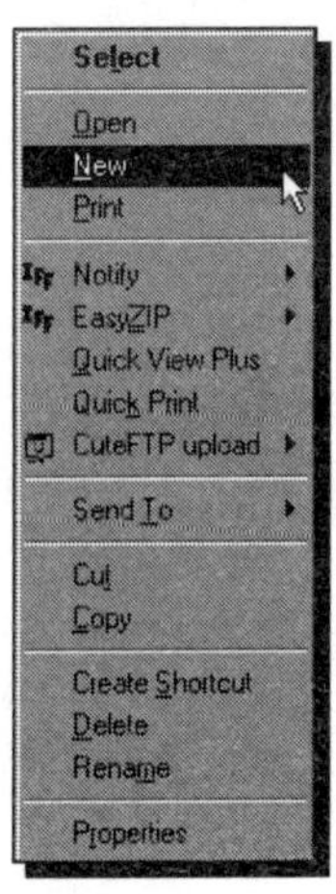

A very useful Windows feature is the ability to carry out almost any file management functions from either the Open or the Save dialogue boxes. Simply select a file, or files, and click the right mouse button (or the left one if you are using it in left-handed mode!) Some of the options, as shown here, are not standard, but you can **Cut**, **Copy**, **Delete** or **Rename** a file, as well as open a list of its **Properties**.

The **New** option, highlighted in our example, is very useful. It is the quickest way we have found to open a new file in a Works application window, as it does not force you to go to the Task Launcher.

Works File Extensions

With Windows you do not need to get involved with file name extensions, and by default, they do not even display. If you see them in our examples it is because we have changed the default settings. Extensions are used by Windows to determine what application (or Works tool) is needed to work with the file. But all the Windows file manipulation dialogue boxes display icons for the different file types.

To help you determine which type of file is used with the Works 2000 tools the filename extensions of the three main application tools are shown with their icons on the next page.

Extension	*Icon*	*Tool*
Wps		Works Word Processor
Wks		Works Spreadsheet
Wdb		Works Database

The Mouse Pointers

In Works 2000 applications, as with all other graphical based programs, the use of a mouse makes many operations both easier and more fun to carry out.

Works 2000 makes use of the mouse pointers available in Windows, some of the most common of which are illustrated below. When a Works application is initially started up the first you will see is the hourglass, which turns into an upward pointing hollow arrow once the individual application screen appears on your display. Other shapes depend on the type of work you are doing at the time.

The hourglass which displays when you are waiting while performing a function.

The arrow which appears when the pointer is placed over menus, scrolling bars, and buttons.

The I-beam which appears in normal text areas of the screen.

The 4-headed arrow which appears when you choose to move a table, a chart area, or a frame.

The double arrows which appear when over the border of a window, used to drag the side and alter the size of the window.

 The Help hand which appears in the Help windows, and is used to access 'hypertext' type links.

Works applications, like other Windows packages, have additional mouse pointers which facilitate the execution of selected commands. Some of these are:

The vertical pointer which appears when pointing over a column in a table or worksheet, used to select the column.

The horizontal pointer which appears when pointing at a row in a table or worksheet, used to select the row.

The slanted arrow which appears when the pointer is placed in the selection bar area of text or a table.

The vertical split arrow which appears when pointing over the area separating two columns, used to size a column.

The horizontal split arrow which appears when pointing over the area separating two rows, used to size a row.

+ The cross which you drag to extend or fill a series.

The draw pointer which appears when you are drawing freehand.

The Works 2000 Help System

With Works 2000 by default you get a help window 'permanently' open on the right side of the screen, as shown on the facing page. The contents of this window will depend on the Works application you are using, the word processor is shown in our example.

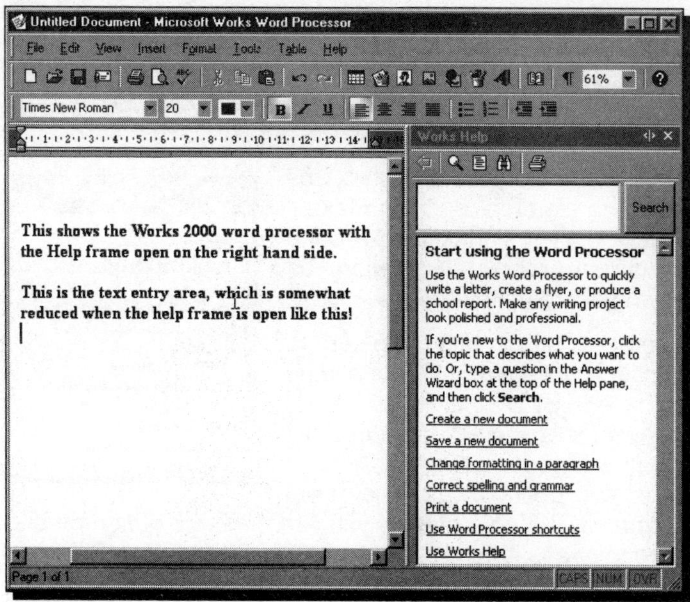

You control the size of the Help pane by clicking this button. It toggles the pane between full and half size.

Click this button to close the Help pane altogether and have much more screen space to work with.

Click the Works Help button to re-open the Help pane with an initial context sensitive display.

There are several ways of using the Help system. If you can see an underlined item in the pane that seems useful, click it to open more details, which should lead to yet more. A little like using a Web browser. Surfing the Help pane!

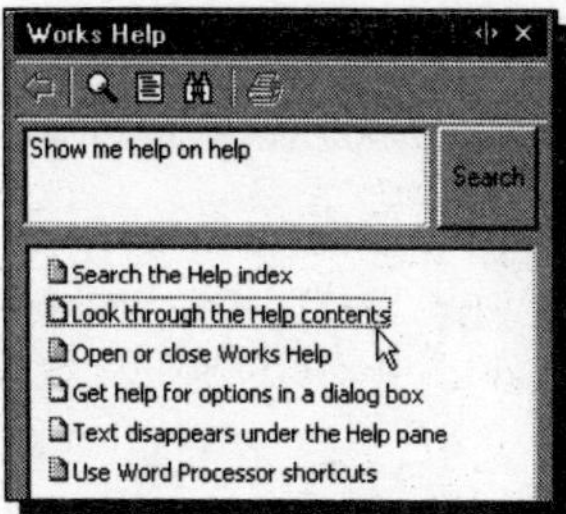

You can also type a complete question in the Answer Wizard text box and click the **Search** button, as we have done here.

This produces a list of options based on the keywords you type in. As before, click on one to open it and read its contents.

Clicking the back button, shown here, takes you back to the previous topic.

If the text box is not open you can click the Answer Wizard button to make it reappear.

The Contents button opens a hierarchical list to make it easy to find your way round the current Works application, as shown here to the right.

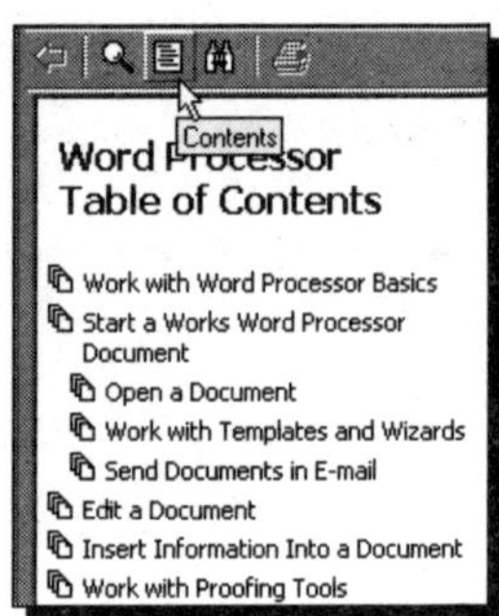

You click on the text of an item to open its contained list. Sometimes you have to go several 'layers' deep, but eventually you will unearth a list with underlined options. Clicking on these will open a page of help information. Unfortunately, if you use the Back button on one of these pages it takes you back to the start of the Contents list. You can use the Related Topics list at the bottom of the pane, but really the whole layout of this section of the Help system is a little amateurish.

When you click the Index button, shown here to the left, an alphabetical keyword list is opened, as on the right.

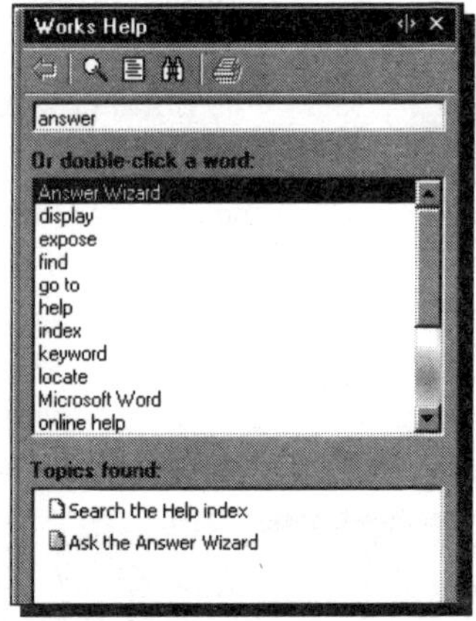

Typing a search keyword in the top text box, or double-clicking one in the list, opens a list of topics in the **Topics found** pane. Clicking one of these will open its data page in the main Help pane.

Whatever subject you choose, the Help window gives useful instructions on how to carry out the operation. Remember that when the mouse pointer turns to a hand you can click on the item below it to open another pane of help information.

Clicking the Print button, when it is available as shown here, opens the Print dialogue box for you to select any options required to send the current Help pane to your printer. Hard copy is sometimes useful for immediate future reference.

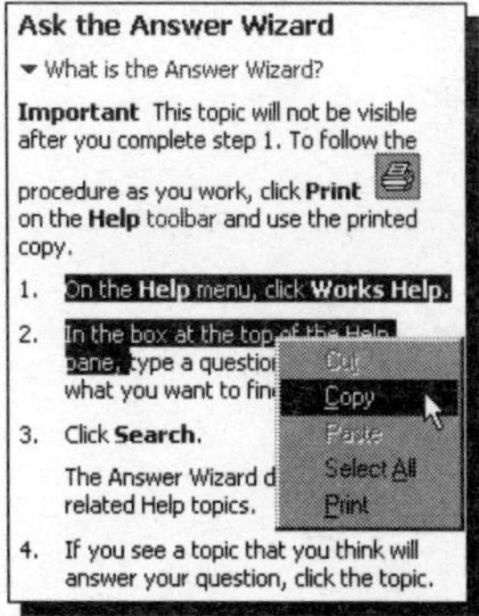

To copy Help information to the Windows clipboard, you should first select it, then click the right mouse button and select **Copy** from the context menu opened, as shown here. You could then paste the text into a word processor file to maybe make your own Help data records.

You can also use this method to send selected data only to the printer, using the **Print** menu option.

You should spend some time exploring the Help system; it is quite detailed, which is just as well as it is the only real source of information about Works 2000 that is provided. Most things are in there, you just have to find them!

Exiting Works

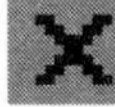

Whenever you are ready to leave a Works 2000 application the procedure is the same whichever tool you are in. You either use the **File**, **Exit** command, click the application's Close button at the top right of the window, or use the <Alt+F4> key strokes. You have to do this with the Task Launcher as well, to completely exit from Works 2000.

As long as any open files have been saved since they were last modified, the application will close. If not you will be given the option to save them, before they are 'lost forever'.

2

Works 2000 Word Processor

The standard Works 2000 package comes equipped with a new and quite impressive word processor almost as powerful as most 'stand alone' versions. It has all the normal editing features, including the ability to insert, delete, erase, search for, replace, and drag and drop copy and move.

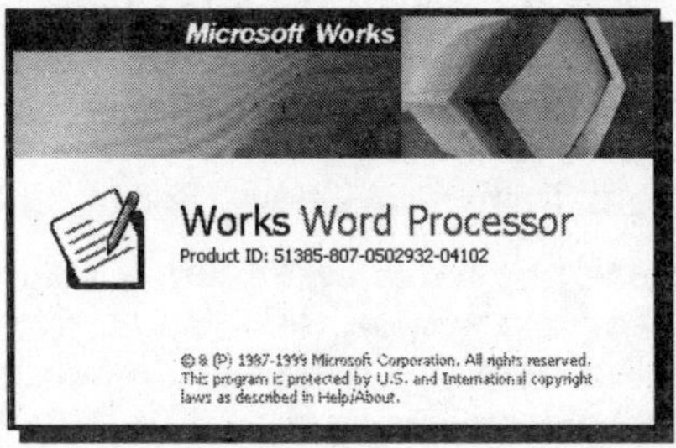

As you would expect, it also allows you to enhance text and create bold, underlined, italic, strike-through, superscript, subscript and other specially formatted text. Being an integrated package it is easy to embed part of a spreadsheet into a document, carry out a mail merge, or send a document to a distant computer using the communications functions.

New Features

New features added to the word processor include:

Automatic spell checking - the program can find and underline spelling mistakes as you type, and give you options to change the words.

Improved mail merge - selects names from the Address Book and other data sources and quickly creates envelopes, labels, and form letters.

Easy-to-use tables - rapidly inserts tables to make lists, or to arrange paragraphs of text and pictures.

Powerful Undo feature - Undoes up to the last 100 typing or formatting actions you've carried out.

Starting the Word Processor

To access the word processor, as we saw in the last chapter, press the **Start a blank Word Processor document** option in the **Programs** tab window of the Task Launcher. Alternatively you can by-pass the Task Launcher by selecting the **Microsoft Works Word Processor** icon, shown here, from the Windows **Start** cascade menu.

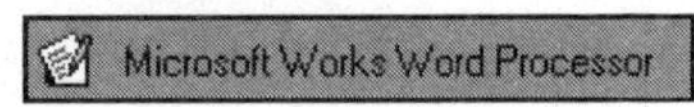

A screen similar to that shown below will appear. Here we have closed the Help window, as it is not very easy to work with it open. But before you do that, make sure you take advantage of what Help has to offer!

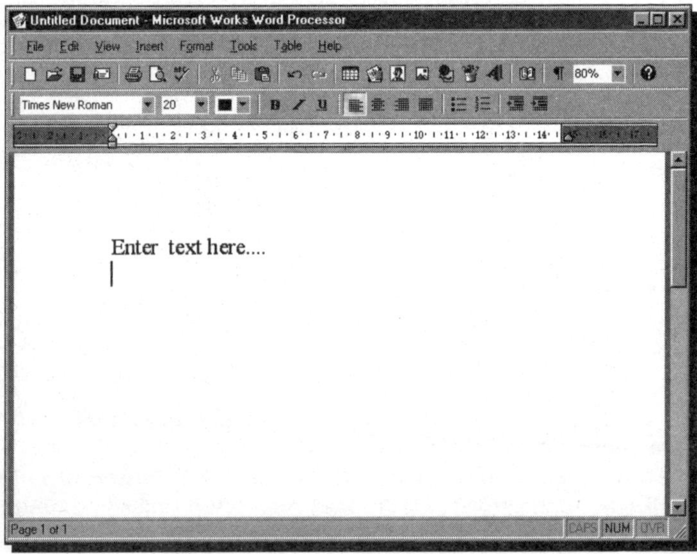

The Word Processor Screen

At the top of this screen is the Title bar, which shows the document title and the application that is open. Below this is the menu bar, which with the word processor, accesses the following sub menus:

We described in the 'Package Overview' how these are accessed with either the mouse, or by pressing the <Alt> key followed by the underlined letter.

The Toolbars

The Standard and Formatting Toolbars occupy the next lines down. If you use a mouse you will find these a big time saver, once you get in the habit of using them. If you prefer, you can turn them off with the **View**, **Toolbars** menu command, as shown here. These are toggle commands, when the '√' shows against a sub-menu option that Toolbar or other screen feature will display, otherwise it will not. The only advantage to be gained by not showing them is you gain extra screen space.

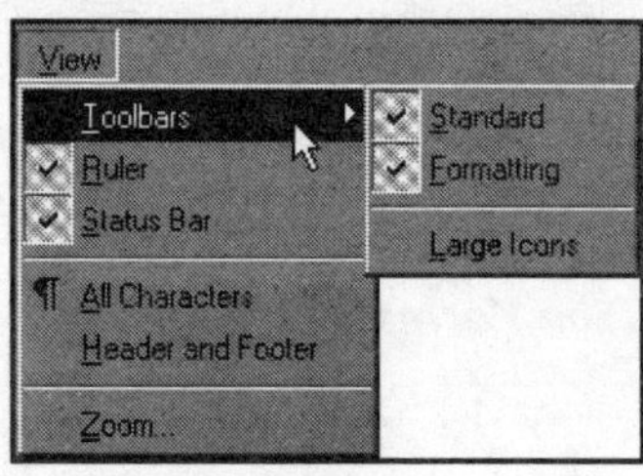

As shown above, you can also choose to have **Large Icons** on your Toolbars, or turn the **Ruler** and **Status Bar** on and off.

When you move the mouse pointer over one of the icons (buttons) on a Toolbar a yellow message box showing its function opens up. To use a Toolbar you simply click the mouse on a button, or icon, and either a standard command will be actioned, or a formatting command will affect all text in the document that is highlighted.

The actions of all the Toolbar buttons are given below and most are explained in more detail as we get into the book.

The Standard Toolbar

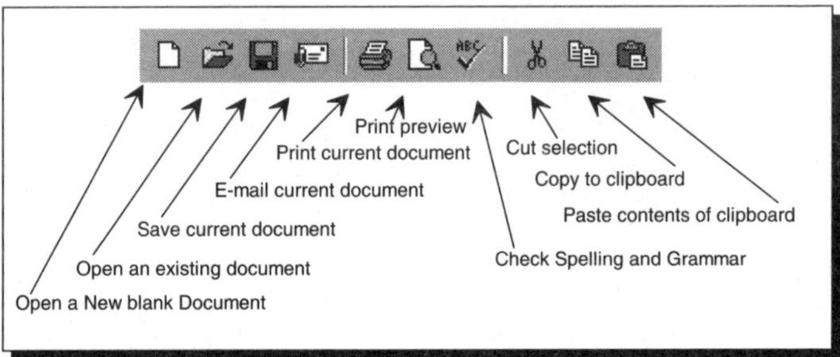

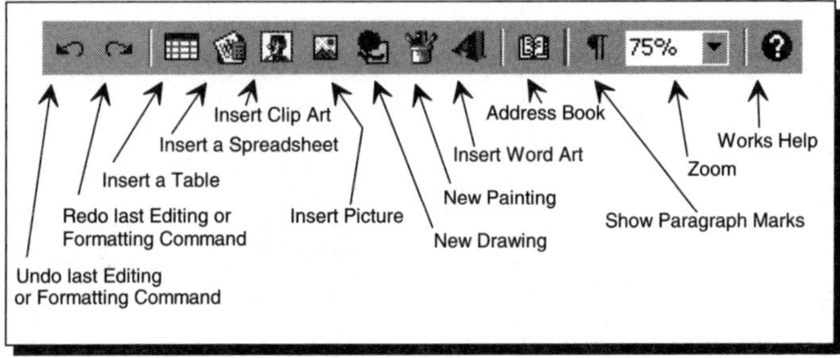

The Formatting Toolbar

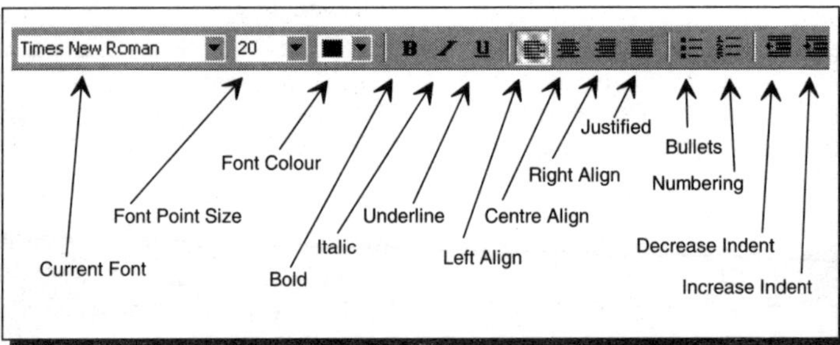

The current font box shows the current typeface. Clicking on the down-arrow button to the right of it allows you to change the typeface of any selected text. The font size box shows the size of selected characters which can be changed by clicking on the down-arrow button next to it and selecting another size from the displayed list. The font colour button lets you change the colour of selected text

Next, are three character formatting buttons which allow you to enhance selected text by emboldening, italicising, or underlining it. The next four buttons allow you to change the justification of a selected paragraph, and the last four help you set the different types of Bullets, Numbering and Indentation options.

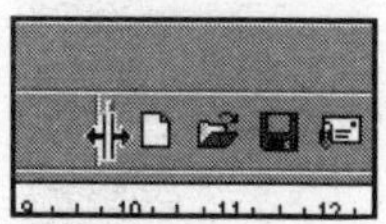

This version of Works does not seem to allow you to change the buttons on the toolbar, but to some extent you can control the positioning of the Toolbars. To do this click and grab one of the vertical lines on the left end of the tool or menu bars, and drag the bar up or down, as shown here. If your screen is wide enough you can place both Toolbars together to give you more editing space.

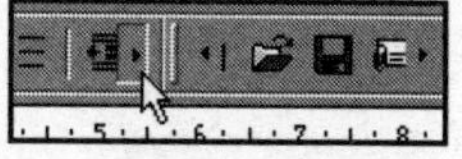

If your screen is too narrow to show all the buttons on a bar small arrow icons will be placed at either end of the bar, as shown in our example. Clicking one of these arrows will scroll the Toolbar buttons through the available space.

The Ruler

Below the Toolbars is the ruler, which appears as a scale across the screen that can be toggled on and off like the Toolbars, with the **View**, **Ruler** command.

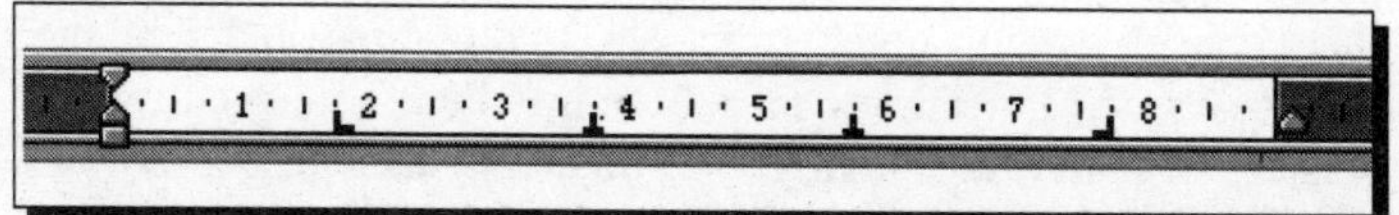

The ruler shows and allows you to change the left and right margin positions and any tab or indent settings active in the paragraph the cursor is in. You change the settings by dragging the markers across the ruler. To add custom tabs to the ruler, you left-click with the mouse pointer to add a left tab and right-click to add a right tab. Double clicking on the ruler opens the Tabs dialogue box which gives you more precise control over the tab settings.

The bottom of the word processing window has a status bar which gives you useful information and shows the status of any keys that are currently locked. This bar can be turned on and off with the **View**, **Status Bar** menu command.

The other scroll bars, boxes and arrows described in the last chapter also surround the working area which makes up the remainder of the screen.

Entering Text

Before going any further, click the mouse in the main text entry area and type the memo text shown below, or something else, to get the feel of Works word processing.

> MEMO TO PC USERS
> Networked Computers
> The microcomputers in the Data Processing room are a mixture of IBM compatible PCs with Pentium processors running at various speeds. They all have 3.5" floppy drives of 1.44MB capacity, and most also have CD-ROM drives. The PCs are connected to various printers via a network; the Laser printers available giving best output.
>
> The computer you are using will have at least a 3.0GB capacity hard disc on which a number of software programs, including the latest version of Windows, have been installed. To make life easier, the hard disc is highly structured with each program installed in a separate folder (directory).

When a new file is opened it is ready for you to begin typing in text. Any time you want to force a new line, or paragraph, just press <Enter>, otherwise the program will sort out line lengths automatically which is known as word wrap. So, you can just carry on typing a complete paragraph without having to press any keys to move to a new line. If you make a mistake, at this stage, press <BkSp> enough times to erase the mistake and retype it.

Now would be a good time to save the document, as described in the previous chapter, press **File, Save As** and type the filename **Memo1** to save in the My Documents folder. Obviously you can change the destination if you want. The program will add the WPS extension for you.

Moving Around a Document

You can move the cursor around a document by clicking the scroll bars and boxes, with the normal direction keys, with the key combinations shown below, or with the **Edit**, **Go To** command, or press <Ctrl+G>. With the last command you can jump to various document features, or to different page numbers.

To move	***Press***
Left one character	←
Right one character	→
Up one line	↑
Down one line	↓
Left one word	Ctrl+←
Right one word	Ctrl+→
Up one paragraph	Ctrl+↑
Down one paragraph	Ctrl+↓
To beginning of line	Home
To end of line	End
To beginning of file	Ctrl+Home
To end of file	Ctrl+End
Up one window	Pg Up
Down one window	Pg Dn

Document Editing

It will not be long when using the word processor before you will need to edit your screen document. This could be to delete unwanted words, to correct a mistake or to add extra text to the document. All these operations are very easy to carry out.

For small deletions, such as letters or words, the easiest method is using the <Del> or <BkSp> keys. With the <Del> key, position the cursor on the first letter to delete and press <Del>; the letter is deleted and the following text moves one space to the left.

With the <BkSp> key, position the cursor immediately to the right of the character to be deleted and press <BkSp>; the cursor moves one space to the left pulling the rest of the line with it and overwriting the character to be deleted.

Word processing is usually carried out in the insert mode. Any characters typed will be inserted at the cursor location and the following text will be pushed to the right, and down, to make room. Pressing the <Ins> key will change you to overstrike mode and the letters 'OVR' will appear on the Status Line. In this mode any text you type will over-write existing text.

To insert blank lines in your text, make sure you are in Insert mode, place the cursor at the beginning of the line where the blank is needed and press <Enter>. The cursor line will move down leaving a blank line. To remove the blank line, position the cursor at its left end and press <Del>.

When larger scale editing is needed, such as using the copy, move and erase operations, the text to be altered must be 'selected', or 'highlighted', before the operation can be carried out. These functions are then available when the **Edit** sub-menu is activated, the Toolbar options used, or Drag and Drop is used.

Selecting Text

The procedure in Works, as in all Windows applications, is that before any operation such as formatting or editing can be carried out on text, it must first be selected. Selected text is highlighted on the screen. This can be carried out in several ways.

Using the menu you can select all the contents of a document, with the **Edit**, **Select All** command.

Using the keyboard, position the cursor on the first character to be selected and either:

- Hold down the <Shift> key while using the direction keys to highlight the required text, then release the <Shift> key, or:
- Press <Ctrl+A> to select the whole document.

With the mouse

- Left click at the beginning of the block and drag the cursor across the block so that whole words of the desired text are highlighted, then release the mouse button.
- With the cursor in a word double-click the left mouse button to select that word.
- Position the cursor in the left window margin (where it will change to a right sloping arrow) and then either click the left button to select the current line, or double-click the left button to select the current paragraph, or triple-click to select the entire document.

We suggest you try out all these methods and find which ones you are most comfortable with.

Copying Blocks of Text

Once text has been selected it can be copied to another location in your present document, to another Works document (as long as it is open), to another Works tool, or to another Windows program.

As with most of the editing and formatting operations there are several ways of doing this. One is by using the **Edit,**

Copy command sequence from the menu, moving the cursor to the start of where you want the copied text, and use the **Edit**, **Paste** command.

You can also use toolbar icons, or quick key combinations. Press the Copy icon, or <Ctrl+C>, once the text to be copied has been selected, and the Paste icon, or <Ctrl+V>, to 'paste' it in the new location. These methods do not require the menu bar to be activated.

To copy the same text again to another location in the document, move the cursor to the new location and Paste it. This operation is called 'pasting' because of the old days (for some of us) with scissors and a glue pot!

When text is copied, or cut, it is actually placed on the Window's clipboard and remains there until replaced by other text.

Moving Blocks of Text

Selected text can be moved to any location on the same document. To do this, 'cut' it to the clipboard by clicking the Cut Toolbar button, or the **Edit**, **Cut** command, or <Ctrl+X>, and then paste it in the new location by clicking the Paste button, with the **Edit**, **Paste** command, or <Ctrl+V>. The moved text will be placed at the cursor location and will force any existing text to make room for it. This operation can be cancelled before the final key command by simply pressing <Esc>.

Drag and Drop Editing

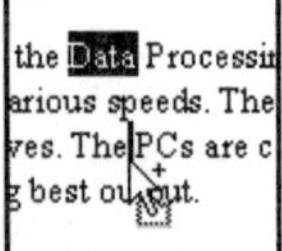

Probably the easiest way to copy and move small blocks of text in a document is with the Drag and Drop feature.

To move the block, drag it with the left mouse button depressed and release the button when the vertical bar is in the required new position. To copy it, hold down the <Ctrl> key while you drag, a small '+' is then added to the pointer, as shown above.

The new text will insert itself where placed, even if the overstrike mode is active. Text moved, or copied, in this way is not placed on the clipboard, so multiple operations are not possible.

Replacing Blocks of Text

One block of text can be 'replaced' by another using either the cut or copy process. Obviously if cut is used the text at the original location will be removed, but not if the copy command is used. The process is the same as an ordinary copy or move, except that the block of text to be replaced must be selected before the final paste command is made.

Deleting Blocks of Text

When text is cut or deleted it is removed from the document. With Works any selected text can be deleted by pressing the <Del> key, or by selecting the **Edit**, **Clear** menu command. This will not, however, place the deleted text on the Windows clipboard, for possible future use. To do this you must use the **Edit**, **Cut** command, the Cut icon, or <Ctrl+X>.

The Undo and Redo Commands

As text is lost with the delete command you should use it with caution, but if you do make a mistake all is not lost as long as you act fairly quickly. Clicking the Undo button, or the **Edit**, **Undo..** command reverses your most recent editing or formatting commands. In fact you can undo up to 100 actions this way, heaven forbid! The Undo process works even after Drag and Drop actions.The quick key sequence for the Undo command is <Ctrl+Z>.

After you undo a command or action, the **Edit**, **Redo..** Menu command and the Redo button, shown here, become active. These both allow you to restore what you've reversed. The quick key sequence for the Redo command is <Ctrl+Y>.

These are very useful features but take care until you get used to them, it is sometimes not easy to work out what is going on.

Page Breaks

The program automatically inserts a page break in a document when a page of typed text is full. There will be places in most multi-page documents where you will want to force a new page to improve the layout. This is done by inserting a manual page break by pressing **Insert**, **Break Page Break**, or just using the key combination <Ctrl+Enter>. Works readjusts all the non-manual page breaks for the remainder of the document. Both types of page break show as a full line across the document. If you click the Show All button as we have done below, it shows the paragraph marks in the document and you can tell the two apart.

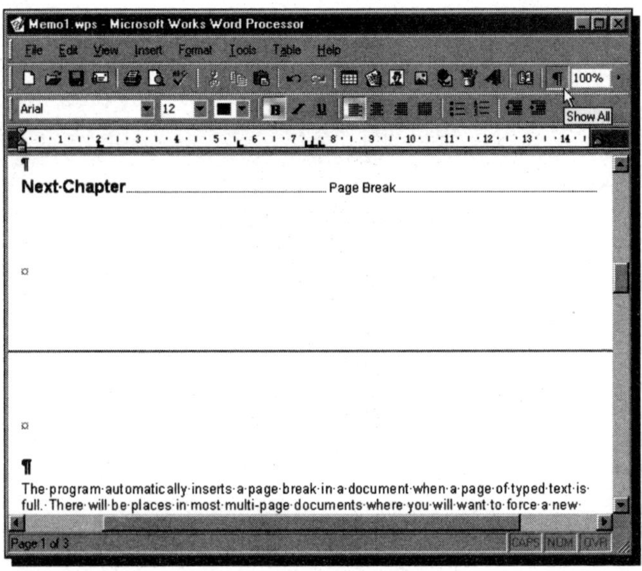

Both display as the line shown above, but the manual break has the '........ Page Break ....' paragraph mark above it.

A manual page break can be deleted by placing the insertion point immediately above it and pressing the <Del> key. An automatic page break cannot be deleted.

Viewing Word Processor Documents

The new Works word processor is fully WYSIWYG (what you see is what you get) with features such as columns, pictures, headers, footers and footnotes appearing in their correct positions. It displays each page in your document as it will look when printed.

The Zoom Command

The Zoom feature allows you to control the amount of the active document that will display on the screen at any time. The zoom size status of a particular document has no effect on the document when it is printed. There are two ways to alter the zoom setting. By clicking the arrow next to the Zoom Toolbar button shown above, or choose **Zoom** from the **View** menu, and then choose the size you want from the dialogue box shown below.

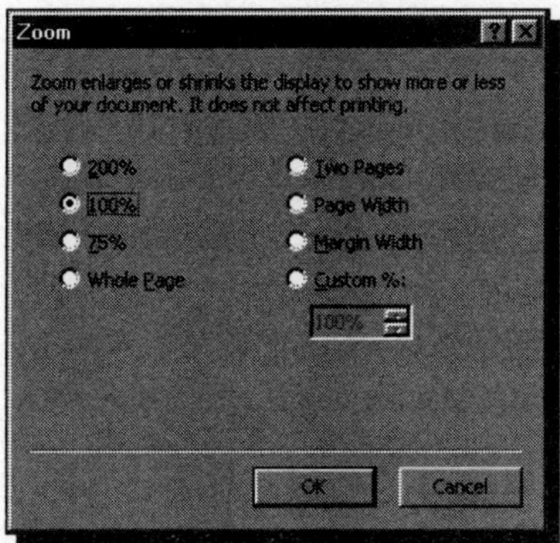

In the Zoom box you have a **Custom %** option in which you can specify any magnification between 25% and 500%.

Other Views

Two other document view types are worth mentioning. Clicking the Print Preview button, or using the **File**, **Print Preview** command, opens a view of your document on the screen exactly as it will be printed. You can't edit text or make any changes in print preview, but you can also zoom the view in and out, and change the page settings. It is well worth using this feature to check your document every time before you print.

The last view available in the word processor is actioned with the **View, Headers and Footers** menu command. This opens the headers area at the top of each page and the footers area at the bottom, so that you can add or edit document headers and footers. Once you have placed either, double-clicking in the header or footer area has the same effect.

Character Enhancement

Another simplistic example will explain the principles of text enhancement. With any word processor it is often easier to type your text in first and worry about the document layout later on. Create a new word processing file and type in the letter text shown below.

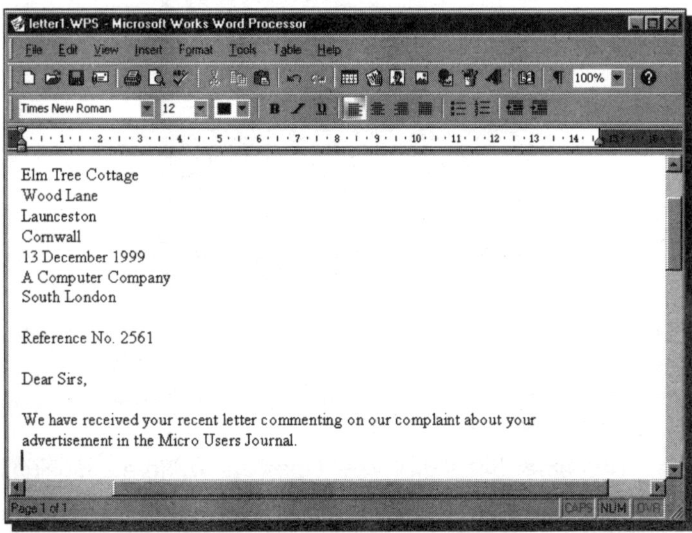

Elm Tree Cottage
Wood Lane
Launceston
Cornwall
13 December 1999
A Computer Company
South London

Reference No. 2561

Dear Sirs,

We have received your recent letter commenting on our complaint about your advertisement in the Micro Users Journal.

The date on line 5 is not just typed in. A code is embedded so that it will give the current date when the letter is printed. This is generated from the dialogue box opened with the **Insert**, **Date and Time** command. Choose the date format you prefer and select the **Automatically update when printed** option. When you have finished, save the document using the **File**, **Save As** command, calling it **Letter1**.

To improve the layout of the letter we will use some of the commands in the **Format** sub-menu and also some of the Toolbar and Quick key options.

First select the top five lines containing the address and date (the easiest way of doing this is to click the mouse alongside line 1, in the left margin, and drag it down to line 5) and then select the **Format**, **Paragraph**, **Indents and Alignment**, command to open the box below. Select the **Alignment** as **Right** as shown and press **OK**.

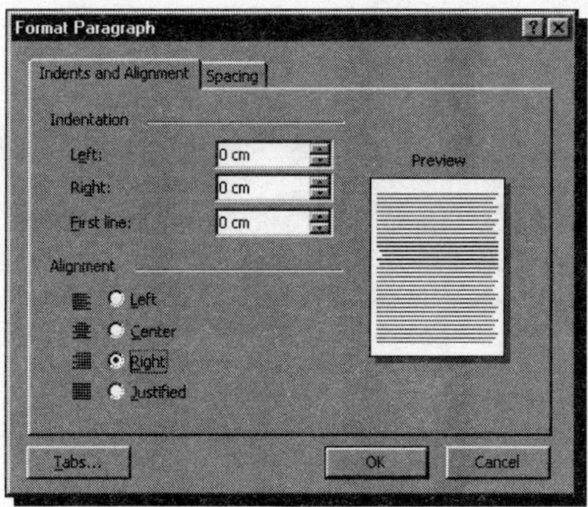

The whole block should now be right justified. By default paragraphs are left justified. While the block is still highlighted press the <Ctrl+L> keys and finally click the Right Align Toolbar icon, shown here. You should now be back with a right justified address.

Then select the Ref... line of text and press **Format**, **Paragraph**, **Indents and Alignment**, **Center** (or the quick keys <Ctrl+E>, or the Center Align Toolbar icon) to centre the line between the left and right margins. While the selection highlight is still active press **Format**, **Font**, **Underline** (or <Ctrl+U>, or the Underline icon on the Toolbar) to underline the reference. By now you have probably accepted that the Toolbar is by far the most convenient way of carrying out these enhancement functions. But often you get more options to choose from when a dialogue box is involved. With the last 'underline' option, for example, you have 16 different types of underlining to choose from! If you repeat the Toolbar click, while the highlight is still active, the feature is turned off again; they act as toggle functions.

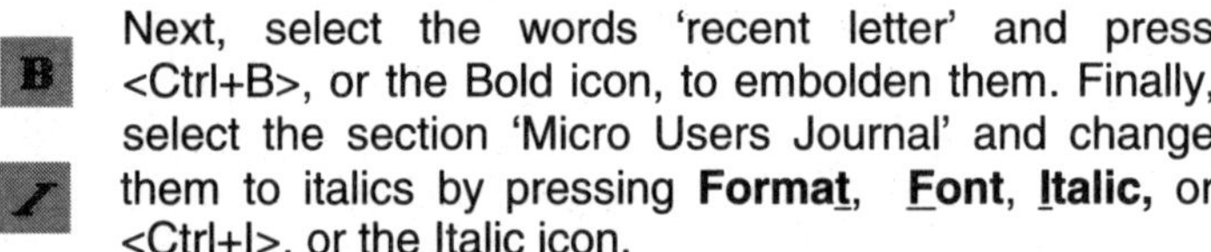

Next, select the words 'recent letter' and press <Ctrl+B>, or the Bold icon, to embolden them. Finally, select the section 'Micro Users Journal' and change them to italics by pressing **Format**, **Font**, **Italic,** or <Ctrl+I>, or the Italic icon.

The letter now looks very different and should be similar to our **Letter2**, shown below.

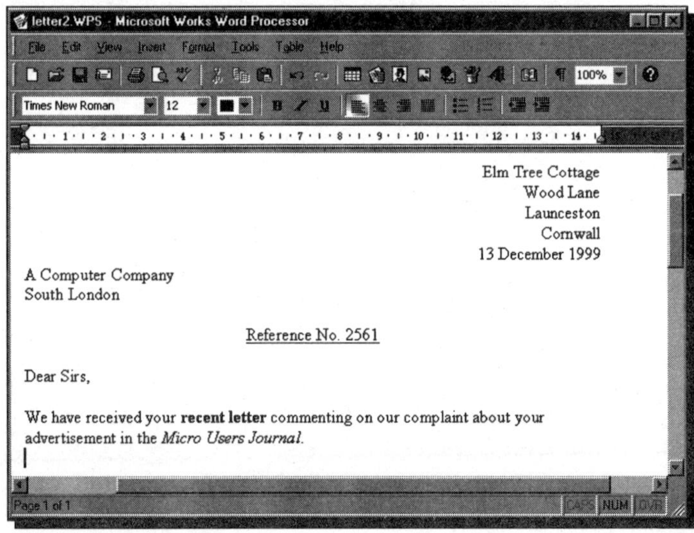

What a difference with only a few keystrokes! Note that when the cursor is in text that has been enhanced, the relevant icon on the Toolbar appears 'depressed'. In the above example the Left Align icon is selected. These status indicators are useful when the enhancements are not obvious from the screen text.

Fonts

A font is a typeface with a specific design. In Works 2000 you can work with and print text in any fonts which are supported by your version of Windows. You can also work with any supported colours, but you can obviously only print them if you have a colour printer.

To change the font, size, colour or enhancements of specific text in a document, first select the text. Choose the **Font** command either from the **Format** menu, or from the 'object menu' opened by right-clicking the document edit area, and make selections in the opened dialogue box, as shown below.

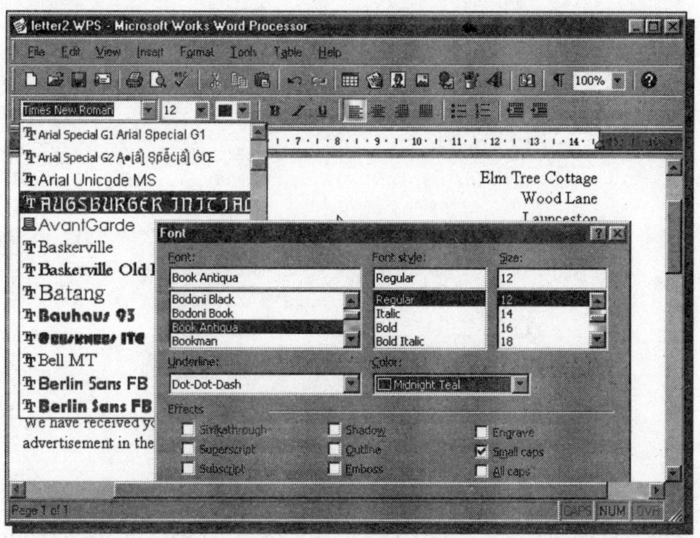

You can also, of course, change the font, size and colour of selected text from the Font, Font Size and Font Color Toolbar icons. Clicking the arrow alongside each of these opens up a menu of available options.

The composite screen on the previous page, shows both methods of changing the font and font size of selected text. You will not be able to get them on the screen at the same time, though, so don't bother trying.

When they are available, the Toolbar icons are by far the best option for carrying out these operations.

Works 2000 measures font sizes in points, where one point is 1/72nd of an inch. You may need to study your printer manual and experiment with these commands to make the most of this Works facility. One thing to remember though is that a printed page usually looks better if you use different fonts and sizes sparingly.

Printing Documents

When Windows was installed on your computer your printers should have been installed as well. Many hundreds of different printers are supported by Windows so, hopefully, you shouldn't have too much trouble getting yours to work. The printer and printing functions are now included in a single Printers folder, which you can open by double-clicking the above icon in the My Computer window. Our Printers folder, shown below, has a list of printers available for use, and an Add Printer icon.

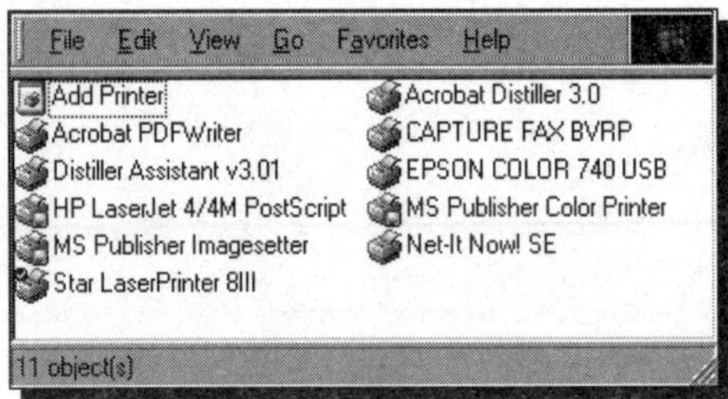

This folder provides an easy way of adding new printers, configuring existing ones, and managing all your print jobs.

Installing a Printer

To 'manually' install a new printer to your set up, double-click the **Add Printer** icon in the Printers window. This opens the Windows Add Printer Wizard, which really makes the installation procedure much easier than it used to be. As with all Wizards you progress from screen to screen by clicking the **Next** button. The first time you do this, you may have to wait a short time, while the printer driver information database is built.

The dialogue box below lets you choose the make and model of printer you want to install.

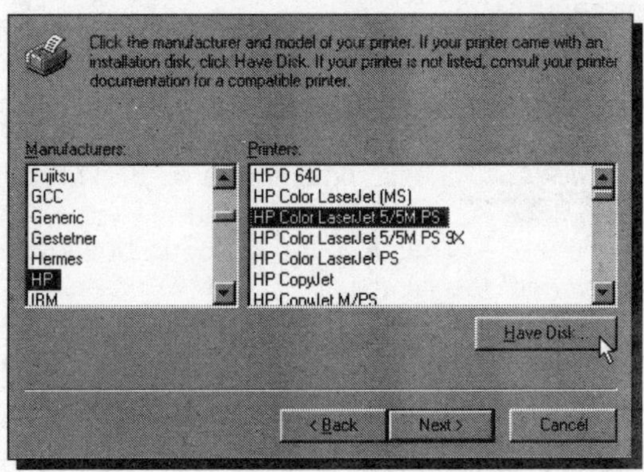

In our case we are setting up a Hewlett Packard (HP in the list) model LaserJet 5/5M PS. If you have a disc of drivers that came with the printer, put it in the floppy drive and click the **Have Disk** button.

You are next asked to select the correct Port. This refers to the socket at the back of your PC which is connected to the printer. For a stand alone set-up this would usually be the LPT1 port. (Short for Line Printer No.1). Next you can customise the printer name, maybe on a network, it would be useful to describe where it is actually located. You can also select whether you want the new printer to be your default, in which case all Windows programs will select it by default.

You should then accept **Yes** to have a test print carried out, to check that all is OK with the installation. When you click the **Finish** button a new icon will be placed in your Printers folder and, as long as the printer is switched on, a test page should be produced. Hopefully, this test should give an impressive demonstration of the printer's capabilities and you will be able to answer **Yes** when asked if the test was successful. If not, click the **No** button, and Windows will attempt to sort out the problem for you.

Configuring a Printer

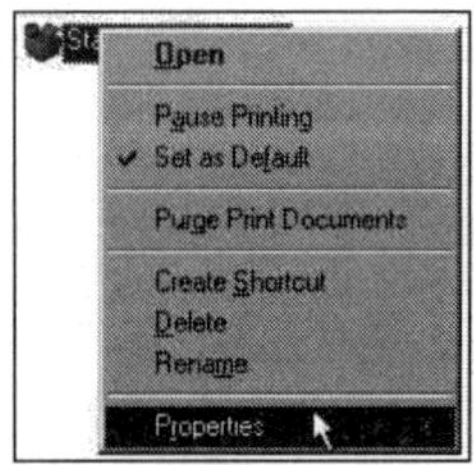

With Windows all configuration for a printer is now consolidated onto a tabbed property sheet that is accessed from its icon in the Printers folder. Right clicking a printer icon opens the object menu, shown on the left, which gives control of the printer's operation. If you click the **Properties** option, the dialogue box shown on the right opens and lets you control all the printer's parameters, such as the printer port (or network path), paper and graphics options, built in fonts, and other device options specific to the printer model. All these settings are fairly self explanatory and as they depend on your printer type we will let you work them out for yourselves.

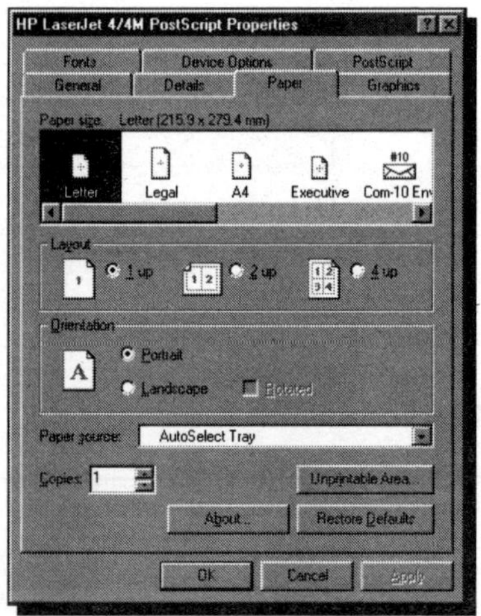

Now your printer is set up you can, at any time, use the **File, Print**

command from the Works document menu bar, or <Ctrl+P>, which both open the 'Print' box, shown below.

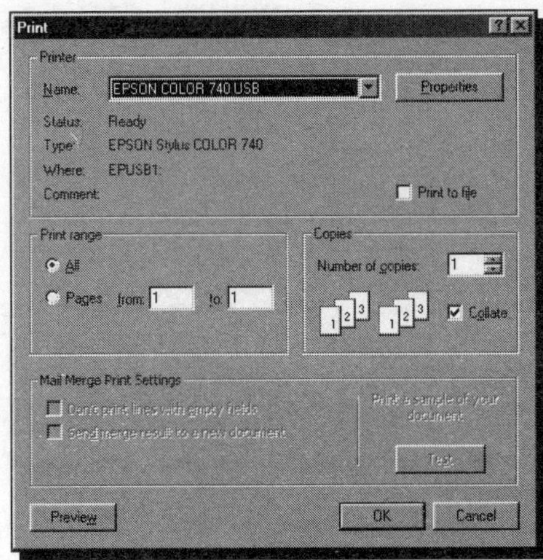

The settings in this box allow you to select which printer is used, the number of copies, and which pages are printed. Finally select **OK**, to send print output from Works to your selected destination, either the printer connected to your computer, or to an encoded file on disc.

The Print icon on the Toolbar sends the current document to the printer using the active settings. It does not give you access to the Print box.

Do remember that, whenever you change printers, the appearance of your document may change, as Works uses the fonts available with the newly selected printer. This can affect the line lengths, which in turn will affect both tabulation and pagination of your document.

Page Setup

The next operation, to make sure your printer is happy with your document settings, is to set up Works for the paper and margin layout you want to use. The **File**, **Page Setup** command opens the tabbed dialogue box shown below. The settings in the three sections of this box are the UK default.

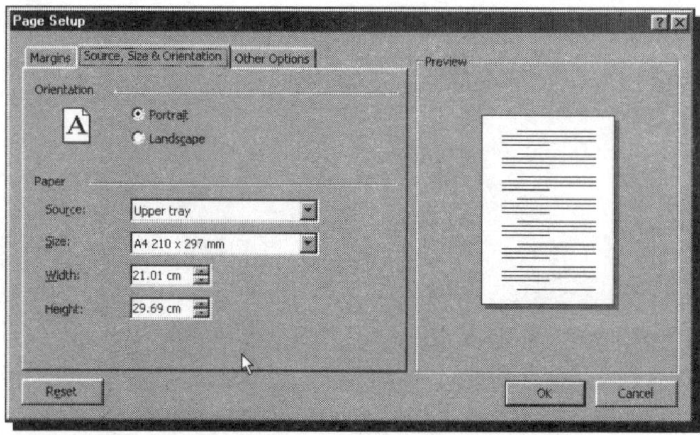

The **Source, Size and Orientation** section, shown above, defaults to A4 size paper (210 x 297 mm). If you want to use a different size paper just select a standard size from the **Size** drop down list, or type in new dimensions for **Width** and **Height**. The default orientation is **Portrait** mode with the height of a page being greater than the width.

The **Margins** section includes settings for **Top, Bottom, Left** and **Right** margins, which are the non-print areas required on each edge of the paper. The **Header** margin is that required between the top of the page and the header line. The **Footer** margin is that between the bottom of the page and the footer line.

The **Other Options** tabbed section gives you control over the **Starting page number** which will normally be '1' unless you break up a piece of work into parts, or chapters, and of the printing of headers and footers, discussed in the next chapter.

Print Preview

Works gives you an easy way of checking what your printer will produce with the **File**, **Print Preview** command, also actioned by clicking the print preview Toolbar button. It lets you see a screen view of what the printed page should look like, similar to that shown below.

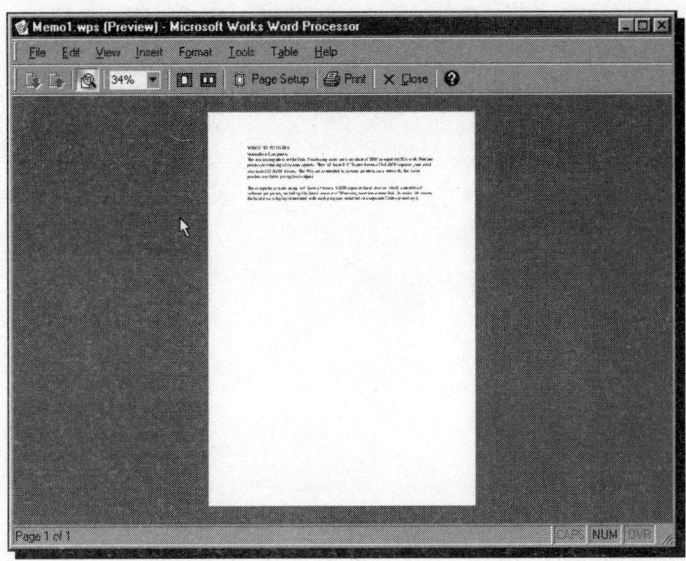

You can zoom in or out with the Magnifier button and then click the mouse pointer over a section of the page, to see your work at different magnification levels, and step through a multi-page document with the Previous or Next buttons.

With a long document you can also click the Multiple Pages button to get an overview of how the whole file will look when printed. To change page settings, such as margins and paper size as discussed earlier, click the Page Setup button.

If you are happy with the preview, press Print to print the document, otherwise press Close to exit Preview. All in all quite an improvement on the previous version of Print Preview.

3

More Advanced WP Features

Paragraph Formatting

Works defines a paragraph, as any text which is followed by a paragraph mark (which appears as a '¶' character on the screen, but only when switched on). So single line titles, as well as long typed text, can form paragraphs. Paragraph markers are not normally shown in Works, but toggling the **View**, **All Characters** command, or the Show All Toolbar button, will toggle them on and off. The example below shows our file **Memo1** with formatting characters switched on. This facility can be very useful when you are laying out a complicated page of data. Note how blank space characters show as a '·' character.

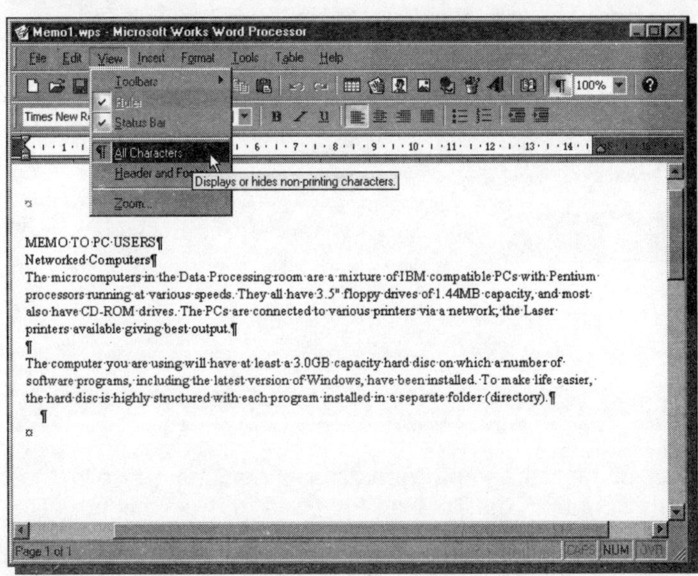

A paragraph marker is placed in a document every time <Enter> is pressed. All paragraph formatting, such as alignment, justification, centring, indenting and line spacing, is stored in the marker for the particular paragraph. If this marker is deleted, or moved, the formatting will be deleted or moved with it.

Indenting Text

Most documents with lists, or numbered sections, will require some form of paragraph indenting. An indent is the space between the margin and the edge of the text in the paragraph. This can be on the left or right side of the page.

Retrieve the file **Memo1** and type '1. ' and '2. ' before the first words of the two main text paragraphs. Select the two paragraphs and press **Format**, **Paragraph**, **Indents and Alignment** to open the dialogue box below.

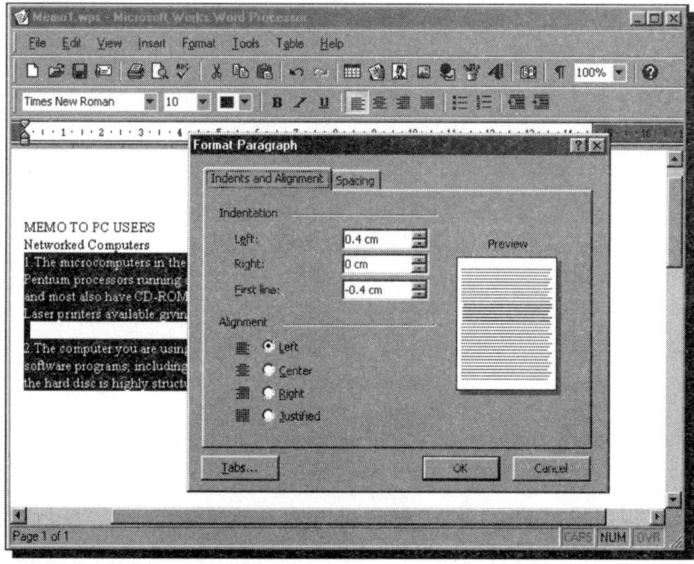

Most of the paragraph formatting operations can either be carried out from the Toolbar, the Ruler, or from this box. The alignment box offers:

Left	Smooth left edge, ragged right
Center	Text centred on line
Right	Smooth right edge, ragged left
Justified	Smooth left and right edges

To create left or right indents for the whole paragraph, type the amount of indent in the respective space, in centimetres. If only the first line is to be indented, type the amount needed in the **First Line**, **Indentation** space.

If you select the **Spacing** tab you will find options to fully control the spacing between lines of text and paragraphs. Under **Line Spacing** you can select several spacing options between single and quadruple. The **Lines Before** and **Lines After** options let you control the amount of white space you want above and below a selected paragraph.

Hanging Indents

The dialogue box on the previous page is set up to produce hanging indents, so that the paragraph numbers show up clearly at the left of the paragraphs.

To do this you should type the same value in the **First Line** box - with a negative sign in front - as that typed in the **Left**, **Indentations** box. When you have finished, and saved the document as **Memo2**, the text area of your screen should look the same as that shown below.

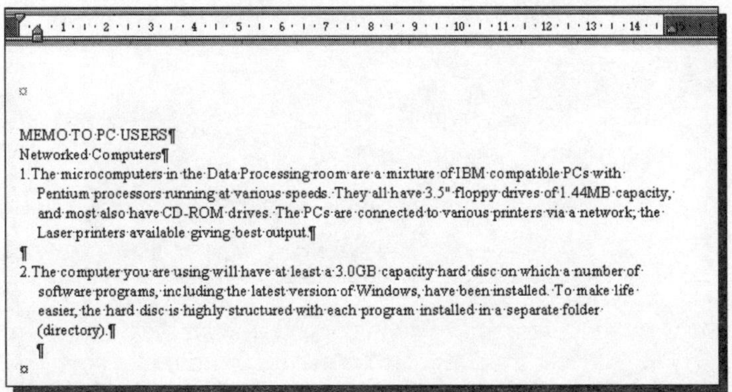

MEMO TO PC USERS¶
Networked Computers¶
1. The microcomputers in the Data Processing room are a mixture of IBM compatible PCs with Pentium processors running at various speeds. They all have 3.5" floppy drives of 1.44MB capacity, and most also have CD-ROM drives. The PCs are connected to various printers via a network; the Laser printers available giving best output.¶
¶
2. The computer you are using will have at least a 3.0GB capacity hard disc on which a number of software programs, including the latest version of Windows, have been installed. To make life easier, the hard disc is highly structured with each program installed in a separate folder (directory).¶
¶

Indenting with the Ruler

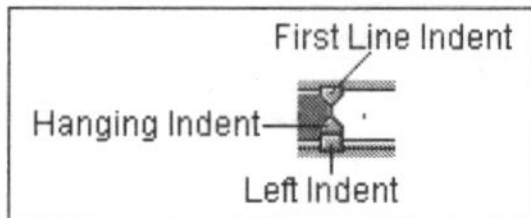

If you look carefully at the Ruler at the top of the screen, after you have placed an indent, you should see that an indent marker has been placed on it. This gives you another way of quickly setting and adjusting indents. You simply drag the marker to the new indent position, as shown by the drop down vertical line, and any selected paragraphs will be indented when you release the mouse button.

Paragraph Borders

As well as the Microsoft Draw and WordArt packages, which are described later, Works 2000 has the facility to place different types of lines, colours and shading patterns in and around selected paragraphs and pages, with the **Format, Borders and Shading** command. An example of the Borders and Shading box and the results of its settings is shown below.

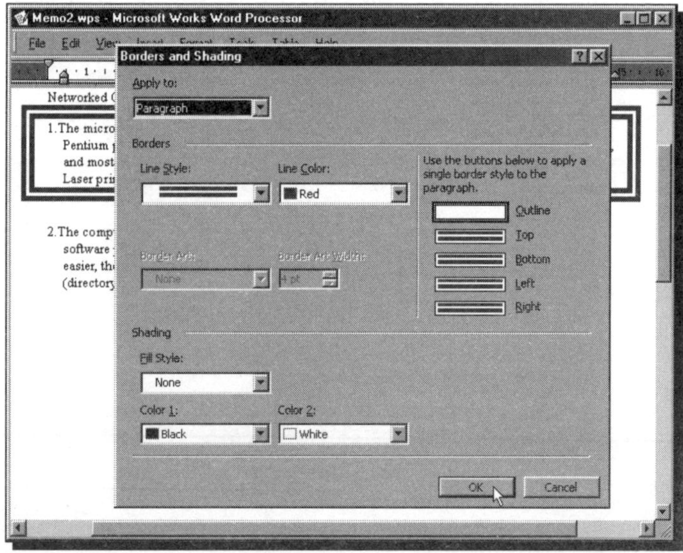

First, select the paragraphs you want to enhance, then in the Borders and Shading box turn on the type of border you want, its **Line Style** and its **Line Color**, (not very English!) and then press <Enter>, or select **OK**. To remove borders you must cancel the selections made in these boxes.

Even if you do not need these features very often, they are well worth exploring.

Text Enhancement

Tab Settings

The Works 2000 word processor defaults to left aligned tabs every 1.27cm, or 0.5in, across the page. For most purposes these will be adequate, but if you need to generate lists, or tables, indexes, etc., the custom tab facility could prove useful. You could, of course, use the Table feature for these as well. There are four types of custom tab stops:

Left	Text aligns to the right of tab
Right	Text aligns to the left of tab
Center	Text centres on tab stop
Decimal	Text aligns at a decimal point

Tabs are shown on the ruler at the top of the screen, as can be seen in our example on the next page.

All default tabs to the left of a new custom tab are removed automatically. You can also select one of four types of leader characters to fill the space to the tab spot. This is useful when preparing contents pages.

Our next example shows part of a contents page which has two **Left** aligned tabs for the subjects, and a **Right** tab with a dot leader for the page numbers. To set custom tab stops, select the required paragraph, or the whole document, and either double click your mouse on the ruler, or choose **Format, Tabs**. A dialogue box like the one shown on the next page will open.

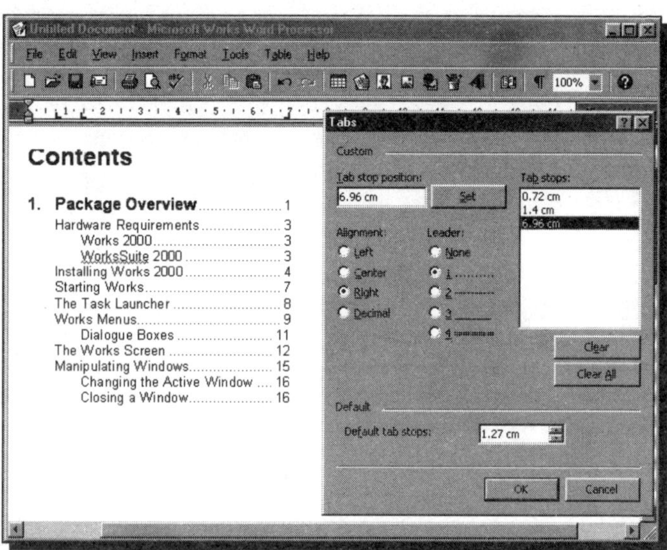

If necessary, type the **Tab stop position** in the text box, select the options needed from the **Alignment** and **Leader** boxes and choose **OK** to place the tab on the ruler. This operation can be repeated for as many tabs as are required. Use the **Clear**, or **Clear All** buttons to remove one tab, or all the tabs, from the ruler.

Tables of figures can be created, and adjusted, by the careful use of tab settings. Use decimal, or right aligned tab stops, for columns of figures. It is an easy matter to readjust the width of columns by resetting the tabs, even after the table has been created.

The Tables feature, discussed later in the chapter, is an easier way of creating such tables however.

Headers and Footers

In a printed document a header is text that appears at the top of each page of the document, whilst a footer appears at the bottom. These can be used to add page numbers, titles, dates and times to your documents.

These are easily added in the Works 2000 word processor by simply typing text, and embedding code, in the WYSIWYG Header and Footer boxes at the top and bottom of the screen page. To place these boxes the first time you need to use the **View**, **Header and Footer** command. Once you have placed one in a document you can double-click in it to access it.

A header is shown in the next example below. This can be added to the file **Memo2** as follows.

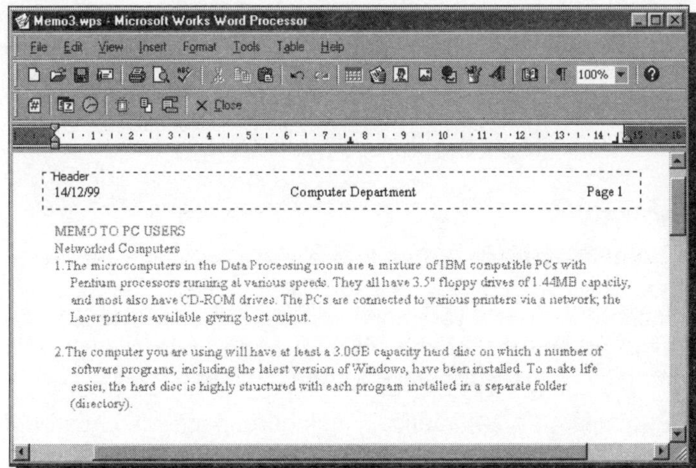

Use the **View**, **Header and Footer** command to open the Header box and right-click on the right end of the Ruler to place a right custom tab. For some reason this version of the Works word processor does not provide this tab automatically. A new Toolbar, as shown above should have been added to the Works window. Move the cursor to the start of the header box and add the date special command by clicking the Insert Date button, or typing <Ctrl+D>, or using the **Insert**, **Date and Time** menu command.

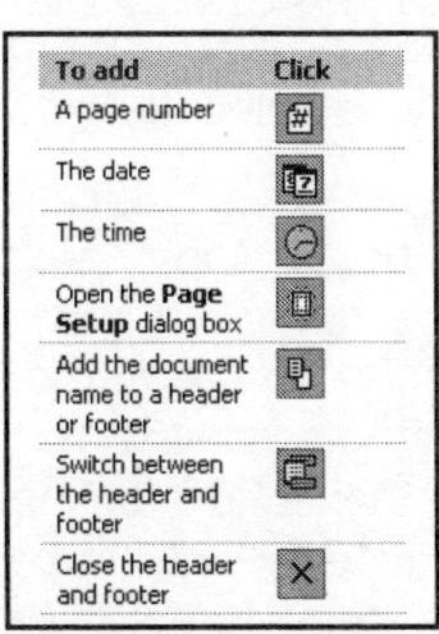

To add	Click
A page number	
The date	
The time	
Open the **Page Setup** dialog box	
Add the document name to a header or footer	
Switch between the header and footer	
Close the header and footer	

With the latter method you can choose the format of the date. This adds today's date to the screen, but will print the current date on paper. Press <Tab> and the cursor is automatically centred on the line. Add a title and press <Tab> again to bring the cursor to the right-hand side of the page. Type 'Page ' followed by the **Insert**, **Page Numbers** command, or click the Insert Page Number button to place the page number, and save as **Memo3**.

Your screen should now look like ours, with the main body of the memo 'greyed out'. Double-clicking there will re-activate the main area and grey out the header box. You could use the **File**, **Print Preview** command to quickly check the printed result. If you want, you can add enhancements, or change the fonts of the header and footer text.

Footnotes

A useful feature in Works is the ability to place reference marks, or numbers, anywhere in a document. Text can be 'attached' to each reference, which will automatically be printed at the end of the relevant page. This operation is carried out with the **Insert**, **Footnote** command.

Footnotes are automatically numbered, and renumbered if edited, but you can also specify other reference marks (such as * or $, for example).

To create a footnote, move the cursor to the position in the document where the reference mark is needed, choose **Insert**, **Footnote,** alter the dialogue box if you want to force a mark instead of a numbered reference, and select **Insert**.

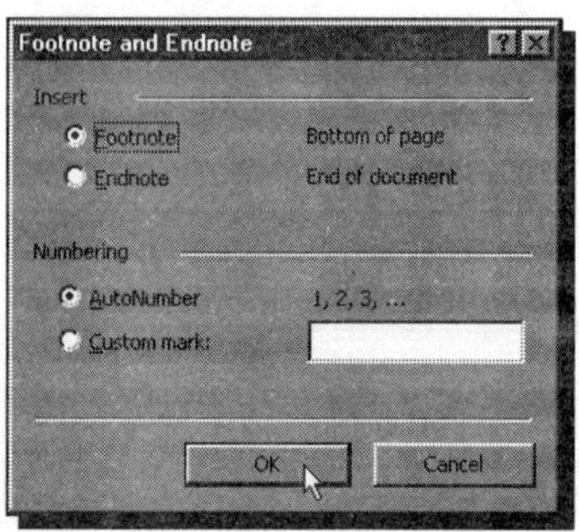

If **Autonumber** is selected in the box, the next consecutive footnote number will be placed at the cursor and the footnote pane will be opened at the bottom of the page. You type the reference text here, and format, or enhance it, if required. You move the cursor back to the document with the mouse when you are ready, or double-click on the reference number.

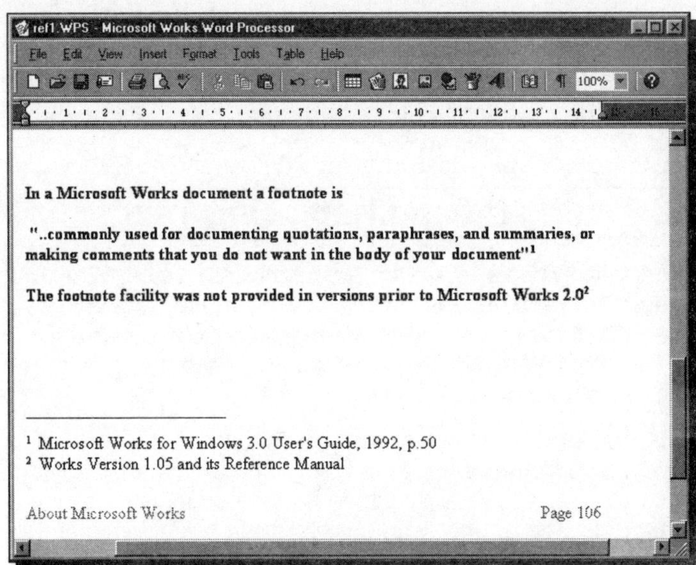

Our example above shows two footnotes placed in the body text, and the note text at the bottom of the page.

Once placed, footnote reference marks are always shown in the document. Footnote text can be edited, the same as any other text and reference marks can also be moved, copied or deleted, with Works looking after the positioning of the attached text.

Endnotes

When you print a document that contains footnotes, they are placed at the bottom of the page holding the reference point. To force your reference text to be printed at the end of the main body of the document text, place them as described above, but check **Endnote** in the Footnotes and Endnotes dialogue box.

Your final printed presentation of these endnotes will be improved if you place blank lines at the end of your document text. Without these the endnote text will be printed immediately under the last line of document text. Any reference heading required should then be placed after these blank lines.

With Works 2000 you can have footnotes and endnotes in the same document, but only one of them can be automatically numbered.

Searching for and Replacing Text

Works allows you to search for specifically selected text, or character combinations. In the search mode, actioned with the **Edit**, **Find** command, it will highlight each occurrence in turn so that you can carry out some action on it, such as change its font or appearance.

In the **Edit**, **Replace** mode you specify what replacement is to be automatically carried out. For example, in a long book chapter you may decide to replace every occurrence of the word 'programme' with the word 'program'. This is very easy to do.

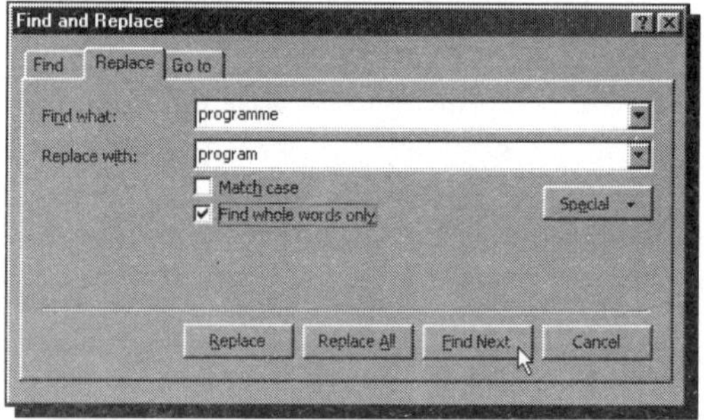

First go to the beginning of the file, as search only operates in a forward direction, then choose **Edit**, **Replace.** In the **Find what** box, type **programme**, and in the **Replace with** box type **program**. To make sure that part words are not selected, choose the **Find whole words only** option, and then click the **Find Next** button. The first match will be highlighted in the document then either choose **Replace**, to change once, or **Replace All** for automatic replacement.

If you select the **Match case** option, only text with the exactly specified case letters will be selected.

The **Special** button gives options for searching for, and replacing, special characters, or a combination of text and special characters (for example, tab or paragraph marks, or white space). White space is a combination of any number of consecutive spaces and tab marks. A very useful example of this is when you have imported columnar data from another file, and the columns are separated with spaces; you can search for white space, and replace it with a tab, to realign the columns.

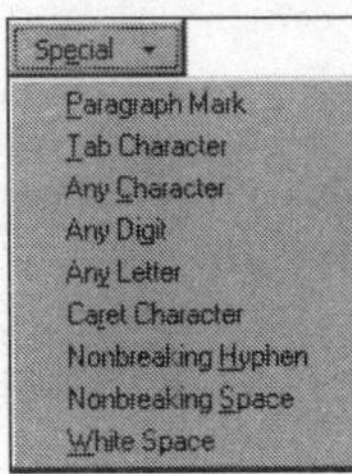

Another example would be searching for a word, which occurs at the beginning of a paragraph, or after a tab. The list below also gives the key combinations of these special characters to enable them to be entered straight into the Find and Replace boxes.

To type the caret (^) character, press <Shift+6>.

To search for, or replace	***Type***
Tab mark	^t
Paragraph mark	^p
Non-breaking space	^s
Non-breaking hyphen	^~
Caret (^)	^^
White space	^w
Any character (wild card)	^?
Any digit	^#
Any letter	^$

Using the Spell Checker

If you have a problem with spelling, the new spell checker in the Works 2000 word processor will be a popular part of the package! As you type text into your document the checker compares every word with the contents of its built-in dictionary. When it finds a word it does not recognise it places a red wavy line under it. If you right-click on such a word, as shown here, you have the choice of accepting a suggested correction, ignoring it, or of adding the word to your dictionary. With the latter option the word will be recognised in the future.

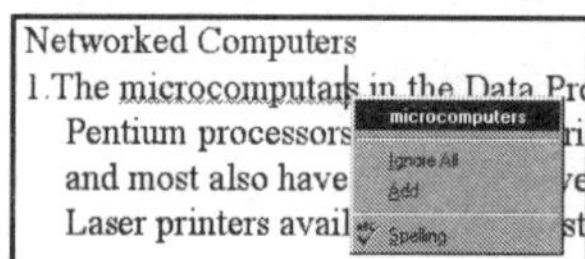

If you select the Spelling option from the above menu, the Spelling and Grammar dialogue box opens, as shown below. Here though, we opened it by clicking the Spelling and Grammar button on the Toolbar, and we could also have used the **Tools**, **Spelling and Grammar** menu command, or the **F7** key.

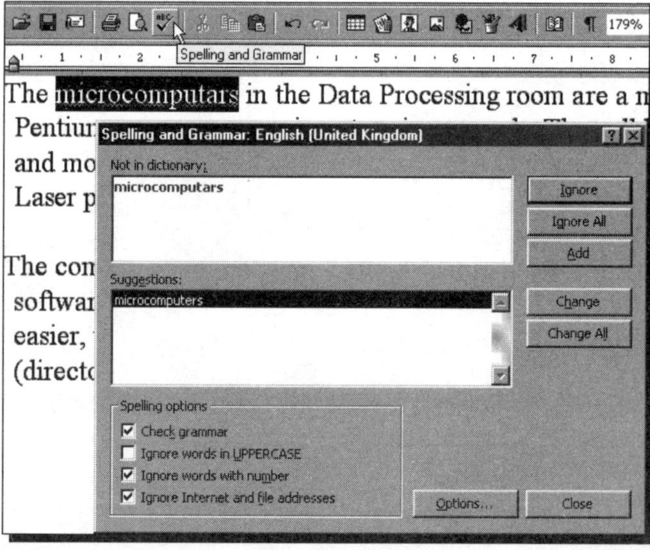

This is the way to check the spelling of a whole document. It will search for wrongly spelled words, words with incorrect capitalisation, incorrect hyphenation, and repeated words, such as 'if if'. It has a large built-in dictionary, and you can add other words that you may need to check for in the future.

A suspect word will be highlighted in the document, and will also be placed in the **Not in dictionary** box. You have several options now:

a. To leave the word unchanged choose **Ignore** for this occurrence, or **Ignore All**.

b. To change the word, edit, or re-type it, in the box, and choose **Change**, or **Change All** to change all instances of that word in the document.

c. Choose from the list of **Suggestions**, and then click **Change**.

d. To add an edited word to the dictionary, choose **Add**.

As long as **Check Grammar** is selected in the **Spelling options** box, Works also checks your grammar at the same time. Grammatical errors are highlighted in green. If you do not understand the flagged error, clicking the **Explain Rule** button will open an explanation box like that shown here.

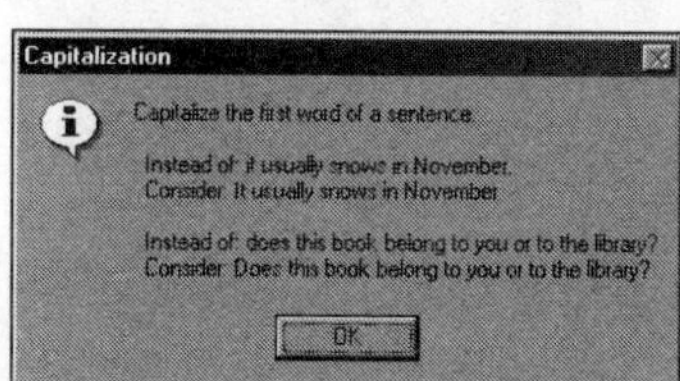

When you have made your choice, the program continues searching the rest of the document. To leave the checker at any time choose **Close**. We found the Spell Checker to be a vast improvement on the previous version of Works.

Using the Thesaurus

To help you with composing your documents Works has a built-in thesaurus. With this you should be able to find a synonym, or word with a similar meaning, for most words.

First double-click the word you want to change to select it, and choose **Tools**, **Thesaurus**, or press the <Shift+F7> keys. This opens the dialogue box shown below.

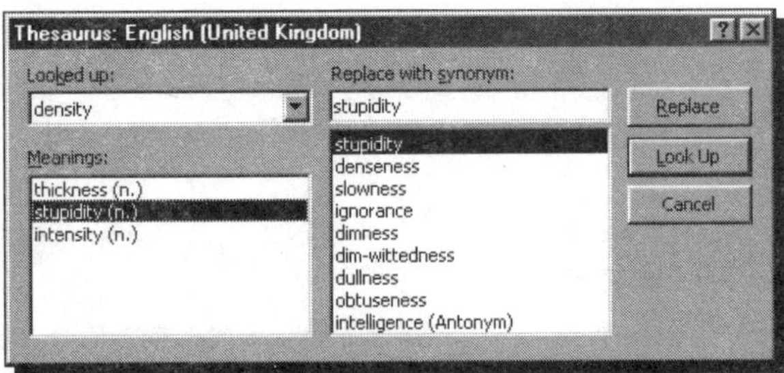

In the **Meanings** box, on the left, are suggestions of the main meanings of the selected word. Depending on the context in the document, you need to select one of these meanings, and then look in the **Replace with synonym** box for a list of possible replacement words.

In the example shown 'density' was the word highlighted in the document. The noun 'stupidity' was selected from the **Meanings** list which produced the eight synonyms shown, and an antonym (opposite meaning). If you select one of the synonyms and press **Look Up** you should get more alternatives to look at.

To replace the original word highlighted in your document, select the best alternative and choose **Replace**.

Word Count

Works includes the facility to count the words in a document. This can be useful if you are working on an assignment that requires a specific number of words. The program considers a word to be any text between two space characters.

To carry out a count use the **Tools**, **Word Count** command. The whole document will be counted, with the exception of text in footnotes, headers and footers.

Adding a Table to a Document

The ability to use Tables is built into most top-range word processors these days. This feature in the Works 2000 word processor has been 'cut down' from previous versions to such an extent that it is now only suitable for creating lists without using tabs.

Tables are used to create adjacent columns of text and numeric data, a table being simply a grid of columns and rows with the intersection of a column and row forming a rectangular box referred to as a 'cell'. Data is placed into individual cells that are organised into columns and rows. You can modify the appearance of table data by applying text formatting and enhancements.

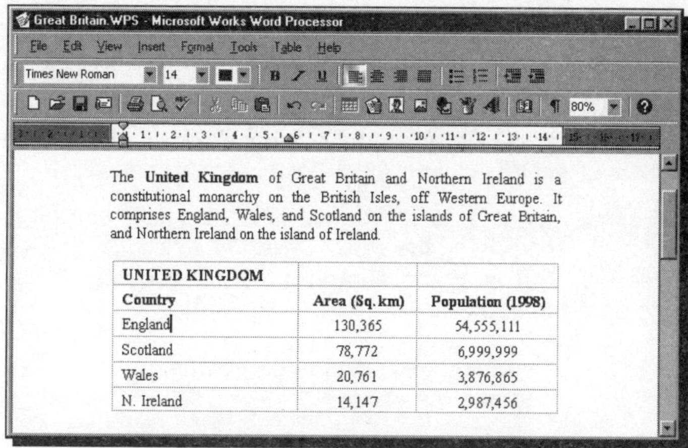

The **United Kingdom** of Great Britain and Northern Ireland is a constitutional monarchy on the British Isles, off Western Europe. It comprises England, Wales, and Scotland on the islands of Great Britain, and Northern Ireland on the island of Ireland.

UNITED KINGDOM		
Country	**Area (Sq.km)**	**Population (1998)**
England	130,365	54,555,111
Scotland	78,772	6,999,999
Wales	20,761	3,876,865
N. Ireland	14,147	2,987,456

As an example we will step through the process of creating the table shown above. To build this geographical, but non-political, example place the insertion point after the document body text and use the **Table Insert Table** command, or click the Insert Table button.

In the opened dialogue box, shown on the next page, enter 7 as the **Number of rows** and 3 in the **Number of columns** as 3. There are 17 different table formats to choose from, but we used 'None' as a starter.

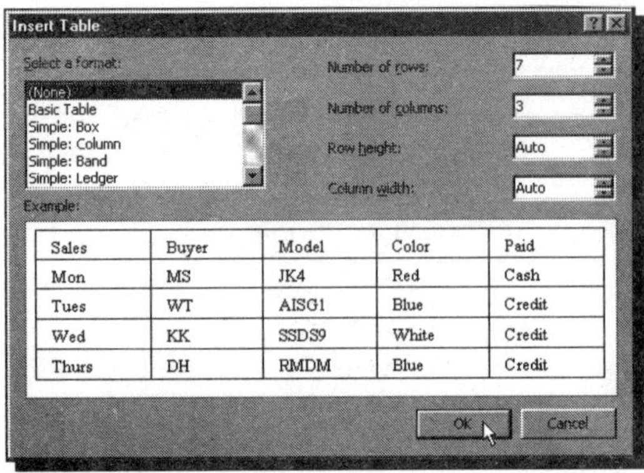

When you are happy with the procedures we suggest you experiment with the other formats.

Pressing **OK** returns you to your document in which a full width table has been placed. If you are in the mood, enter the data as shown. To format the column titles you can select the whole of the second row by moving the pointer to the left of it and clicking when it changes to a right sloping arrow. Then click the Bold and Centre Align Toolbar icons.

Format any other data that needs it and finally turn off the gridlines, by selecting the whole table, right-clicking on it, and selecting **Borders and Shading** from the context menu. This opens the box shown below.

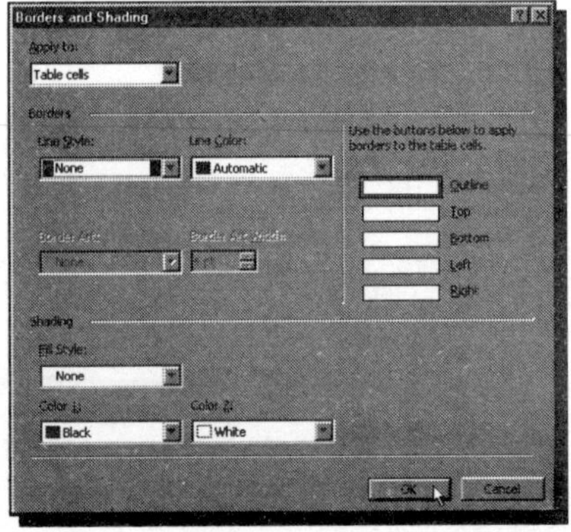

Make sure that **Table cells** is selected in the **Apply to** drop-down box, select **None** in the **Line Style** drop-down box, and then click on each of the **Outline**, **Top**, **Bottom**, **Left** and **Right** buttons in turn. We will leave it to you to experiment with the other features in this box.

Inserting a Spreadsheet

The reason the Tables feature has been so down-graded seems to be that you can now embed a spreadsheet into your document, using the **Insert**, **Spreadsheet** menu command, or Toolbar button. Inserting a spreadsheet gives you access to the functionality of a spreadsheet without leaving the document.

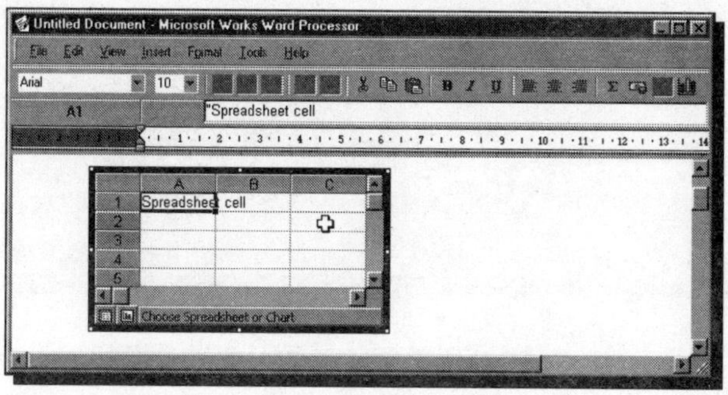

A new, blank spreadsheet appears in the document, as shown above. To start typing data, double-click the spreadsheet, which then becomes 'active', and the Spreadsheet toolbar and menus replace those of the Word Processor.

To view the data in a chart, if there is one in the spreadsheet, click Chart at the bottom of the spreadsheet frame. To view the data in the spreadsheet again, click Spreadsheet at the bottom of the frame.

To return to the Word Processor document, click outside the spreadsheet or chart. A useful feature, but you may have to spend some time in the spreadsheet chapters of this book to get the best out of it.

Using a Text Box

A Text Box lets you place text with a different size, orientation, or format anywhere within the body of a document, and have the document text wrap around it, as shown in our example below.

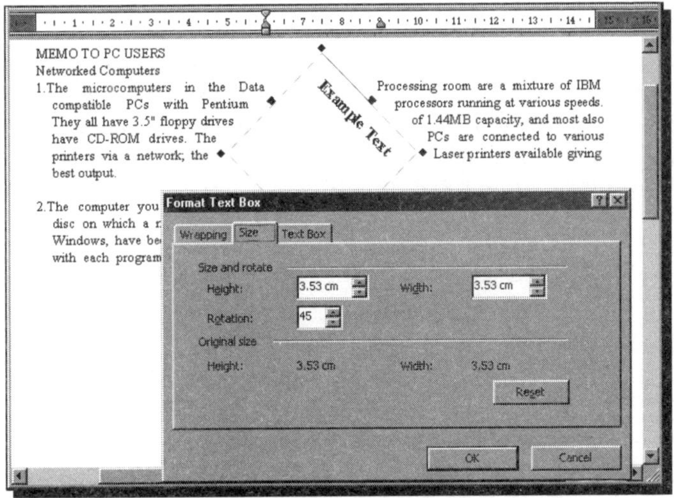

Here we have used the **Insert**, **Text Box** command, typed some text into the Text Box, and dragged it to its final position by clicking and dragging it when the mouse pointer changes to that shown here.

The **Format**, **Text Box** command opens the dialogue box above. Options in the **Size** tabbed sheet give you complete control of the Text Box size and also lets you rotate it, as in our example above. The **Wrapping** tab options give you control of how the document text 'wraps' around the Text Box, and the **Text Box** tab options let you control the Text Box internal margins. Quite a useful feature.

****

That completes our coverage of the Works 2000 word processor, but the next chapter on Microsoft's Accessories is equally applicable to this program as well as to Word 2000.

4

Microsoft's Accessories

Works 2000 installs several accessories which you can use with either of the word processors provided with the two different versions. We describe some of these accessories in this chapter, but you should be aware that they may behave slightly differently depending on which versions of the word processors you have. In fact, some of these accessories are available to any program by using its **Insert**, **Object** menu command, but in our discussions that follow we use the standard Works 2000 word processor to explain them.

Adding a Note to your Document

A very useful facility is the ability to add 'pop-up' notes anywhere in your documents. To do this, place the cursor where you want a Note to be placed, action the **Insert**, **Object** command and select **Microsoft Note-It** from the opened dialogue box, as shown below. This opens the Microsoft Note-It box on the next page.

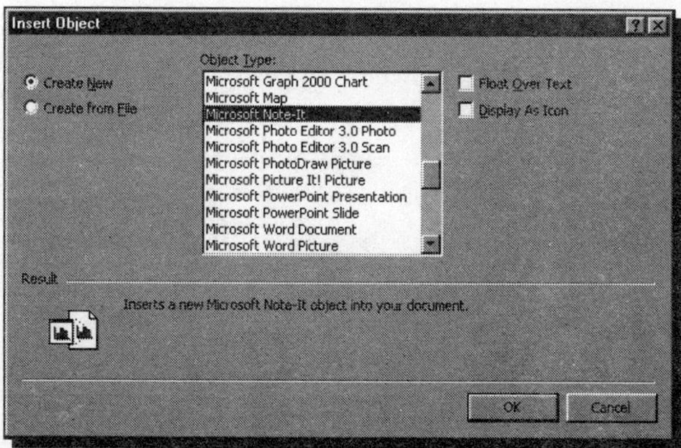

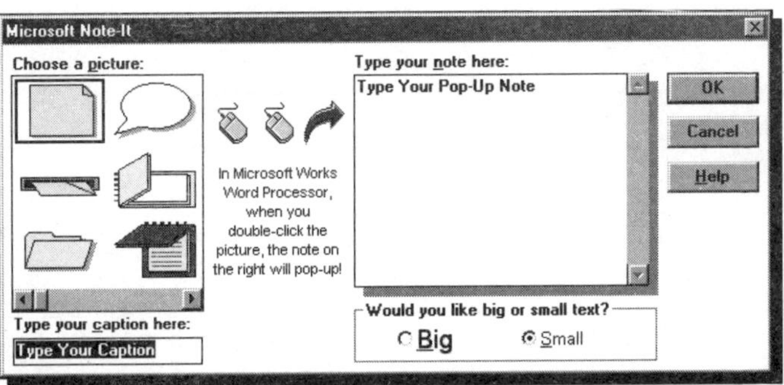

The **Choose a picture** box gives you the amazing choice of 58 different note types. If it turns you on, you can liven up your document no end! To place a caption under the displayed note, type the required text in the **Type your caption here** text box. The main text to be 'hidden' in the note is typed in the **Type your note here** box. Select the size of Note text you want from the **Big** and **Small** options and finally press **OK** to place your note.

At any time in the future the note text can be read by double clicking on the note, as shown in our example below.

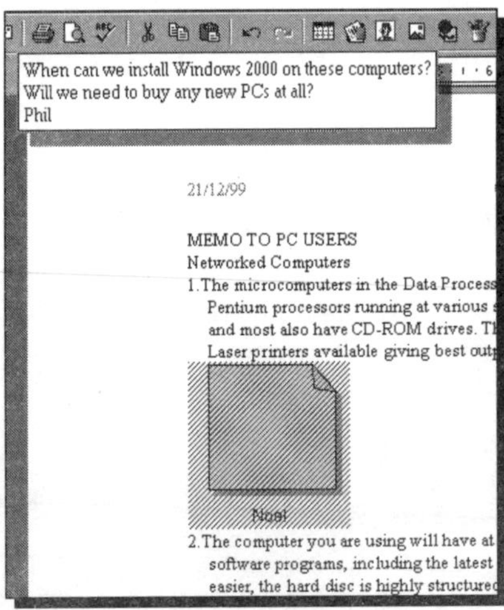

Notes can be very useful if several people are editing a document and they want to make comments for the others to see. Each person would then choose a different shape of note icon, which would be recognisable by the rest of the team.

Adding WordArt to your Document

The WordArt facility lets you easily create quite eye-catching title lines for your documents. To use it, place the insertion point where you want the heading and use the **Insert**, **Object**, **WordArt** command, or click the WordArt Toolbar icon. Type your heading text and note that a new Toolbar has been added to the screen, as shown below.

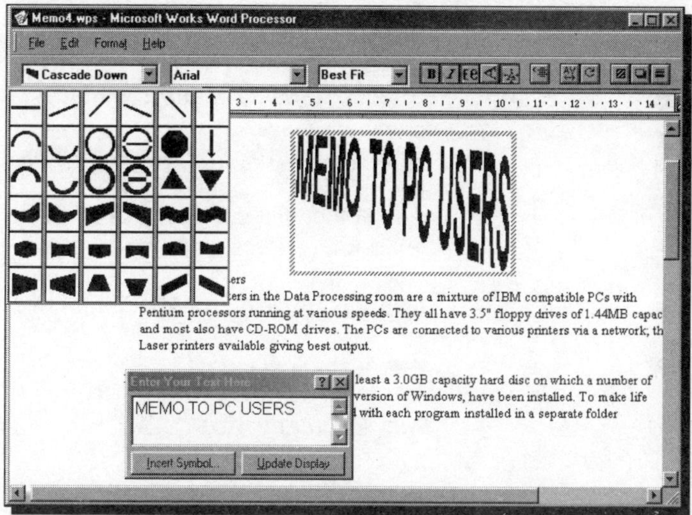

This also shows the shapes available in the drop down menu opened on the left of the bar. The buttons on the Toolbar are used to design the look of your WordArt text, as follows:

Click	*To*
Plain Text (drop-down)	Choose a shape for WordArt
Arial (drop-down)	Change the font
Best Fit (drop-down)	Change the font size
B	Make text bold
I	Make text italic
Ee	Make letters all the same height, regardless of their capitalisation
	Flip letters on their side
	Stretch text to the edges of the frame
	Choose how text aligns in a frame
	Change the spacing between letters
	Adjust the shape of the text, or rotate text within a frame
	Change the colour or shading of text
	Add a shadow to text
	Add a border to text

When your heading looks the way you want, simply click the pointer outside the dialogue box to return to your document, which should now have the new heading placed on it. You can edit a WordArt graphic at any time by double-clicking it.

WordArt has its own Help system built in, which is well worth looking into.

Adding Graphics to a Document

It is a very easy matter to add a ClipArt drawing to your documents. Works comes with a folder (or more) of professional graphics for you to use. They are added by clicking the Insert Clip Art button, or with the **Insert**, **Picture**, **ClipArt** command, which opens a Microsoft Clip Gallery shown below.

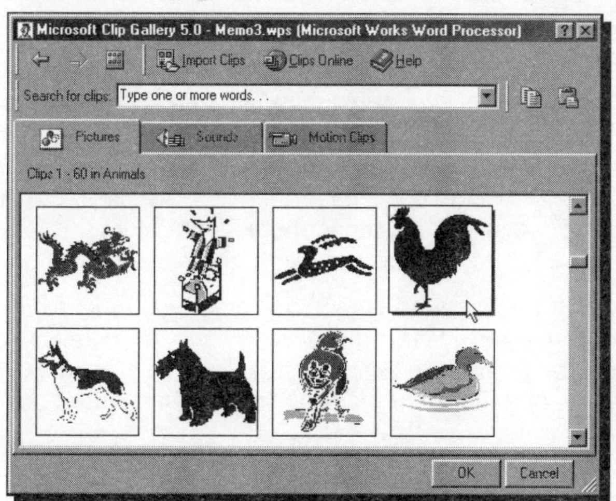

This dialogue box allows you to select a category of Clip Art pictures which then displays various graphics held under this category. We selected Animals, then the cockerel, and clicked the **Insert clip** button, pointed to here, which brought the graphic into our document.

The **Format**, **Object**, **Wrapping** commands allow you to select the wrapping style for the inserted object. Once you have done this, the graphic is 'released' and you can then move it, otherwise it remains locked in the inserted position. The display on the next page shows the result of selecting the **Tight** option of wrapping. Pointing to the inserted graphic, changes the mouse pointer to a four-headed arrow which allows you to move the graphic to the required position. Note that the graphic was inserted in the document without the need for a containing frame, which allows for better wrapping around it.

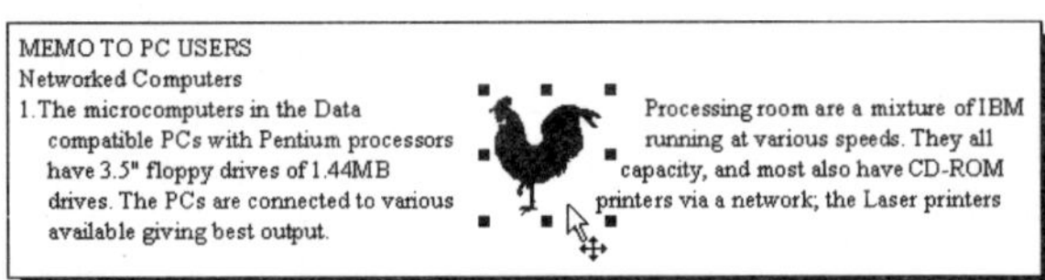

Inserting a Graphic File Image

If you have a graphic image or photograph saved in file format (maybe from the Internet, a digital camera or scanner) it is easy to add this to a document. Use the **Insert**, **Picture**, **From File** command, or click the Insert Picture Toolbar button shown here, and select the file from the opened dialogue box.

As with any inserted object in Works, you have to use the **Format**, **Object**, **Wrapping** commands and select either **Square** or **Tight** before you can then move a picture around the page, otherwise it remains locked in the inserted position.

Microsoft Draw

To create a new drawing in your document, place the insertion point where you want the drawing and use the **Insert**, **Picture**, **New Drawing** command, or click the New Drawing Toolbar button shown here. This opens Microsoft Draw, places a frame in the document for the new drawing, and opens the Autoshapes, floating toolbar as shown at the top of the next page.

You can then use the Drawing tools to create, or edit, a graphic consisting of lines, arcs, ellipses, rectangles, and even text boxes. These can either exist in their own right, or be additions to a picture or object.

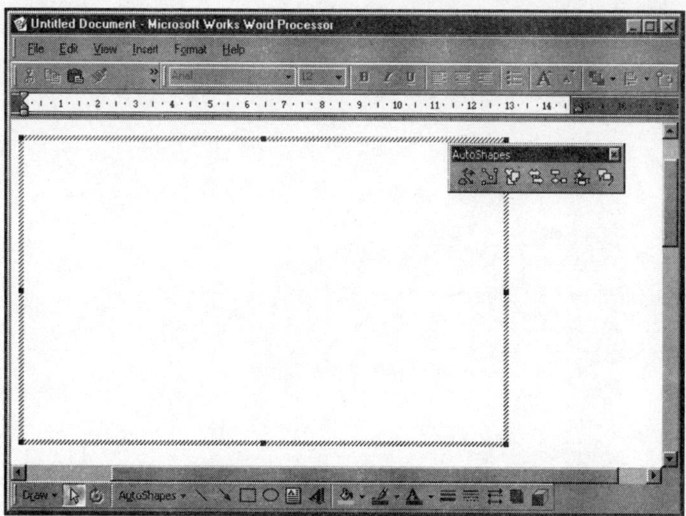

The Draw Help System

If you action the **Help** menu command while Microsoft Draw is in control of your document, you can access a 'normal' Windows help window, as shown below. This gives very detailed help information on the package, unlike most of the Works 2000 help windows! Progress?

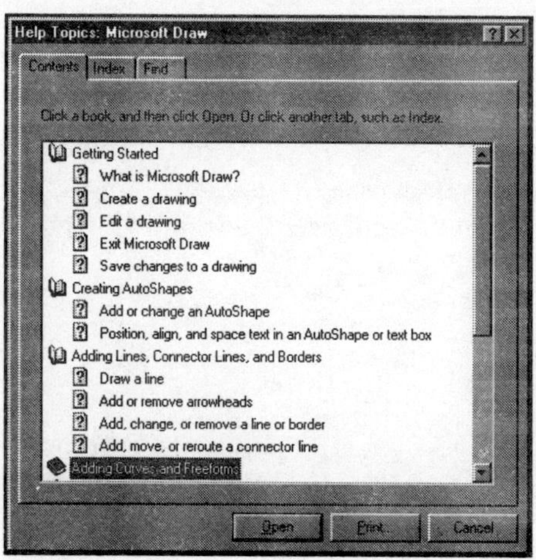

The Draw Toolbar

The various buttons on the Draw toolbar have the following functions:

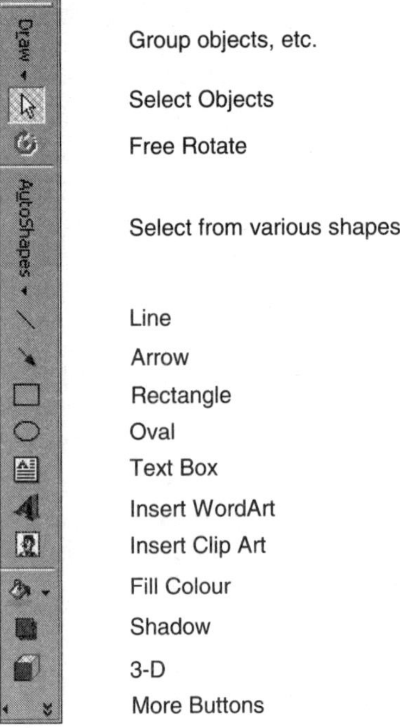

Amongst the many features available from the toolbar are:

AutoShapes – the additional AutoShape categories, such as connectors, block arrows, flowchart symbols, stars and banners, callouts, and action buttons make drawing diagrams much easier.

Bezier curves – used to easily create exact curves with pinpoint precision.

3-D effects – allow you to transform 2-D shapes into realistic 3-D objects with new 3-D effects, such as changing the lighting perspective of a 3-D object.

Perspective shadows – allow you to select from a wide range of shadows with perspective, and you can adjust the depth and angle of each shadow to make pictures more realistic.

Connectors – used to create diagrams and flowcharts with new straight, angled, and curved connectors between the shapes; when shapes are moved, the connectors remain attached and automatically reposition themselves.

Arrowhead styles – allow you to change the width and height of arrowheads for maximum effect.

Object alignment – allow you to distribute and space objects evenly, both horizontally and vertically.

Precise line-width control – allows you increased control over the width of lines by selecting pre-set options or customised line widths.

Image editing – lets you easily adjust the brightness or contrast of a picture.

Transparent background – allows you to insert a bit map on your slides or Web pages so as to appear to be part of the design by turning background colours into transparent areas.

Creating a Drawing

The effects of the drawing tools can be superimposed either on the document area or on top of a graphic. The result is that you can annotate drawings and pictures to your heart's desire.

To create an object, click on the required Drawing button, such as the **Oval** or **Rectangle**, position the mouse pointer where you want to create the object on the screen, and then drag the mouse to draw the object. Hold the <Shift> key while you drag the mouse to create a perfect circle or square. If you do not hold <Shift>, Draw creates an oval or a rectangle.

You can use the **AutoShapes** toolbar or button to select from a variety of pre-drawn **Lines**, **Basic Shapes**, etc. First click on the desired line or shape, then position the mouse pointer where you want to create the object on the screen and click the left mouse button to fix it in that position.

Editing a Drawing

To select an object, click on it. Draw displays white handles around the object selected.

You can move an object, or multiple objects, within a draw area by selecting them and dragging to the desired position. To copy an object, click at the object, then use the **Edit, Copy** / **Edit, Paste** commands.

To size an object, position the mouse pointer on a white handle and then drag the handle until the object is the desired shape and size.

To delete an object, select it and press the <Del> key. To delete a drawing, hold the <Shift> key down and click each object in turn that makes up the drawing, unless they are grouped or framed, then press <Del>.

Using Layered Drawings

You can right-click an object, select the **Order** option from the displayed shortcut menu, then use the **Bring to Front** or **Send to Back** sub-menu options to determine the order of layered drawings. Drawings, or pictures, layered on top of each other can create useful visual effects, provided you remember that the top drawing and/or picture obscures the one below it, as shown below.

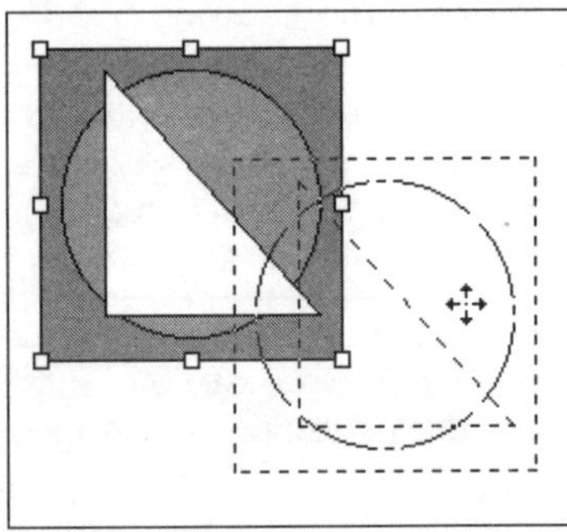

Here we have used Draw's Rectangle, Oval, and the AutoShapes, Right Angle options to draw the three displayed shapes. The order you draw these is not important as you can use the Bring to Front and Send to Back options to rearrange them to your taste. We then selected each shape in turn, and used the Fill Color button to give them different shades from the displayed options to the right.

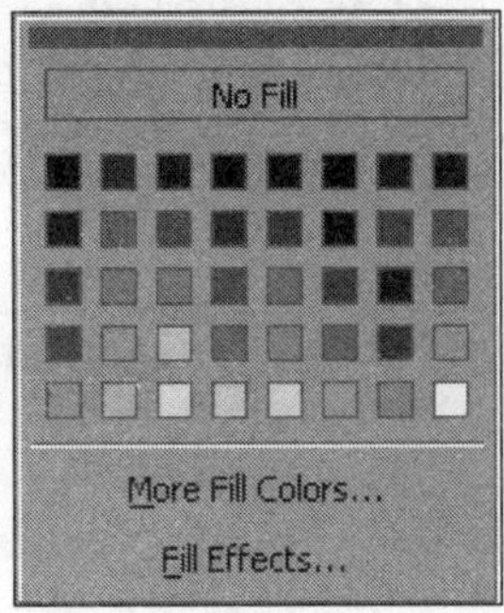

Finally, we selected each shape, while holding down the <Shift> key, then used the **Draw** button and clicked **Group** from the displayed menu to lock them together, before attempting to move the whole group down and to the right (you can tell they are grouped because attempting to move them, moves the whole group, shown above in a dotted outline).

We strongly recommend you to experiment with these and other options, like us you will almost certainly surprise yourself with the results.

Inserting a New Painting

To create a new painting in your document, place the insertion point where you want it and use the **Insert**, **Picture**, **New Painting** command, or click the New Painting Toolbar button shown here. This places a frame and opens Microsoft Paint, as shown below.

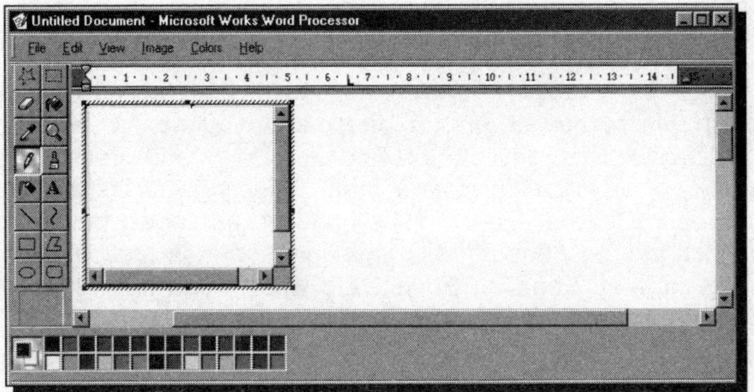

We do not have space here to describe the Paint program, which is actually one of Windows own accessories. If you do want more help on the package may we suggest you look at either of our books *Windows 98 explained* (BP 456), or *Windows 95 explained* (BP 400). Both are also published by BERNARD BABANI (publishing) Ltd.

Microsoft Equation

Another useful facility, for engineers and scientists (why should artists have all the fun?), is the ability to add equations anywhere in your documents. To do this, place the cursor where you want the equation, action the **Insert**, **Object** command and select 'Microsoft Equation 3.0' from the **Object type** list. This displays the Equation Editor shown below.

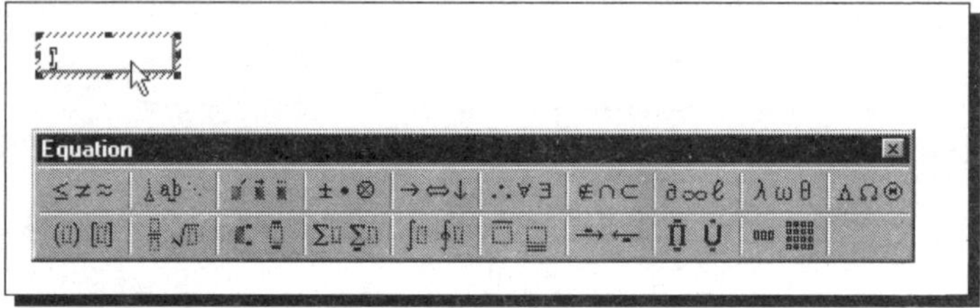

This allows you to build mathematical equations which can then be embedded in your document.

Inserting an Equation

If building equations is not your cup of tea, you can safely skip this section. If, on the other hand, you want to learn to build equations, activate the Equation Editor and press **F1** to display the following Help screen. Selecting the first option, reveals a further list of topics under it, as shown below, of which the most important to look up first are: 'Equation Editor Basics' and 'Equation Editor, and what it can do'. The first tells you about the Equation Toolbar and how you can use it.

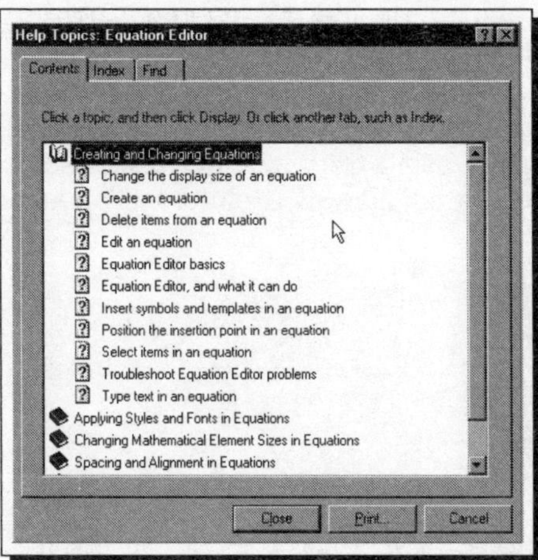

The top row of the Equation Editor toolbar has buttons for inserting more than 150 mathematical symbols, many of which are not available in the standard Symbol font.

To insert a symbol in an equation, click a button on the top row of the toolbar, as shown on the composite screen dump below, and then click the specific symbol from the palette that appears under the button.

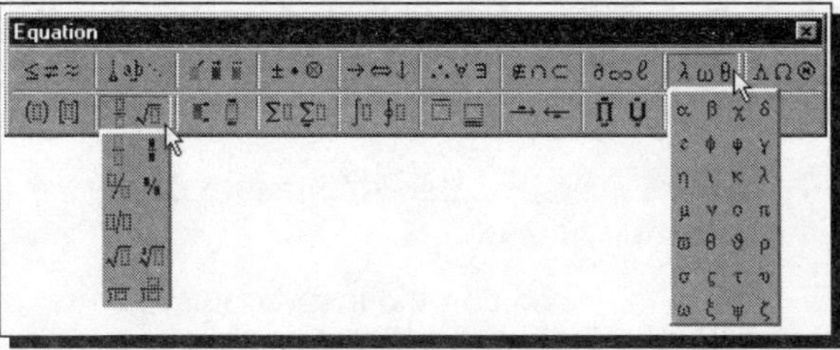

The bottom row of the Equation Editor toolbar has buttons for inserting templates or frameworks that contain such symbols as fractions, radicals, summations, integrals, products, matrices, and various fences or matching pairs of symbols such as brackets and braces. There are about 120 templates, grouped on palettes, many of which contain slots - spaces into which you type text and insert symbols.

Templates can be nested, by inserting them in the slots of other templates, to build complex hierarchical formulae.

As an example, we will take you through the steps required, when using the Equation Editor, to construct the equation for the solution of a quadratic equation, as shown below.

$$x = \frac{-b \pm \sqrt{\{b^2 - 4ac\}}}{2a}$$

To construct this equation, place the insertion pointer at the required place in your document, activate the Equation Editor, and follow the steps listed below. The templates and symbols you require from the Equation Editor are shown to the right of the appropriate step.

- Type ***x =*** followed by selecting the template shown here from the lower second button. 
- Type ***–b*** followed by selecting the ± symbol from the upper fourth button. 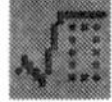
- Select the square root template shown here from the lower second button. 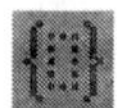
- Select the brackets template shown here from the lower first button. 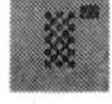
- Type ***b*** followed by selecting the template from the lower third button. 
- Type **2** and re-position the insertion pointer as shown here, and then type ***–4ac***. 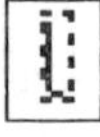
- Position the insertion pointer at the denominator and type ***2a***.

Obviously, the Equation Editor is capable of a lot more than we have covered here, but this simple example should serve to get you started. Try it, it's simpler than it looks.

5

Microsoft Word 2000 Basics

Users of WorksSuite 2000 have Microsoft Word 2000 as their word processor. This can be started in several ways, by clicking the Windows **Start** button then selecting **Programs** and clicking on the 'Microsoft Word' item on the cascade menu, by clicking a Word icon on the Windows Desktop shown here, or by double-clicking on a Word document file icon. In the latter case the document will be loaded into Word at the same time.

You can also start Word 2000 from the **Programs** window of the WorksSuite Task Launcher, shown below. Selecting **Word** in the Programs list opens an extensive list of Tasks which can step you through the process of starting different documents. To open a blank document click the **Start a blank Word document** link located above the Task list.

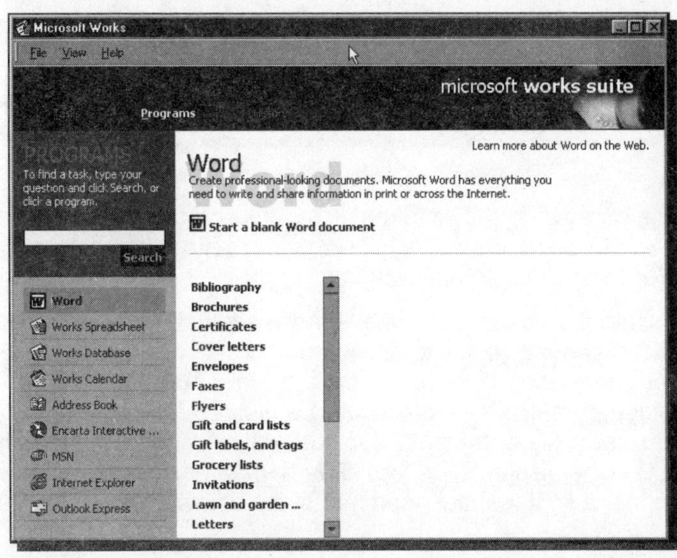

The Word Screen

The opening 'blank' screen of Word 2000 is shown below. It is perhaps worth spending some time looking at the various parts that make up this screen. Word follows the usual Microsoft Windows conventions and if you are familiar with these you can skip through this section. Otherwise a few minutes might be well spent here.

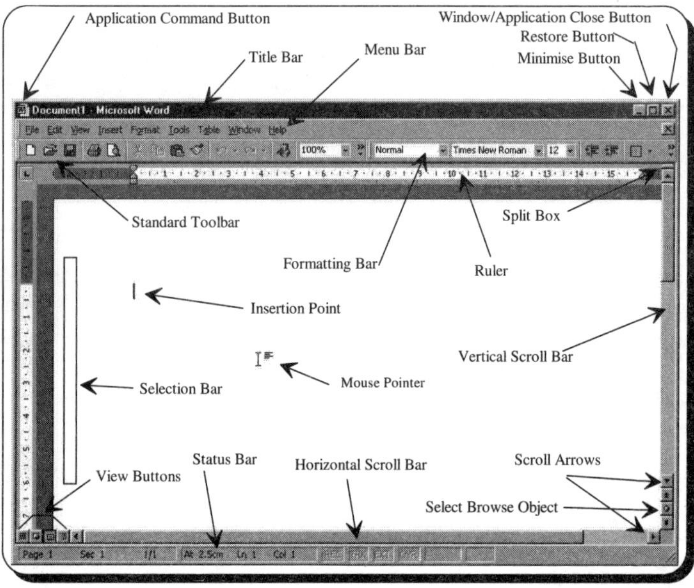

The window as shown takes up the full screen area available. If you click on the application restore button, you can make Word show in a smaller window.

Note that in this case, the Word window displays an empty document with the title 'Document1', and has a solid 'Title bar', indicating that it is the active application window. Although multiple windows can be displayed simultaneously, you can only enter data into the active window (which will always be displayed on top). Title bars of non active windows appear a lighter shade than that of the active one.

The Word screen is divided into several areas which have the following functions:

Area	***Function***
Command buttons	Clicking on the command button, (see upper-left corner of the Word window), displays a pull-down menu which can be used to control the program window. It allows you to restore, move, size, minimise, maximise, and close the window. 
Title Bar	The bar at the top of a window which displays the application name and the name of the current document.
Minimise Button	When clicked on, this button minimises a document to an icon, or the application to the Windows Taskbar.
Restore Button	When clicked on, this button restores the active window to the position and size that was occupied before it was maximised. The restore button is then replaced by a Maximise button, as shown here, which is used to set the window to full screen size.  
Close button	The extreme top right button that you click to close a window. 
Menu Bar	The bar below the Title bar which allows you to choose from several menu options.

	Clicking on a menu item displays the pull-down menu associated with that item.
Standard Toolbar	The bar below the Menu bar which contains buttons that give you mouse click access to the functions most often used in the program. These are grouped according to function.
Formatting Bar	The buttons on the Formatting Bar allow you to change the attributes of a font, such as italic and underline, and also to format text in various ways. The Formatting Bar contains three boxes; a style box, a font box and a size box which show which style, font and size of characters are currently being used. These boxes give access to other installed styles, fonts and character sizes.
Ruler	The area where you can see and set tabulation points and indents.
Split Box	The area above the top vertical scroll button which when dragged allows you to split the screen. 
Scroll Bars	The areas on the screen that contain scroll boxes in vertical and horizontal bars. Clicking on these bars allows you to control the part of a document which is visible on the screen.
Scroll Arrows	The arrowheads at each end of each scroll bar at which you can click to scroll the screen up and down one line, or left and right 10% of the screen, at a time.

Selection Bar	The area on the screen in the left margin of the Word window (marked here with a box for convenience), where the mouse pointer changes to an arrow that slants to the right. Clicking the left mouse button once selects the current line, while clicking twice selects the current paragraph.
Insertion pointer	The pointer used to specify the place of text insertion.
Views Buttons	Clicking these buttons changes screen views quickly.
Status Bar	The bottom line of the document window that displays status information.

The Standard Toolbar

This is located below the Menu bar at the top of the Word screen and contains command buttons. To action a command, left-click its button with the mouse. Not only can you control what buttons show on the various toolbars, but as you work with Word the buttons you use most often are displayed on them automatically.

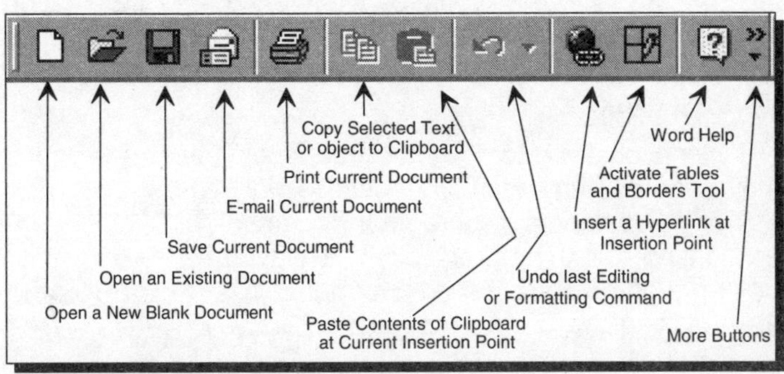

The use of these Standard Toolbar buttons will be discussed in great detail, with worked examples, in the next chapter.

The Formatting Bar

This is located to the right of or below the Standard Toolbar, and is divided into sections that contain command buttons, as shown below.

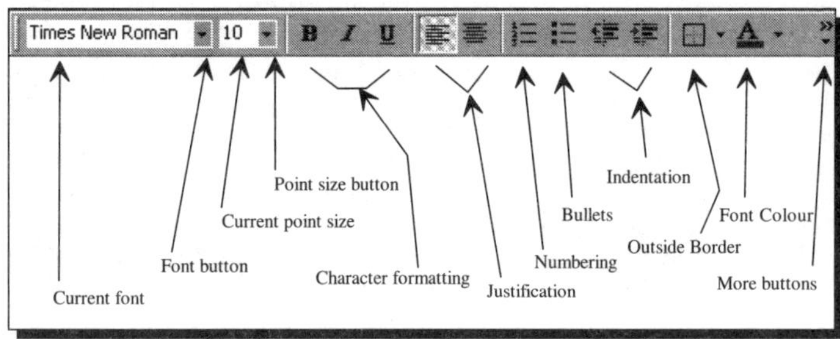

The Current font box shows the current typeface. Clicking on the down-arrow button to the right of it allows you to change the typeface of any selected text. The Current point size box shows the size of selected characters which can be changed by clicking on the down-arrow button next to it and selecting another size from the displayed list.

Next, are three character formatting buttons which allow you to enhance selected text by emboldening, italicising, or underlining it. The next two buttons allow you to change the justification of a selected paragraph, and the next four help you set the different types of Numbering and Indentation options. The last two buttons allow you to add an Outside Border to selected text or objects, and change the font colour of selected text.

Clicking on the More Buttons area, opens up the menu shown here with additional options for justifying selected paragraphs and highlighting text. The first option displays the name of the current style (Normal) in a box. Clicking the down-arrow against this box, opens up a menu of default paragraph styles with their font sizes. Once the Style box is opened, from then on, it appears to the left of the Font box, replacing other formatting icons.

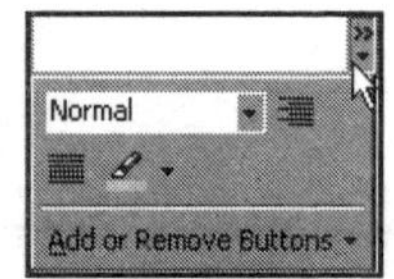

The Status Bar

This is located at the bottom of the Word window and is used to display statistics about the active document.

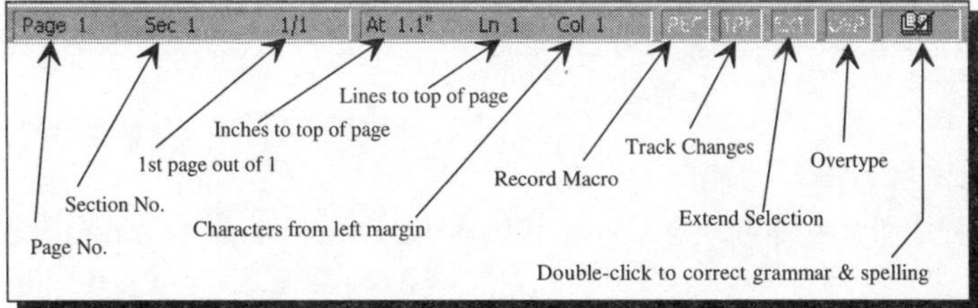

For example, when a document is being opened, the Status bar displays for a short time its name and length in terms of total number of characters. Once a document is opened, the Status bar displays the statistics of the document at the insertion point; here it is on Page 1, Section 1, 1 character from the left margin.

Double-clicking the left of the status bar displays the Find and Replace dialogue box, as shown below.

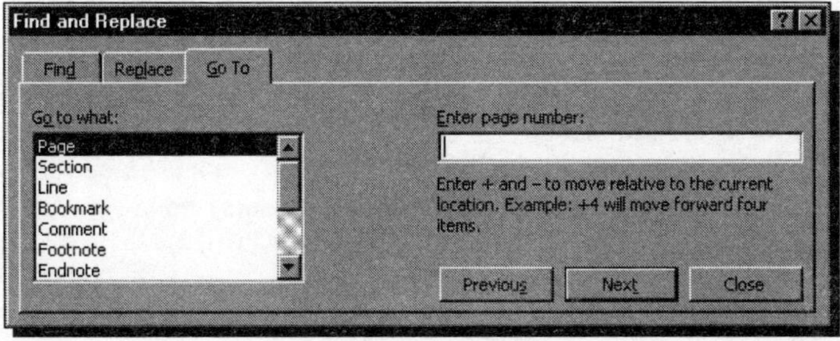

This is shown with the **Go To** tab selected. You can choose which page, section line, etc., of the document to go to, or you can use the other tabs to **Find** and **Replace** text (more about this later).

Double-clicking the other features on the Status bar will activate these features.

Creating Word Documents

When the program is first used, all Word's features default to those shown on page 84 (apart from showing the ruler). It is quite possible to use Word in this mode, without changing any main settings, but it is also possible to customise the package to your needs.

Entering Text

In order to illustrate some of Word's capabilities, you need to have a short text at hand. We suggest you type the memo displayed below into a new document. At this stage, don't worry if the length of the lines below differ from those on your display.

As you type in text, any time you want to force a new line, or paragraph, just press <Enter>. While typing within a paragraph, Word sorts out line lengths automatically (known as 'word wrap'), without you having to press any keys to move to a new line. If you make a mistake while typing, press the <BkSp> key enough times to erase the mistake and start again.

MEMO TO PC USERS
Networked Computers
The microcomputers in the Data Processing room are a mixture of IBM compatible PCs with Pentium processors running at various speeds. They all have 3.5" floppy drives of 1.44MB capacity, and most also have CD-ROM drives. The PCs are connected to various printers via a network; the Laser printers available giving best output.

The computer you are using will have at least a 3.0GB capacity hard disc on which a number of software programs, including the latest version of Windows, have been installed. To make life easier, the hard disc is highly structured with each program installed in a separate folder (directory).

Moving Around a Document

You can move the cursor around a document with the normal direction keys, and with the key combinations listed below.

To move	*Press*
Left one character	←
Right one character	→
Up one line	↑
Down one line	↓
Left one word	Ctrl+←
Right one word	Ctrl+→
To beginning of line	Home
To end of line	End
To paragraph beginning	Ctrl+↑
To paragraph end	Ctrl+↓
Up one screen	PgUp
Down one screen	PgDn
To top of previous page	Ctrl+PgUp
To top of next page	Ctrl+PgDn
To beginning of file	Ctrl+Home
To end of file	Ctrl+End

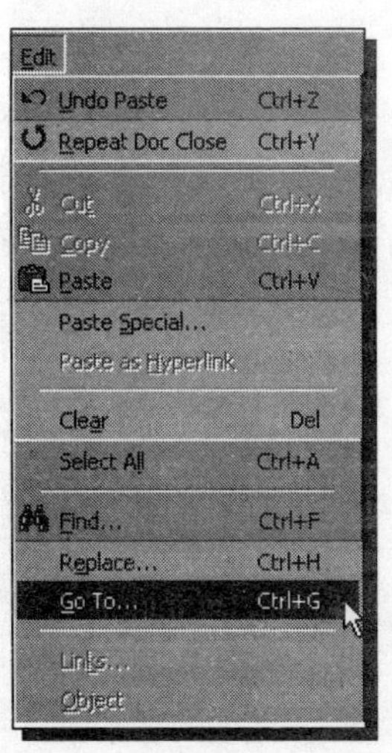

To jump to a specified page number in a multi-page document, either double-click the left of the status bar to display the Find and Replace dialogue box, then click the Go To tab, or use the **Edit**, **Go To** command (or <Ctrl+G>), shown here and to be explained shortly.

Obviously, you need to become familiar with the above methods of moving the cursor around a document, particularly if you are not using a mouse and you spot an error in a document which needs to be corrected, which is the subject of the latter half of this chapter.

Templates and Paragraph Styles

As we saw under the Formatting Bar section earlier, when you start Word for the first time, the Style box contains the word **Normal**. This means that all the text you have entered, at the moment, is shown in the Normal paragraph style which is one of the styles available in the NORMAL template. Every document produced by Word has to use a template, and NORMAL is the default. A template contains, both the document page settings and a set of formatting instructions which can be applied to text.

Changing Paragraph Styles

To change the style of a paragraph, do the following:

- Place the cursor (insertion pointer) on the paragraph in question, say the title line
- Left click the Style Status button, and select the **Heading 1** style.

The selected paragraph reformats instantly in bold, and in Arial typeface of point size 16.

With the cursor in the second line of text, select **Heading 3** which reformats the line in Arial 13. Your memo should now look presentable, as shown below.

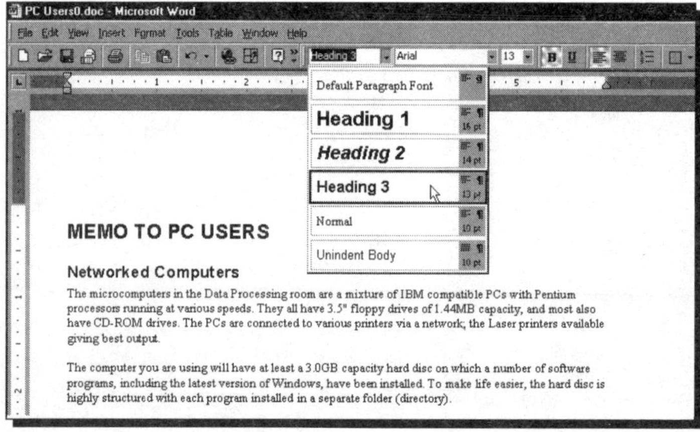

Document Screen Displays

Word provides four display views, Normal, Web Layout, Print Layout, and Outline, as well as the options to view your documents in a whole range of screen enlargements by selecting **Zoom**. You control all these viewing options with the **View** sub-menu, shown here, and when a document is displayed you can switch freely between them. When first loaded the screen displays in Print Layout view.

The view options have the following effect, and can also be accessed by clicking the View buttons on the left of the Status bar.

Normal Layout

A view that simplifies the layout of the page so that you can type, edit and format text quickly. In normal view, page boundaries, headers and footers, backgrounds, drawing objects, and pictures that do not have the '**In line with text**' wrapping style do not appear.

Web Layout

A view that optimises the layout of a document to make online reading easier. Use this layout view when you are creating a Web page or a document that is viewed on the screen. In Web layout view, you can see backgrounds, text is wrapped to fit the window, and graphics are positioned just as they are in a Web browser.

Print Layout

Provides a WYSIWYG (what you see is what you get) view of a document. The text displays in the typefaces and point sizes you specify, and with the selected attributes.

This view is useful for editing headers and footers, for adjusting margins, and for working with columns and drawing objects. All text boxes or frames, tables, graphics, headers, footers, and footnotes appear on the screen as they will in the final printout.

Outline Layout

Provides a collapsible view of a document, which enables you to see its organisation at a glance. You can display all the text in a file, or just the text that uses the paragraph styles you specify. Using this mode, allows you to quickly rearrange large sections of text. Some people like to create an outline of their document first, consisting of all the headings, then to sort out the document structure and finally fill in the text.

With large documents, you can create what is known as a *Master* document by starting with an Outline View, and then designate headings in the outline as sub-documents. When you save the master document, Word assigns names to each sub-document based on the text you use in the outline headings. You can also convert an existing document to a master document and then divide it into sub-documents, or you can add existing documents to a master document to make them sub-documents.

In a master document, you can quickly change the top-level structure of the document by adding, removing, combining, splitting, renaming, and rearranging sub-documents. You can also create a table of contents, index, cross-references, and headers and footers for all of the sub-documents. The master document's template applies to all the sub-documents, so the entire document has a consistent design. Printing a master document is a fast way to print all the sub-documents without opening them individually. A Master document can be thought of as a 'container' for a set of separate files or sub-documents.

Full Screen

Selecting the **View, Full Screen** command, displays a clean, uncluttered screen; the Toolbars, Ruler, Scroll bars, and Status bar are removed. To return to the usual screen, click the **Close Full Screen** button on the icon which appears at the bottom of your screen when in this mode.

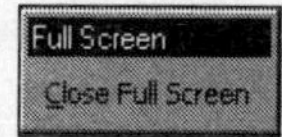

Zoom

Selecting the **View, Zoom** command, displays the Zoom dialogue box (we only show the left side of it here), in which you can change the viewing magnification factor from its default value of 100%.

Changing Default Options

Modifying Margins

To change the standard page margins for your entire document from the cursor position onward, or for selected text (more about this later), do the following:

- Select the **File, Page Setup** command
- Click the left mouse button at the **Margins** tab on the displayed dialogue box, shown below.

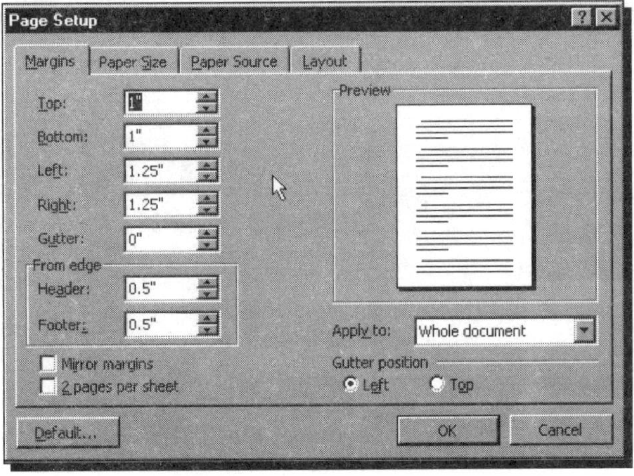

The 'Preview' page to the right of the box shows how your changes will look on a real page.

Changing the Default Paper Size

To change the default paper size from the size set during installation to a different size, do the following:

- Select the **File, Page Setup** command
- Click the left mouse button at the **Paper Size** tab on the displayed dialogue box

- Click the down-arrow against the **Paper Size** box to reveal the list of available paper sizes
- Change the page size to your new choice, and press the **Default** button and confirm that you wish this change to affect all new documents based on the Normal template.

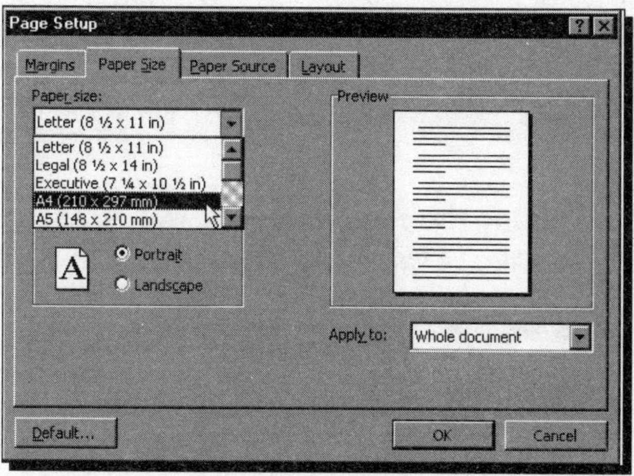

Check that the paper size matches that in your printer, otherwise you may get strange results. The orientation of the printed page is normally **Portrait** (text prints across the page width), but you could choose to change this to **Landscape** which prints across the page length, as long as your printer can print in landscape.

All changes you can make to your document from the Page Setup dialogue box can be applied to either the whole document or to the rest of the document starting from the current position of the insertion pointer. To carry out such changes click the down-arrow button against the **Apply to** box and choose appropriately from the drop-down menu list.

Modifying the Paper Source

Clicking on the third Page Setup tab, displays yet another dialogue box, part of which is shown here, from which you can select the paper source. You might have a printer that holds paper in trays, in which case you might want to specify that the first page (headed paper perhaps), should be taken from one tray, while the rest of the paper should be taken from a different tray.

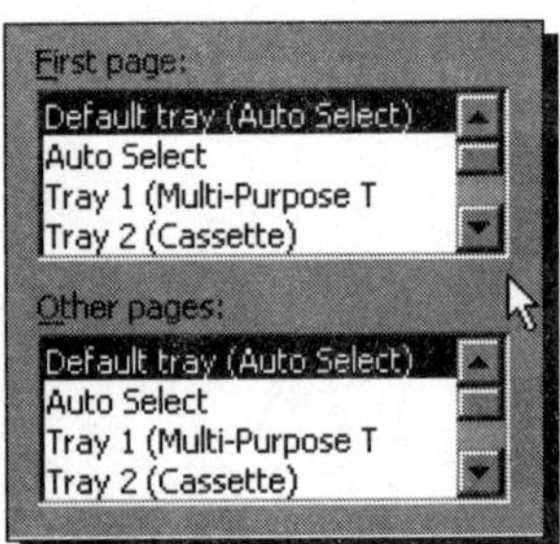

Modifying the Page Layout

Clicking the last Page Setup tab displays the Layout box, part of which is shown here. From this dialogue box you can set options for headers and footers, section breaks, vertical alignment and whether to add line numbers or borders.

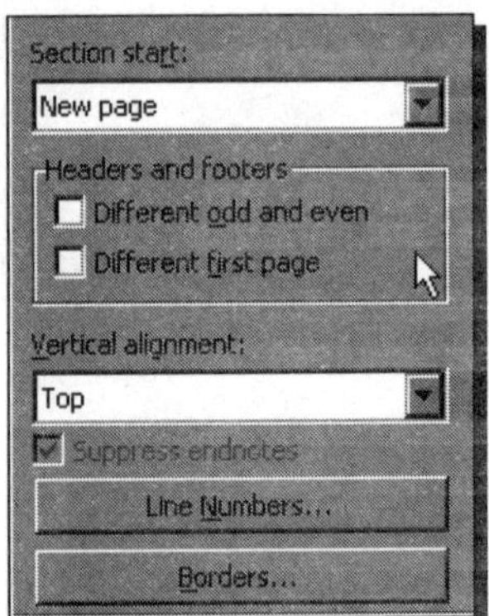

The default for **Section Start** is 'New Page' which allows the section to start at the top of the next page. Pressing the down arrow against this option, allows you to change this choice.

In the Headers and Footers section of the dialogue box, you can specify whether you want one header or footer for even-numbered pages and a different header or footer for odd-numbered pages. You can further specify if you want a different header or footer on the first page from the header or footer used for the rest of the document. Word can align the top line with the 'Top' margin, but this can be changed with the **Vertical Alignment** option.

Changing Other Default Options

You can also change the default options available to you in Word 2000, by selecting the **Tools, Options** command. Using the displayed Options dialogue box below, you can, amongst other things, do the following:

- Specify the default **View** options. For example, you can select whether non-printing formatting characters, such as Tabs, Spaces, and Paragraph marks, are shown or not.
- Adjust the **General** Word settings, such as background re-pagination, display of the recently used file-list, and selection of units of measurement.
- Adjust the **Print** settings, such as allowing background printing, reverse print order, or choose to print comments with documents.
- Change the **Save** options, such as selecting to always create a backup copy of your work.

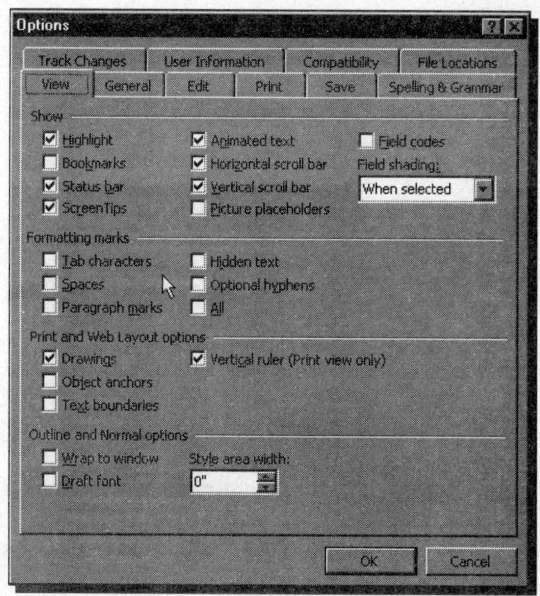

Saving to a File

To save a document to disc, use either of the commands:

- **File, Save** (or click the Save toolbar icon) which is used when a document has previously been saved to disc in a named file; using this command saves your work under the existing filename automatically without prompting you.
- **File, Save As** command which is used when you want to save your document with a different name from the one you gave it already.

Using the **File, Save As** command (or the very first time you use the **File, Save** command when a document has no name), opens the following dialogue box:

Note that the first 255 characters of the first paragraph of a new document is highlighted in the **File name** field box and the program is waiting for you to type a new name. Any name you type (less than 255 characters) will replace the existing name. Filenames cannot include any of the following keyboard characters: /, \, >, <, *, ?, ", |, :, or ;. Word adds the file extension **.doc** automatically and uses it to identify its documents.

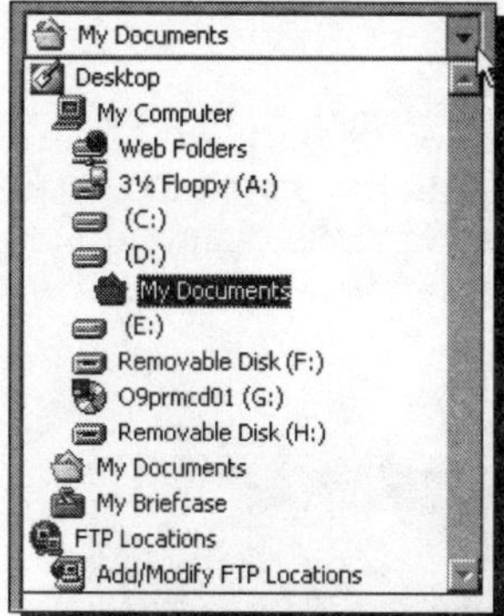

You can select a drive other than the one displayed, by clicking the down arrow against the **Save in** text box at the top of the Save As dialogue box. You can also select a folder in which to save your work. If you do not have a suitably named folder, then you can create one using the Create New Folder button on the Save As dialogue box, shown below.

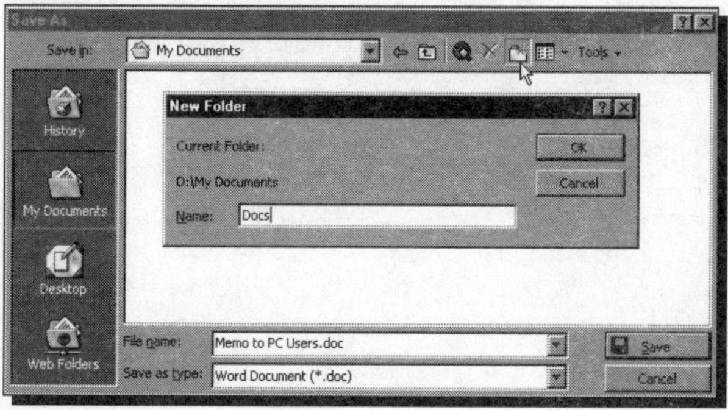

We used this facility to create a folder called **Docs** within the **My Documents** folder.

To save our work currently in memory, we selected the **Docs** folder in the **Save in** field of the Save As dialogue box, then moved the cursor into the **File name** box, and typed **PC Users 1**. We suggest you do the same.

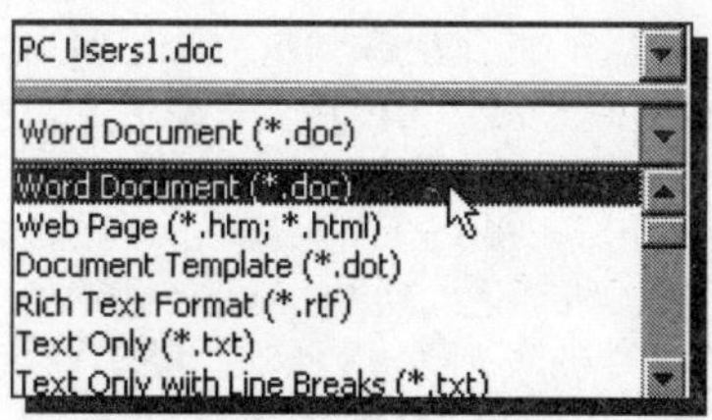

By clicking the **Save as type** button at the bottom of the Save As dialogue box, you can save the Document Template, or the Text Only parts of your work, or you can save your document in a variety of other formats, including Rich Text, and Web Page (HTML).

Selecting File Location

You can select where Word is to look automatically for your document files when you first choose to open or save a document by selecting the **Tools, Options** command, click the File Locations tab of the displayed Options dialogue box, and modifying the location of the document files, as shown below.

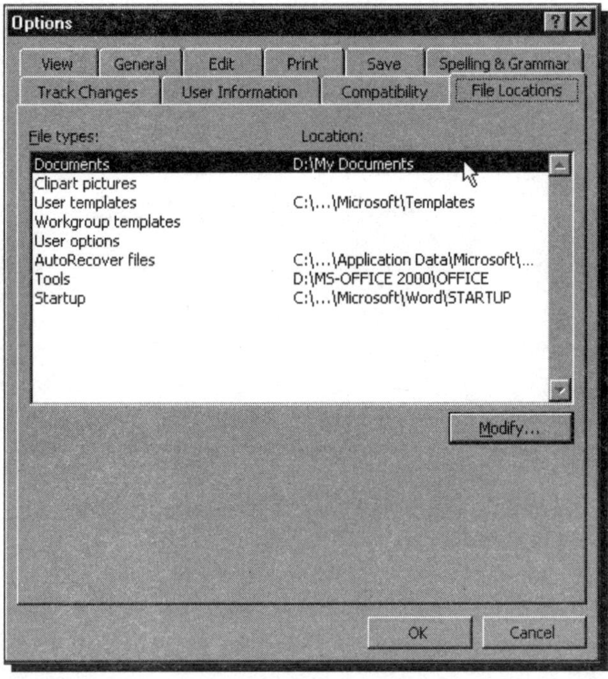

As you can see, the default location of other types of files is also given in the above dialogue box.

Microsoft suggests that you store documents, worksheets, presentations, databases, and other files you are currently working on, in the **My Documents** folder. This, of course, is a matter of preference, so we leave it to you to decide. We prefer to create sub-folders within the **My Documents** folder and save files from the same application in one sub-folder.

Document Properties

A useful feature in Word is the facility to add document properties to every file by selecting the **File, Properties** command. A Properties box, as shown below, opens for you to type additional information about your document.

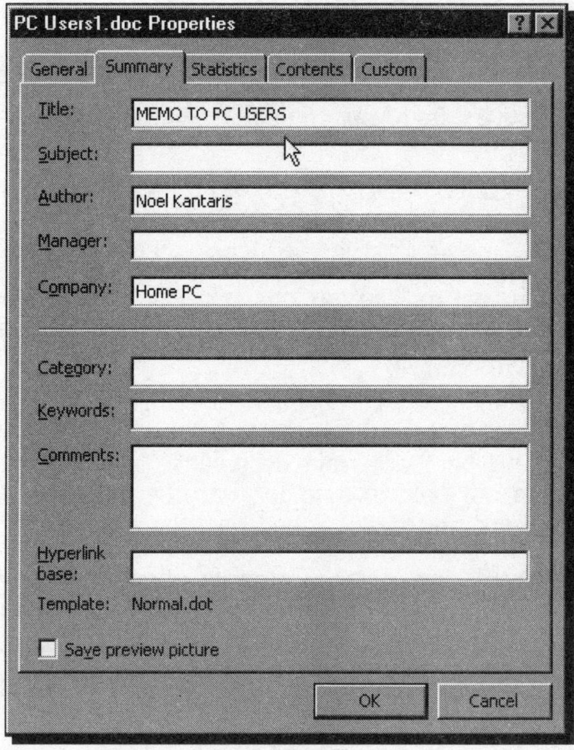

In this box you can select to add a manager, company, or category name to group files together for ease of retrieval.

To do this on a more regular basis, make sure that the **Prompt for Document Properties** box in the Save Options dialogue box (use the **Tools, Options** command and click the Save tab of the Options dialogue box) is selected and appears ticked.

Closing a Document

There are several ways to close a document in Word. Once you have saved it you can click its 'X' close button, or double-click on the Document Control button at the left end of the menu bar; you would usually use these when you have several files open together.

If you want to close the current document, and then open a new one or a different one, do the following:

- Choose **File, Close** to close the current document (remove it from your computer's memory) before using either
- **File, New** (or clicking) to create a new file, or
- **File, Open** (or clicking) to use an existing file.

If the document (or file) has changed since the last time it was saved, you will be given the option to save it before it is removed from memory.

If a document is not closed before a new document is opened, then both documents will be held in memory, but only one will be the current document. To find out which documents are held in memory, use the Taskbar, or the **Window** command to reveal the following menu options:

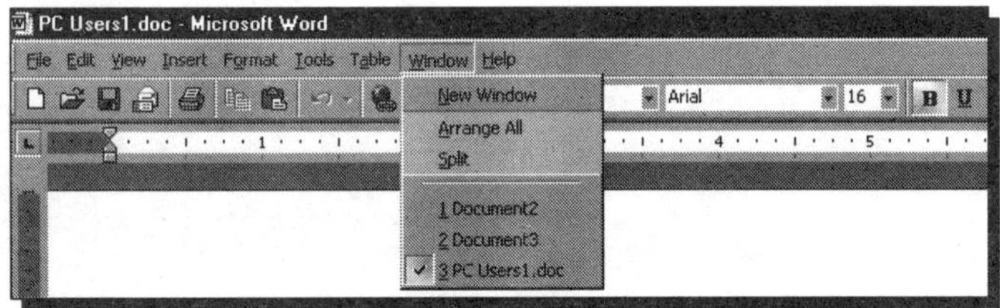

In this case, the third document in the list is the current document, and to make another document the current one, either type the document number, or point at its name and click the left mouse button.

To close a document which is not the current document, use the **Window** command, make it current, and close it with one of the above methods.

Using the Office Assistant

The Office Assistant is a source of help information in Word 2000, whatever you are doing the Assistant will help you.

To find out how it works, start Word 2000, then click the Office Assistant button, shown here, type the word ***help*** in the displayed 'What would you like to do?' box, shown to the left, and left-click the **Search** button.

A list of help topics is then displayed, as shown to the right. To see more topics, left-click the small triangle at the bottom of the list with the caption 'See more', to display additional topics, as shown below.

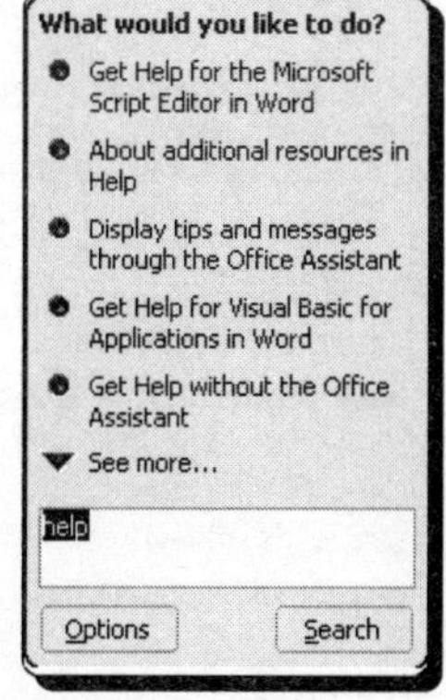

To find out how you can use the Office Assistant, click the 'Ways to get assistance while you work' option which causes the display of the screen shown on the next page. From this latter screen you can find out all there is to know about the Office Assistant.

The Office Assistant, as its name might suggest is part of Microsoft Office 2000, as of course is Word 2000 itself. It can be very entertaining, but we must admit that we find it a little annoying and have it turned off. The Word Help system is still available from either the **Help** menu command, or with the **F1** key.

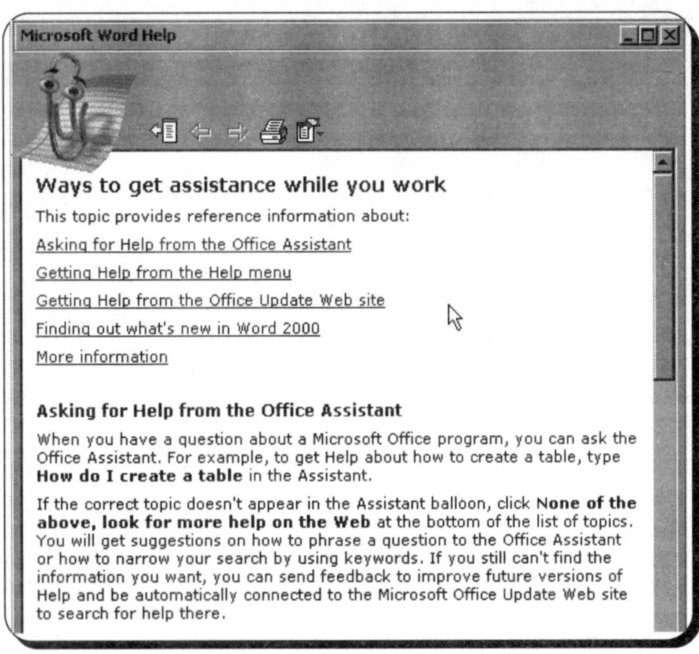

Note the Web browser type buttons at the top of the screen. These allow you to carry out the following functions:

	Show - click this button to display the help screen tabs which allow you to access Help's Contents, Answer Wizard, and Index.
	Back - if more than one help screen has been opened, click this button to go back to the previously opened help screen.
	Forward - if you have moved back to a previous help screen, click this button to move forward through opened help screens.
	Print - click this button to print the contents of the current help screen.
	Options - click this button to open up a menu of options which control all of the above facilities plus the ability to select the Internet Options dialogue box.

Customising the Office Assistant

You can customise the Office Assistant to a great degree. Not only can you change the way it responds to your enquiries, but you can also switch it off once you have mastered a particular Office application.

To see the default options settings of the Office Assistant, activate it, left-click on it, and left-click the **Options** button on the displayed box, shown here.

Doing this, causes the following dialogue box to be displayed on your screen:

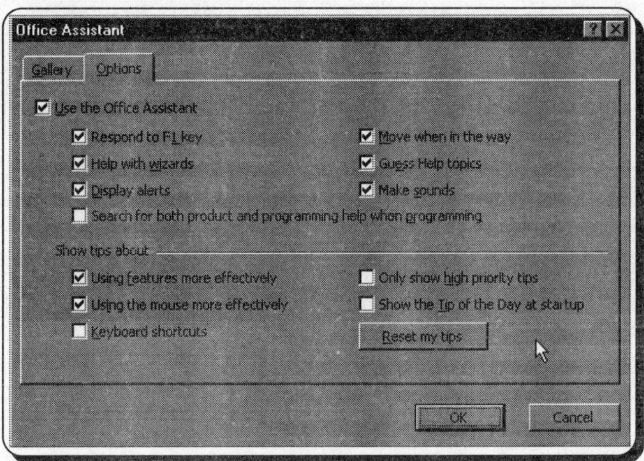

As you can see, it is possible to choose from several options. To change the shape of your Office Assistant (there are eight shapes to choose from - see next page), either left-click the Gallery tab of the above dialogue box, or right-click the Office Assistant and select the **Choose Assistant** option from the displayed menu, as shown here.

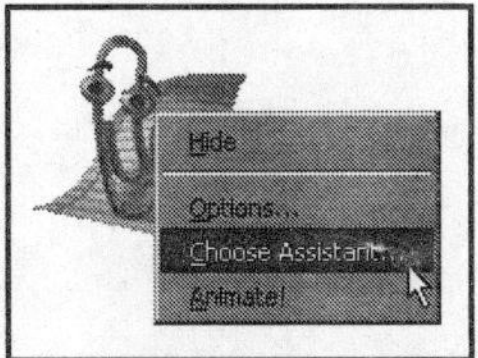

Either action displays the following dialogue box in which you can select your preferred Assistant shape by left-clicking the **Next** button.

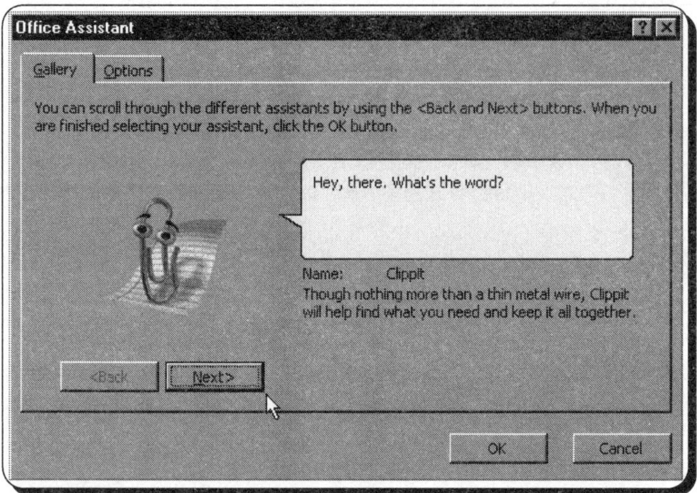

The shapes of the available Assistants are as follows:

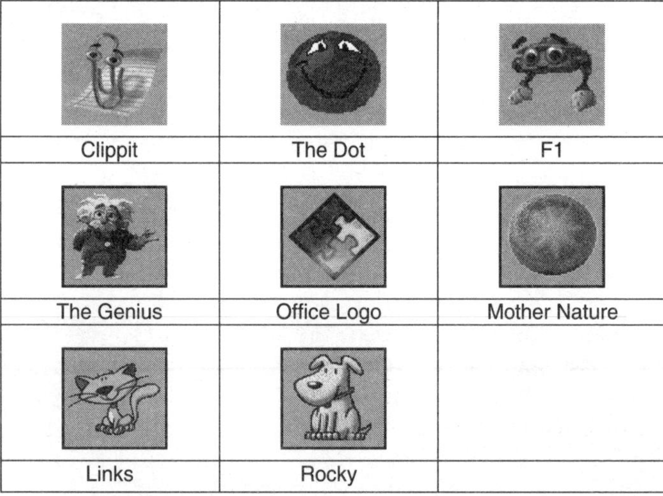

Clippit	The Dot	F1
The Genius	Office Logo	Mother Nature
Links	Rocky	

6

Editing Word Documents

It will not be long, when using Word, before you will need to edit your document. One of the first things you will notice is that misspelled words are unobtrusively underlined in a red wavy line and that ungrammatical phrases are similarly underlined in green. To demonstrate this facility, use the **File, New** command (or click) to create a new file, and type the words 'Computors are fun to usr', exactly as misspelled here. What should appear on your screen is shown below, but with the misspelled words underlined in a red wavy line.

Right-clicking the first word allows you to correct it, as shown here. To correct such a word, left-click on 'Computers'. You even have a choice of English. Next, place the cursor on 'usr' and right-click once more to display:

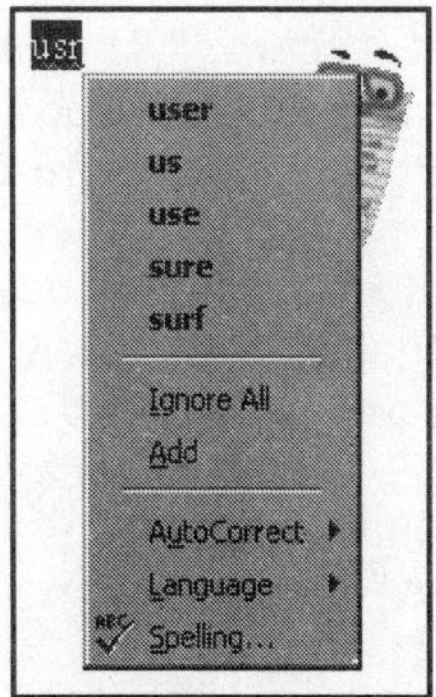

This is possibly the most timesaving enhancement in editing misspelled words as you type. The spell and grammar checker will be discussed later in more detail.

Other editing could include deleting unwanted words or adding extra text in the document. All these operations are very easy to carry out. For small deletions, such as letters or words, the easiest method to adopt is the use of the <Del> or <BkSp> keys.

With the <Del> key, position the cursor on the left of the first letter you want to delete and press <Del>. With the <BkSp> key, position the cursor immediately to the right of the character to be deleted and press <BkSp>. In both cases the rest of the line moves to the left to take up the space created by the deleting process.

Word processing is usually carried out in the insert mode. Any characters typed will be inserted at the cursor location (insertion point) and the following text will be pushed to the right, and down, to make room. To insert blank lines in your text, place the cursor at the beginning of the line where the blank line is needed and press <Enter>. To remove the blank line, position the cursor on it and press <Del>.

When larger scale editing is needed you have several alternatives. You could first 'select' the text to be altered, then use the **Cut**, **Copy** and **Paste** operations available in the **Edit** sub-menu, or click on the Toolbar button alternatives shown here.

Another method of copying or moving text is to use the 'drag and drop' facility which requires you to highlight a word, grab it with the left mouse button depressed, and drop it in the required place in your text. This facility will also be discussed shortly in some detail.

Adding Buttons to the Standard Toolbar

When you first use Word, the **Cut** button shown above is not on the default Standard Toolbar. To place it there, first click the **More Buttons** icon, then the **Add or Remove Buttons**, and from the displayed menu select the one required, as shown to the left. From then on, the selected button appears on the Toolbar, but may displace other buttons.

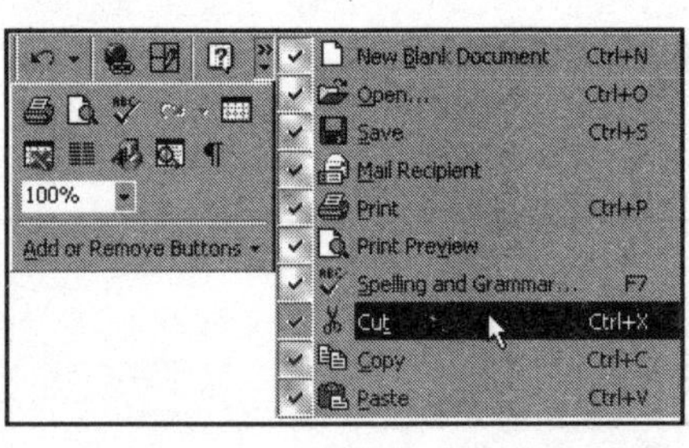

Selecting Text

The procedure in Word, as with most Windows based applications, is first to select the text to be altered before any operation, such as formatting or editing, can be carried out on it. Selected text is highlighted on the screen. This can be carried out in two main ways:

A. Using the keyboard, to select:

• A block of text.	Position the cursor on the first character to be selected and hold down the <Shift> key while using the arrow keys to highlight the required text, then release the <Shift> key.
• From the present position to the end of the line.	Use <Shift+End>.
• From the present cursor position to the beginning of the line.	Use <Shift+Home>.
• From the present cursor position to the end of the document.	Use <Shift+Ctrl+End>.
• From the present cursor position to the beginning of the document.	Use <Shift+Ctrl+Home>.

B. With the mouse, to select:

• A block of text.	Press down the left mouse button at the beginning of the block and while holding it pressed, drag the cursor across the block so that the desired text is highlighted, then release the mouse button.
• A word.	Double-click within the word.
• A line.	Place the mouse pointer on the selection bar, just to the left of the line, and click once (for multiple lines, after selecting the first line, drag the pointer in the selection bar).
• A sentence.	Hold the <Ctrl> key down and click in the sentence.
• A paragraph.	Place the mouse pointer in the selection bar and double-click (for multiple paragraphs, after selecting the first paragraph, drag the pointer in the selection bar) or triple-click in the paragraph.
• The whole document.	Place the mouse pointer in the selection bar, hold the <Ctrl> key down and click once.

Copying Blocks of Text

Once text has been selected it can be copied to another location in your present document, to another Word document, or to another Windows application, via the clipboard. As with most of the editing and formatting operations there are several alternative ways of doing this, as follows:

- Use the **Edit, Copy** command sequence from the menu, to copy the selected text to the Windows clipboard, moving the cursor to the start of where you want the copied text to be placed, and using the **Edit, Paste** command.

- Use the quick key combinations, <Ctrl+Ins> (or <Ctrl+C>) to copy and <Shift+Ins> (or <Ctrl+V>) to paste, once the text to be copied has been selected. This does not require the menu bar to be activated.

- Use the 'Copy to clipboard' and 'Paste from clipboard' Standard Toolbar buttons; you can of course only use this method with a mouse.

To copy the same text again to another location, or to any open document window or application, move the cursor to the new location and paste it there with any of these methods. It is stored on the clipboard until it is replaced by the next Cut, or Copy operation.

- Selected text can be copied by holding the <Ctrl> key depressed while dragging the mouse with the left button held down. The drag pointer is an arrow with an attached square - the vertical dotted line showing the point of insertion. The new text will insert itself where placed, even if the overstrike mode is in operation. Text copied by this method is not placed on the clipboard, so multiple copies are not possible as with other methods.

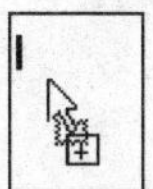

Moving Blocks of Text

Selected text can be moved to any location in the same document by either of the following:

- Using the **Edit, Cut**, command or <Shift+Del> (or <Ctrl+X>).
- Clicking the 'Cut to clipboard' Standard Toolbar button, shown here.

Next, move the cursor to the required new location and use either of the following procedures:

- The **Edit, Paste** command.
- Any other paste actions as described previously.

The moved text will be placed at the cursor location and will force any existing text to make room for it. This operation can be cancelled by simply pressing <Esc>. Once moved, multiple copies of the same text can be produced by other **Paste** operations.

Selected text can be moved by dragging the mouse with the left button held down. The drag pointer is an arrow with an attached square - the vertical dotted line showing the point of insertion.

Deleting Blocks of Text

When text is 'cut' it is removed from the document, but placed on the clipboard until further text is either copied or cut. With Word any selected text can be deleted by pressing **Edit, Cut,** or clicking the 'Cut to Clipboard' Standard Toolbar icon, shown here, or by pressing the <Del>, or <BkSp> keys. However, using **Edit, Cut**, allows you to use the **Edit, Paste** command, but using the <Del> or <BkSp> keys, does not.

The Undo Command

As text is lost with the delete command, you should use it with caution, but if you do make a mistake all is not lost as long as you act promptly. The **Edit, Undo** command or <Ctrl+Z> (or <Alt+BkSp>) reverses your most recent editing or formatting commands.

You can also use the Undo Standard Toolbar button, shown here, to undo one of several editing or formatting mistakes (press the down arrow to the right of the button to see a list of your recent changes, as shown here).

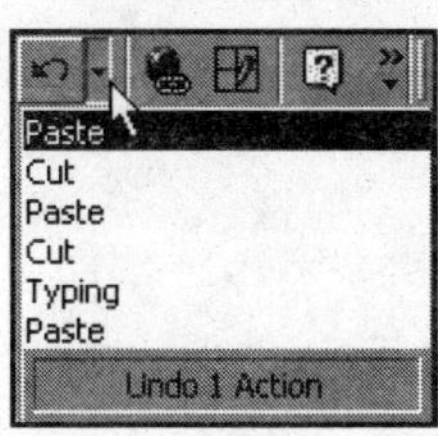

Undo does not reverse any action once editing changes have been saved to file. Only editing done since the last save can be reversed.

Finding and Changing Text

Word allows you to search for specifically selected text, or character combinations. To do this use the **Find** or the **Replace** option from the **Edit** command sub-menu.

Using the **Find** option (<Ctrl+F>), will highlight each occurrence of the supplied text in turn so that you can carry out some action on it, such as change its font or appearance.

Using the **Replace** option (<Ctrl+H>), allows you to specify what replacement is to be automatically carried out. For example, in a long article you may decide to replace every occurrence of the word 'microcomputers' with the word 'PCs'.

To illustrate the **Replace** procedure, either select the option from the **Edit** sub-menu or use the quick key combination <Ctrl+H>. This opens the Find and Replace dialogue box shown on the next page.

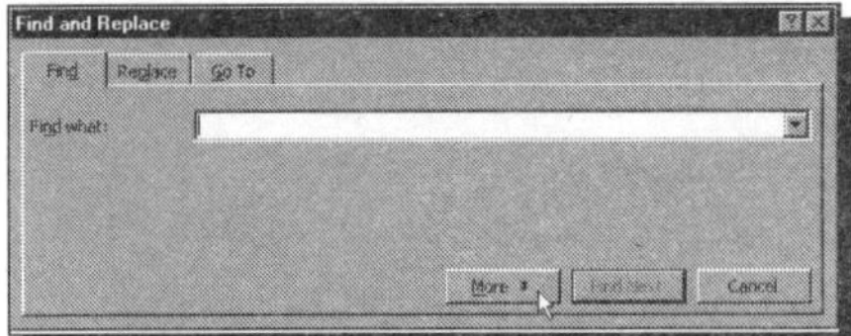

Clicking the **More** button displays the top half of the composite screen dump shown below.

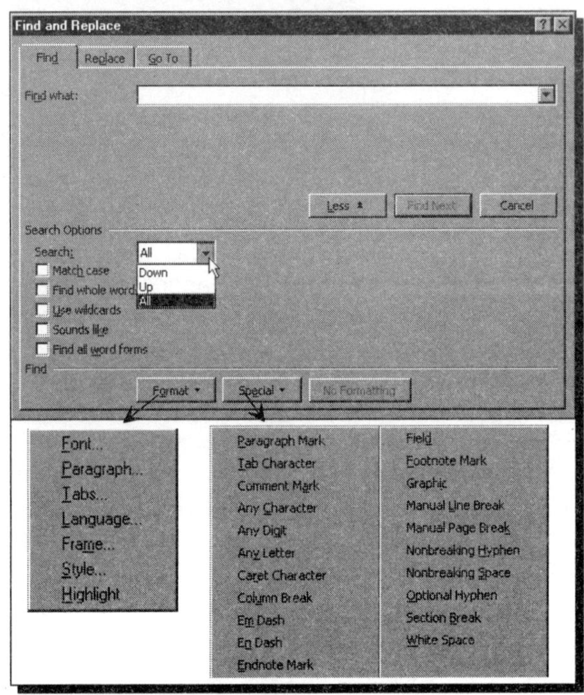

Towards the bottom of the dialogue box, there are five check boxes; the first two can be used to match the case of letters in the search string, and/or a whole word, while the last three can be used for wildcard, 'sounds like' or 'word forms' matching.

The two buttons, **Format** and **Special**, situated at the bottom of the dialogue box, let you control how the search is carried out. The lists of available options, when either of these buttons is pressed, are displayed above. You will of course only see one or the other, but not both as shown here.

You can force both the search and the replace operations to work with exact text attributes. For example, selecting:

- The **Font** option from the list under **Format**, displays a dialogue box in which you select a font (such as Arial, Times New Roman, etc.); a font-style (such as regular, bold, italic, etc.); an underline option (such as single, double, etc.); and special effects (such as strike-through, superscript, subscript, etc.).

- The **Paragraph** option, lets you control indentation, spacing (before and after), and alignment.

- The **Style** option, allows you to search for, or replace, different paragraph styles. This can be useful if you develop a new style and want to change all the text of another style in a document to use your preferred style.

Using the **Special** button, you can search for, and replace, various specified document marks, tabs, hard returns, etc., or a combination of both these and text, as listed in the previous screen dump.

Below we list only two of the many key combinations of special characters that could be typed into the **Find what** and **Replace with** boxes when the **Use wildcards** box is checked.

Type	*To find or replace*
?	Any single character within a pattern. For example, searching for nec?, will find neck, connect, etc.
*	Any string of characters. For example, searching for c*r, will find such words as cellar, chillier, etc., also parts of words such as character, and combinations of words such as connect, cellar.

Page Breaks

The program automatically inserts a 'soft' page break in a document when a page of typed text is full. To force a manual, or hard page break, either type <Ctrl+Enter> or use the **Insert**, **Break** command and select **Page Break** in the dialogue box, as shown to the left.

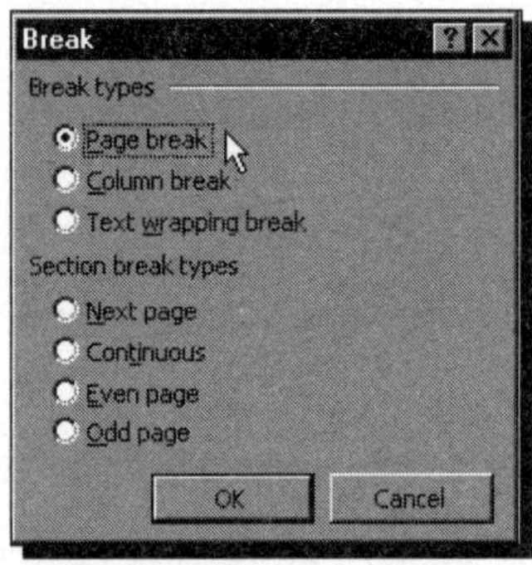

Pressing **OK** places a series of dots across the page to indicate the page break (this can only be seen in Normal View), as shown below. If you are in Print View, the second paragraph below appears on the next page. To delete manual page breaks place the cursor on the line of dots, and press the <Del> key. In Print View, place the cursor at the beginning of the second page and press the <BkSp> key.

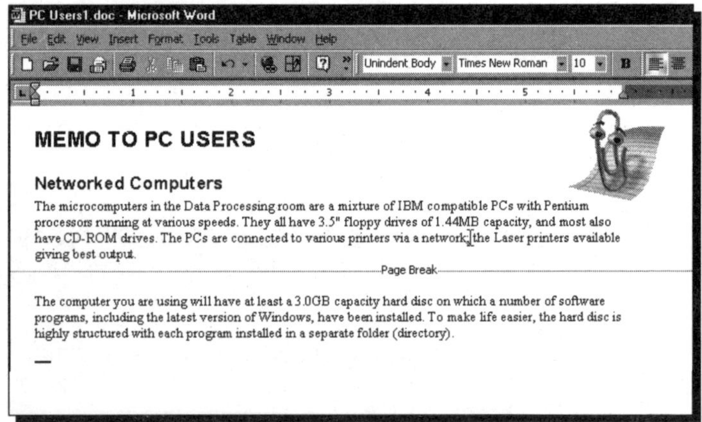

Soft page breaks which are automatically entered by the program at the end of pages, cannot be deleted.

Using the Spell Checker

The package has a very comprehensive spell checker which whenever it thinks it has found a misspelled word, underlines it with a red wavy line. To correct your document, right-click such words for alternatives.

However, the spell checker can also be used in another way. To spell check your document, either click the 'Spelling' button on the Standard Toolbar, shown here, or use the **Tools**, **Spelling and Grammar** command (or **F7**) to open the dialogue box shown below (if necessary, use the **Tools, Language, Set Language** command, select the correct dictionary and click the **Default** button).

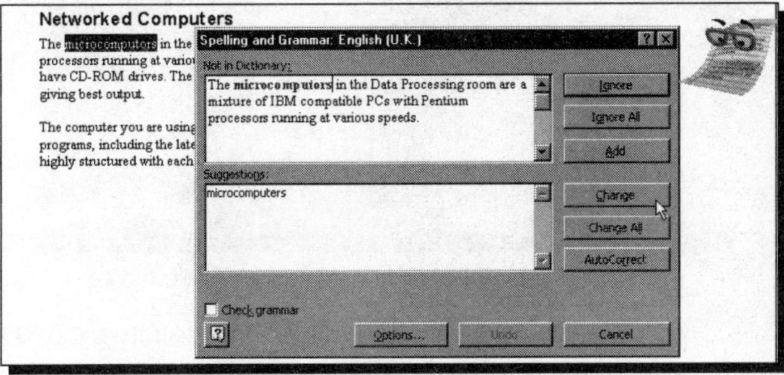

Word starts spell checking from the point of insertion onwards. If you want to spell check the whole document, move the insertion pointer to the beginning of the document before starting. If you want to check a word or paragraph only, highlight it first. Once Word has found a misspelled word, you can either correct it in the Not in Dictionary box, or select a word from the **Suggestions** list.

The main dictionary cannot be edited. However, the system has the ability to add specialised and personal dictionaries with the facility to customise and edit them. If you are using a personal dictionary and choose **Add**, the specified word is added to that dictionary.

Using the Thesaurus

If you are not sure of the meaning of a word, or you want to use an alternative word in your document, then the thesaurus is an indispensable tool. To use the thesaurus, simply place the cursor on the word you want to look up and select **Tools, Language, Thesaurus** command (or press the <Shift+**F7**> key combination). As long as the word is recognised, the following dialogue box will open.

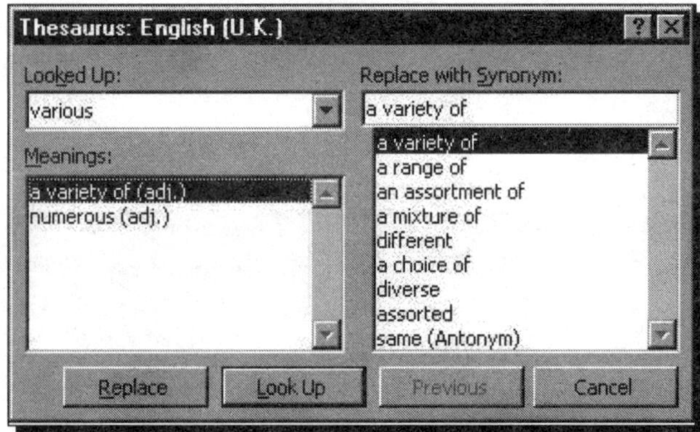

This is very powerful tool. You can see information about an item in the **Meanings** list, or you can look up a synonym in the **Replace with Synonym** list. To change the word in the **Looked Up** text box, select an offered word in either the **Meanings** or the **Replace with Synonym** list box, or type a word directly into the **Replace with Synonym** text box, and press the **Replace** button.

You can use the thesaurus like a simple dictionary by typing any word into the **Replace with Synonym** box and clicking the **Look Up** button. If the word is recognised, lists of its meaning variations and synonyms will be displayed. Pressing the **Replace** button will place the word into the document.

Printing Documents

When Windows was first installed on your computer the printers you intend to use should have been selected, and the SETUP program should have installed the appropriate printer drivers. Before printing for the first time, you would be wise to ensure that your printer is in fact properly installed. To do this, click on **Start** then select **Settings** and click the **Printers** menu option to open the Printers dialogue box shown below.

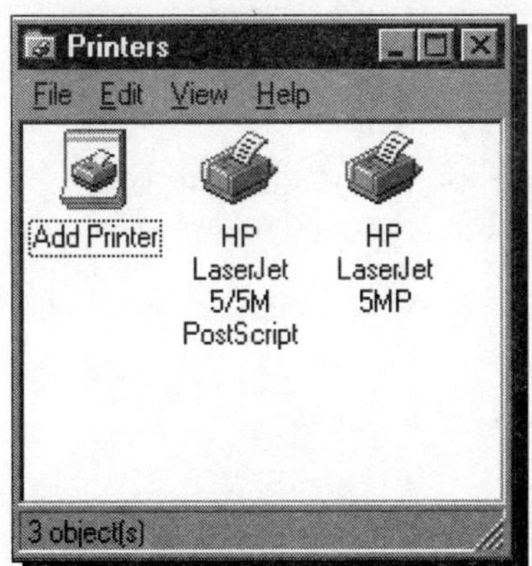

Here, two printer drivers have been installed; an HP LaserJet 5MP as the 'default' printer and an HP LaserJet 5/5M PostScript. In our case these are both configured to output to a printer via the parallel port LPT1. This refers to the socket at the back of your PC which is connected to your printer. LPT1 is short for Line Printer No. 1. Your selections may, obviously, not be the same.

To see how a printer is configured (whether to print to the parallel port or to a file), select it by clicking its icon, use the **File, Properties** command and click the Details tab of the displayed dialogue box.

Opening a Word Document

Next, return to or reactivate Word and, if the document you want to print is not in memory, either click the 'Open' button on the Standard Toolbar, or use the **File, Open** command, to display the Open dialogue box shown overleaf.

Use this dialogue box to locate the file (document) you want to print, which will be found on the drive and folder (directory) on which you saved it originally. Select it and click the **Open** button (or double-click its name), to load it into your computer's memory.

To print your document, do one of the following:

- Click the Print icon on the Standard Toolbar, shown here, which prints the document using the current defaults.

- Use the **File, Print** command which opens the 'Print' box, shown below.

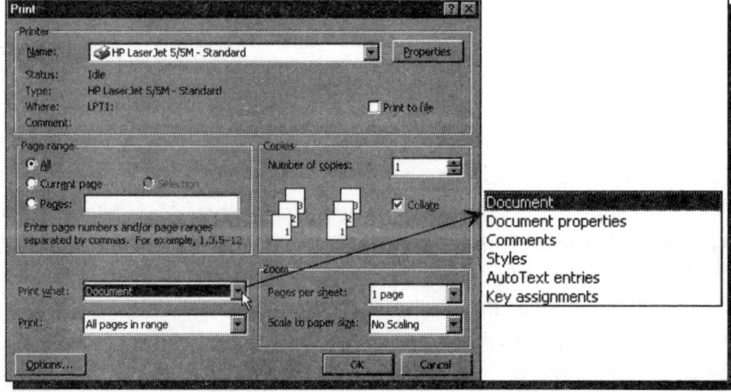

The settings in the Print dialogue box allow you to select the number of copies, and which pages, you want printed. You can also select to print the document, the summary information relating to that document, comments, styles, etc., as shown in the drop-down list also on the previous page.

You can even change the selected printer by clicking the down arrow against the **Printer Name** box which displays the available printers on your system.

Clicking the **Properties** button on the Print dialogue box, displays the Properties dialogue box for the selected printer, shown below, which allows you to select the paper size, orientation needed, paper source, etc.

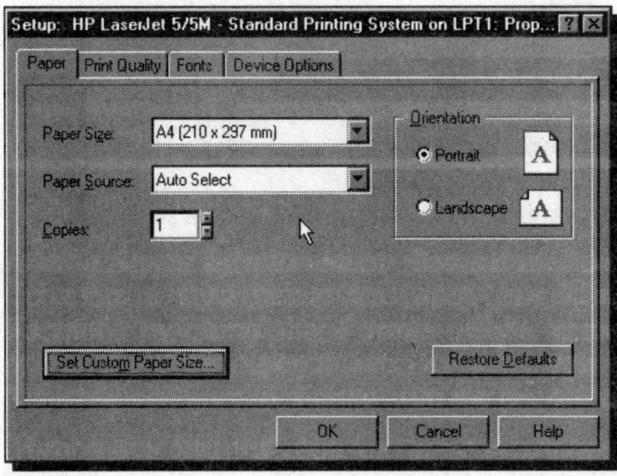

The **Options** button on the Print dialogue box, gives you access to some more advanced print options, such as printing in reverse order, with or without comments, print hidden text or field codes, etc., as shown on the next page.

Clicking the **OK** button on these various multilevel dialogue boxes, causes Word to accept your selections and return you to the previous level dialogue box, until the Print dialogue box is reached. Selecting **OK** on this first level dialogue box, sends print output from Word to your selection, either the printer connected to your computer, or to an encoded file on disc. Selecting **Cancel** or **Close** on any level dialogue box, aborts the selections made at that level.

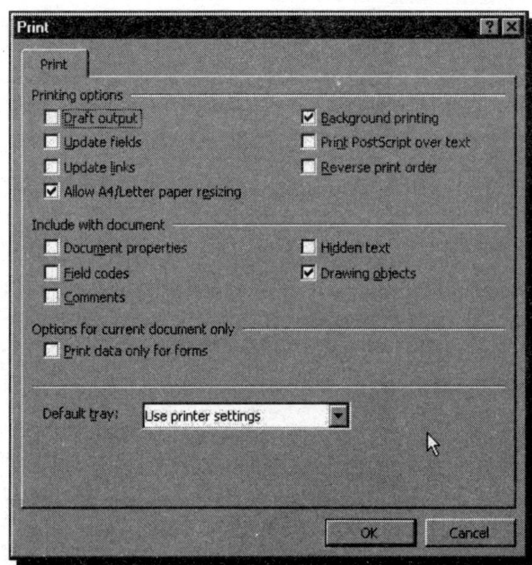

Do remember that, whenever you change printers, the appearance of your document may change, as Word uses the fonts available with the newly selected printer. This can affect the line lengths, which in turn will affect both the tabulation and pagination of your document.

Before printing to paper, click the Print Preview icon (if not on the Standard Toolbar, click the More Buttons icon or use the **File, Print Preview** command, to see how much of your document will fit on your selected page size. This depends very much on the chosen font. Thus, this option allows you to see the layout of the final printed page, which can save a few trees and equally important to you, a lot of frustration and wear and tear on your printer. To return to your working document from a print preview display, click the **Close** button on its menu bar.

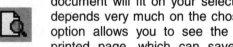

Other enhancements of your document, such as selection of fonts, formatting of text, and pagination, will be discussed in the next chapter.

7

Formatting Word Documents

Formatting involves the appearance of individual words or even characters, the line spacing and alignment of paragraphs, and the overall page layout of the entire document. These functions are carried out in Word in several different ways.

Primary page layout is included in a document's Template and text formatting in a Template's styles. Within any document, however, you can override Paragraph Style formats by applying text formatting and enhancements manually to selected text. To immediately cancel manual formatting, select the text and use the **Edit, Undo** command, or (<Ctrl+Z>). The selected text reverts to its original format. In the long term, you can cancel manual formatting by selecting the text and using the <Shift+Ctrl+N> key stroke. The text then reverts to its style format.

Formatting Text

If you use TrueType fonts, which are automatically installed when you set up Windows, Word uses the same font to display text on the screen and to print on paper. The screen fonts provide a very close approximation of printed characters. TrueType font names are preceded by TT in the Font box on the Formatting Bar and in the Font dialogue box which displays when you use the **Format, Font** command.

If you use non-TrueType fonts, then use a screen font that matches your printer font. If a matching font is not available, or if your printer driver does not provide screen font information, Windows chooses the screen font that most closely resembles the printer font.

Originally, the title and subtitle of the **PC Users1** memo, were selected from the default Normal style as 'Heading 1' and 'Heading 3', which were in the 16 and 13 point size Arial typeface, respectively, while the main text was typed in 10 point size Times New Roman.

To change this memo into what appears on the screen dump displayed below, first select the title of the memo and format it to italics, 18 point size Arial and centre it between the margins, then select the subtitle and format it to 14 point size Arial. Both title and subtitle are in bold as part of the definition of their respective paragraph style. Finally select each paragraph of the main body of the memo in turn, and format it to 12 point size Times New Roman. If you can't access these font styles, it will probably be because your printer does not support them, in which case you will need to select other fonts that are supported.

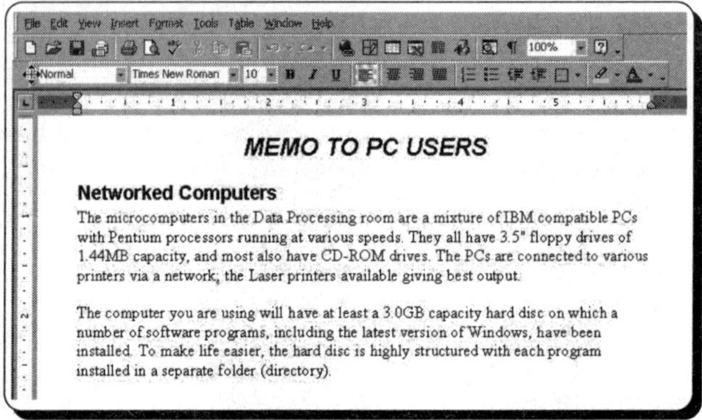

All of this formatting can be achieved by using the buttons on the Formatting Bar (see also the section entitled 'Paragraph Alignment').

As you can see, by moving the Formatting Bar from its former position (to the right of the Standard Toolbar) to just below it (see next section on how to do this), we have exposed more buttons.

Save the result under the new filename **PC Users2**, using the **File, Save As** command.

Moving Toolbars

As we have seen, the default buttons appearing on the two Toolbars below the Menu Bar have distinctive functions. The one to the left is Standard Toolbar, while the one to the right is the Formatting Bar. Each of these two Toolbars is preceded by a vertical handle. Moving the mouse pointer on such a handle, changes it into a small four-headed 'moving' pointer, as shown below.

It is in fact possible to move individual Toolbar sets to any part of the screen, and also change the buttons contained in each. As an example, we will move the Formatting Bar and place it below the Standard Toolbar. To do so, move the mouse pointer on to the vertical handle preceding the set you want to move, and when it changes into the small four-headed pointer press the left mouse button and drag it below its current position. Releasing the mouse button, fixes the bar into its new position, as shown below.

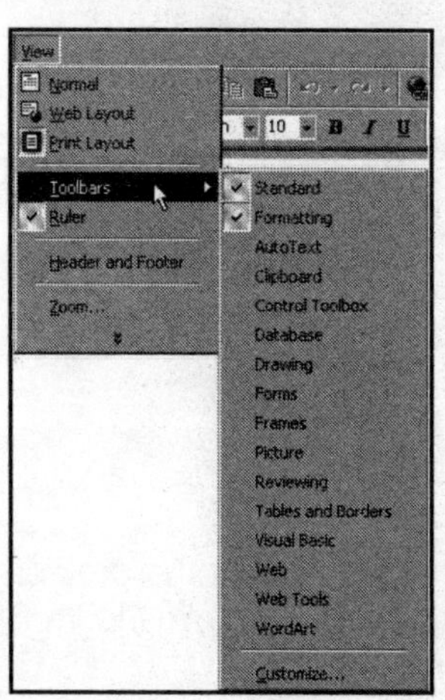

As you can see, additional buttons have appeared on both bars, which previously could not be seen.

To see additional sets of Toolbars, use the **View, Toolbars** command to open up a menu of options, as shown to the left. You can toggle these on and off by clicking on their names. Be careful, however, how many of these you activate, as they take valuable screen space.

Text Enhancements

In Word all manual formatting, including the selection of font, point size, style (bold, italic, highlight, strike-through, hidden and capitals), colour, super/subscript, and various underlines, are carried out by first selecting the text and then executing the formatting command.

The easiest way of activating the formatting commands is from the Formatting Bar. Another way is to use the **Format**, **Font** command, which displays the following dialogue box:

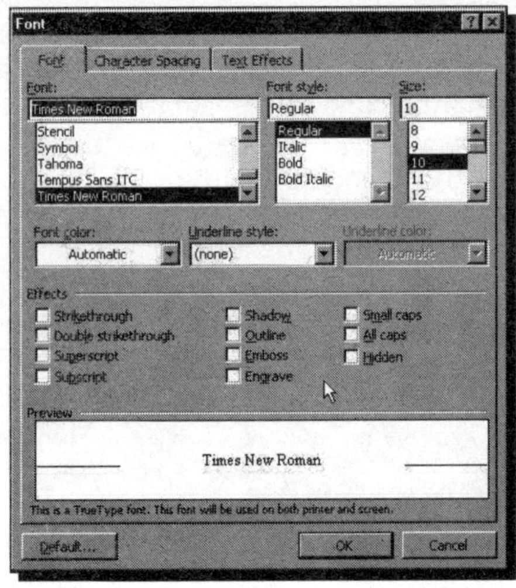

Yet another method is by using quick keys, some of which are listed below:

To Format	***Type***
Bold	Ctrl+B
Italic	Ctrl+I
Underline	Ctrl+U
Word underline	Ctrl+Shift+W
Double underline	Ctrl+Shift+D

There are quick keys to do almost anything, but the problem is remembering them! The ones listed here are the most useful and the easiest to remember.

Paragraph Alignment

Word defines a paragraph, as any text which is followed by a paragraph mark, which is created by pressing the <Enter> key. So single line titles, as well as long typed text, can form paragraphs.

The paragraph symbol, shown here, is only visible in your text if you have selected it from the Standard Toolbar, or used <Ctrl+*>.

Word allows you to align a paragraph at the left margin (the default), at the right margin, centred between both margins, or justified between both margins. As with most operations there are several ways to perform alignment in Word. Three such methods are:

- Using buttons on the **Formatting Bar**.
- Using keyboard short cuts, when available.
- Using the **Format**, **Paragraph** menu command.

The table below describes the buttons on the Formatting Bar and their keystroke shortcuts.

Buttons on Formatting Bar	***Paragraph Alignment***	***Keystrokes***
	Left	<Ctrl+L>
	Centred	<Ctrl+E>
	Right	<Ctrl+R>
	Justified	<Ctrl+J>

The display below shows the dialogue box resulting from using the **Format**, **Paragraph** command in which you can specify any **Left, Right**, or **Special** indentation required.

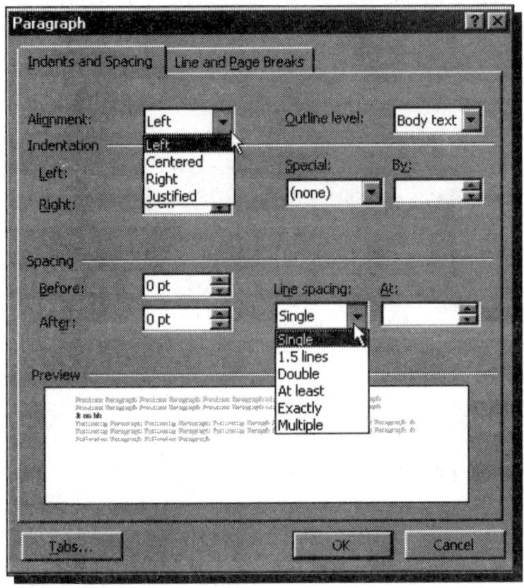

Paragraph Spacing

The above Paragraph dialogue box can also be used to display a paragraph on screen, or print it on paper, in single-line, 1½-line, or double-line spacing. You can even set the spacing to any value you want by using the **At Least** option, as shown on the above screen dump, then specify what interval you want.

The available shortcut keys for paragraph spacing are as follows:

To Format	***Type***
Single-spaced lines	Ctrl+1
One-and-a-half-spaced lines	Ctrl+5
Double-spaced lines	Ctrl+2

Whichever of the above methods is used, formatting can take place either before or after the text is entered. If formatting is selected first, then text will type in the chosen format until a further formatting command is given. If, on the other hand, you choose to enter text and then format it afterwards, you must first select the text to be formatted, then activate the formatting.

Word gives you the choice of 4 units to work with, inches, centimetres, points or picas. These can be selected by using the **Tools**, **Options** command, choosing the **General** tab of the displayed Options dialogue box, and clicking the down arrow against the **Measurement units** list box, shown open here, which is to be found at the bottom of the dialogue box. We selected to work in centimetres from now on.

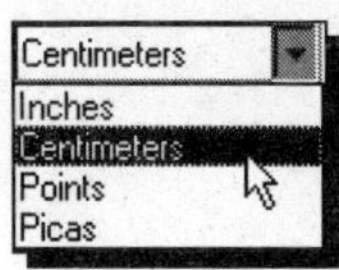

Indenting Text

Most documents will require some form of paragraph indenting. An indent is the space between the margin and the edge of the text in the paragraph. When an indent is set (on the left or right side of the page), any justification on that side of the page sets at the indent, not the page border.

To illustrate indentation, open the file **PC Users2**, select the first paragraph, and then choose the **Format**, **Paragraph** command. In the **Indentation** field, select 2.5cm for both **Left** and **Right**, as shown on the next page. On clicking **OK**, the first selected paragraph is displayed indented. Our screen dump shows the result of the indentation as well as the settings on the Paragraph dialogue box which caused it.

You can also use the Formatting Bar buttons, shown below, to decrease or increase the indent of a selected text.

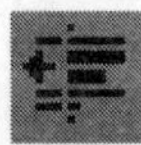

Use this button to decrease indent.

Use this button to increase indent.

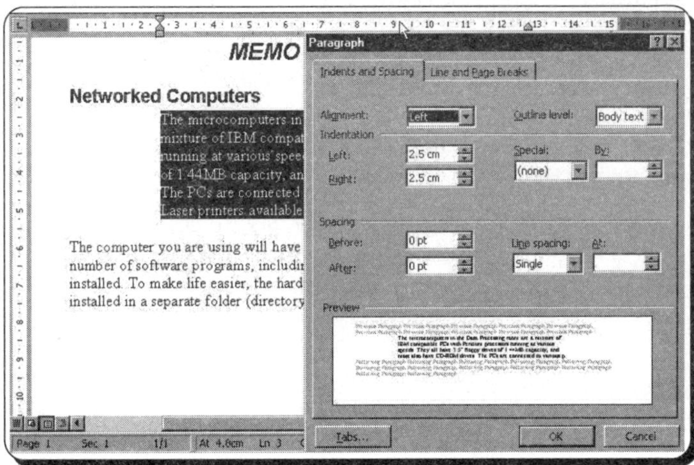

The **Indentation** option in the Paragraph dialogue box, can be used to create 'hanging' indents, where all the lines in a paragraph, including any text on the first line that follows a tab, are indented by a specified amount. This is often used in lists to emphasise certain points.

To illustrate the method, use the **PC Users1** file and add at the end of it the text shown below. After you have typed the text in, save the enlarged memo as **PC Users3**, before going on with formatting the new information.

In Windows you can work with files in three different ways:

Name Description

My Computer Use the My Computer utility which Microsoft have spent much time and effort making as intuitive as possible.

Explorer Use the Windows Explorer, a much-improved version of the older File Manager.

MS-DOS Use an MS-DOS Prompt window if you prefer to and are an expert with the DOS commands.

Saving the work at this stage is done as a precaution in case anything goes wrong with the formatting - it is sometimes much easier to reload a saved file (using the **File, Open** command), than it is to try to unscramble a wrongly formatted document!

Next, highlight the last 4 paragraphs above, use the **Format**, **Paragraph** command, and select 'Hanging' under **Special** and 3 cm under **By**. On clicking the **OK** button, the text formats as shown in the composite screen dump below, but it is still highlighted. To remove the highlighting, click the mouse button anywhere on the page. The second and following lines of the selected paragraphs, should be indented 3 cm from the left margin.

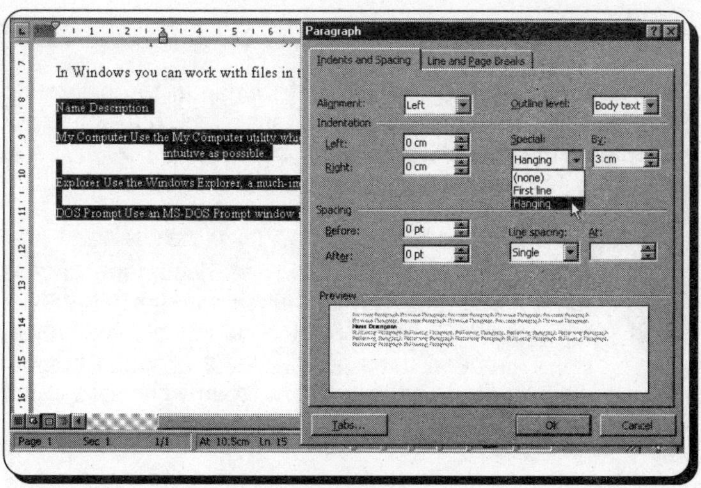

This is still not very inspiring, so to complete the effect we will edit the first lines of each paragraph as follows:

Place the cursor in front of the word 'Description' and press the <Tab> key once. This places the start of the word in the same column as the indented text of the other paragraphs. To complete the effect place tabs before the words 'Use' in the next three paragraphs, until your hanging indents are correct, as shown on the next page.

In Windows you can work with files in three different ways:

Name	Description
My Computer	Use the My Computer utility which Microsoft have spent much time and effort making as intuitive as possible.
Explorer	Use the Windows Explorer, a much-improved version of the older File Manager.
MS-DOS	Use an MS-DOS Prompt window if you prefer to and are an expert with the DOS commands.

This may seem like a complicated rigmarole to go through each time you want the hanging indent effect, but with Word you will eventually set up all your indents, etc., as styles in templates. Then all you do is click in a paragraph to produce them.

When you finish formatting the document, save it under its current filename either with the **File, Save** command (<Ctrl+S>), or by clicking the Save button. This command does not display a dialogue box, so you use it when you do not need to make any changes to the saving operation.

Inserting Bullets

Bullets are small characters you can insert, anywhere you like, in the text of your document to improve visual impact. In Word there are several choices for displaying lists with bullets or numbers. As well as the two Formatting Bar buttons, others are made available through the **Format, Bullets and Numbering** command, which displays the following dialogue box.

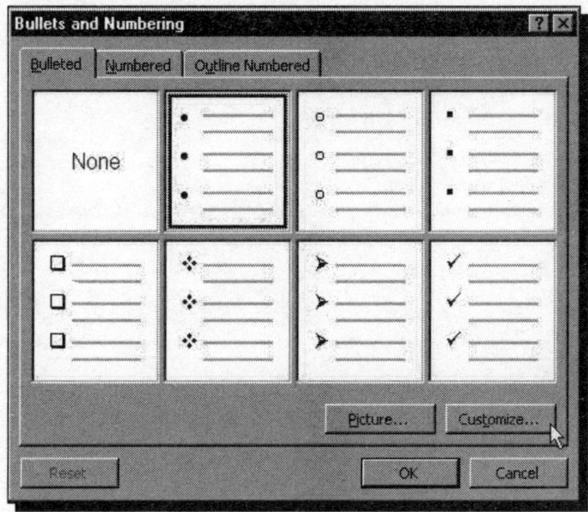

You can select any of the bullets shown here, and then you could click the **Customize** button to change the shape and size of the bullet, or the indentation.

Further, by pressing the **Bullet** button on the Customized Bulleted List dialogue box which would be displayed, you could select any character from the Symbol typeface or other available typefaces.

If you select the **Numbered** or **Outline Numbered** tab, a similar dialogue box is displayed, giving you a choice of several numbering or outline (multilevel) systems.

Once inserted, you can copy, move or cut a bulleted line in the same way as any other text. However, you can not delete a bullet with the <BkSp> or <Del> keys.

Formatting with Page Tabs

You can format text in columns by using tab stops. Word has default left tab stops every 1.27 cm from the left margin, as shown here. This symbol appears on the left edge of the ruler (see below).

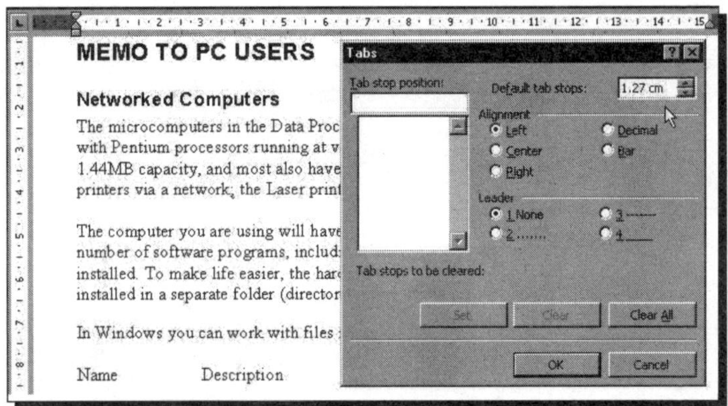

To set tabs, use either the **Format**, **Tabs** command which produces the Tab dialogue box, or click on the tab symbol on the left of the Ruler which cycles through the available tab stops.

The tab stop types available have the following function:

Button Name	*Effect*
Left	Left aligns text after the tab stop.
Centre	Centres text on tab stop.
Right	Right aligns text after the tab stop.
Decimal	Aligns decimal point with tab stop.

To clear the ruler of tab settings press the **Clear All** button in the Tabs dialogue box. When you set a tab stop on the ruler, all default tab stops to the left of the one you are setting are removed. In addition, tab stops apply either to the paragraph containing the cursor, or to any selected paragraphs.

The easiest way to set a tab is to click on the tab type button you want and then point and click at the required position on the lower half of the ruler. To remove an added tab, point to it, click and drag it off the ruler.

If you want tabular text to be separated by characters instead of by spaces, select one of the three available characters from the **Leader** box in the Tabs dialogue box. The options are none (the default), dotted, dashed, or underline. The Contents pages of this book are set with right tabs and dotted leader characters.

Note: As all paragraph formatting, such as tab stops, is placed at the end of a paragraph, if you want to carry the formatting of the current paragraph to the next, press <Enter>. If you don't want formatting to carry on, press the down arrow key instead.

Formatting with Styles

We saw earlier on page 92, how you can format your work using Paragraph Styles, but we confined ourselves to using the default **Normal** style only. In this section we will get to grips with how to create, modify, use, and manage styles.

As mentioned previously, a Paragraph Style is a set of formatting instructions which you save so that you can use it repeatedly within a document or in different documents. A collection of Paragraph Styles can be placed in a Template which could be appropriate for, say, all your memos, so it can be used to preserve uniformity. It maintains consistency and saves time by not having to format each paragraph individually.

Further, should you decide to change a style, all the paragraphs associated with that style reformat automatically. Finally, if you want to provide a pattern for shaping a final document, then you use what is known as a Template. All documents which have not been assigned a document template, use the **Normal.dot** global template, by default.

Paragraph Styles

Paragraph Styles contain paragraph and character formats and a name can be attached to these formatting instructions. From then on, applying the style name is the same as formatting that paragraph with the same instructions.

You can create a style by example, using either the Formatting Bar or the keyboard, or you can create a style from scratch, before you use it, by selecting the **Format, Style** menu command. By far the simplest way of creating a style is by example.

Creating Paragraph Styles by Example: Previously, we spent some time manually creating some hanging indents in the last few paragraphs of the **PC Users3** document. To create a style from this previous work, place the insertion pointer in one of these paragraphs, say, in the 'Name Description' line, and highlight the entire name of the existing style in the Formatting Bar's Style box, as shown below.

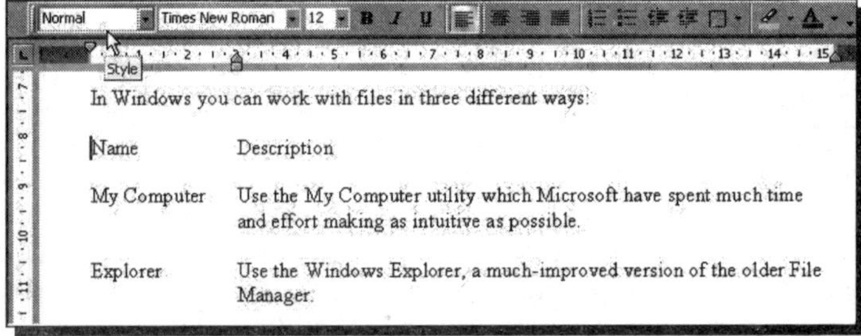

Then, type the new style name you want to create, say, 'Hanging Indent', and press <Enter>.

Finally, highlight the last three paragraphs with hanging indents and change their style to the new 'Hanging Indent', by clicking the mouse in the Style box button and selecting the appropriate style from the displayed list, as shown below. Save the result as **PC Users4**.

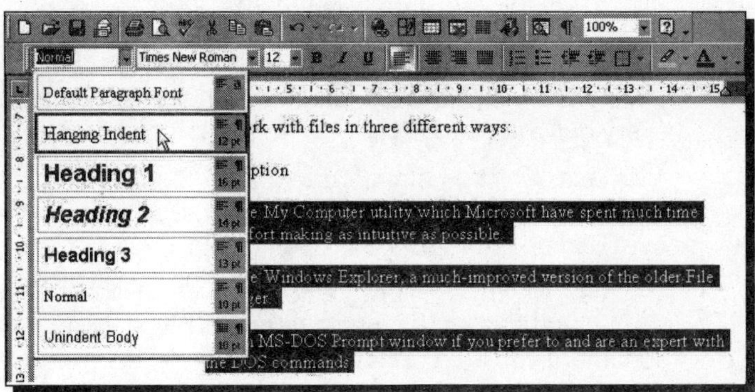

Creating Styles with the Menu Command: You can create, or change, a style before you apply any formatting to a paragraph, by using the **Format**, **Style** command. This displays the Style dialogue box, in which you can choose which style you want to change from the displayed **Styles** list.

Having selected the style you want to change (or not, as the case may be), click the **Modify** button which produces the Modify Style dialogue box. From here you can create a new style, or modify an existing style, by changing the formatting of characters, borders, paragraphs, and tab stops. You can even select which style should follow your current style.

Finally, have a look at Word's built-in styles by selecting **Style Gallery** from the **Format, Theme** menu. There are over sixty available styles, one of which might suit your type of document. Try them with the **PC Users4** file open, as it reformats your document on a viewing pane.

Word Document Templates

A Word 2000 template provides the overall pattern of your final document. It is much more powerful than a Works 2000 template, and can contain:

- Styles to control your paragraph and formats.
- Page set-up options.
- Boilerplate text, which is text that remains the same in every document.
- AutoText, which is standard text and graphics that you could insert in a document by typing the name of the AutoText entry.
- Macros, which are programs that can change the menus and key assignments to comply with the type of document you are creating.
- Customised shortcuts, toolbars and menus.

If you don't assign a template to a document, then the default **Normal.dot** template is used by Word. To create a new document template, you either modify an existing one, create one from scratch, or create one based on the formatting of an existing document.

Creating a Document Template

To illustrate the last point above, we will create a simple document template, which we will call **PC User**, based on the formatting of the **PC Users4** document. But first, make sure you have defined the 'Hanging Indent' style as explained earlier.

To create a template based on an existing document do the following:

- Open the existing document.
- Select the **File, Save As** command which displays the Save As dialogue box, shown overleaf.

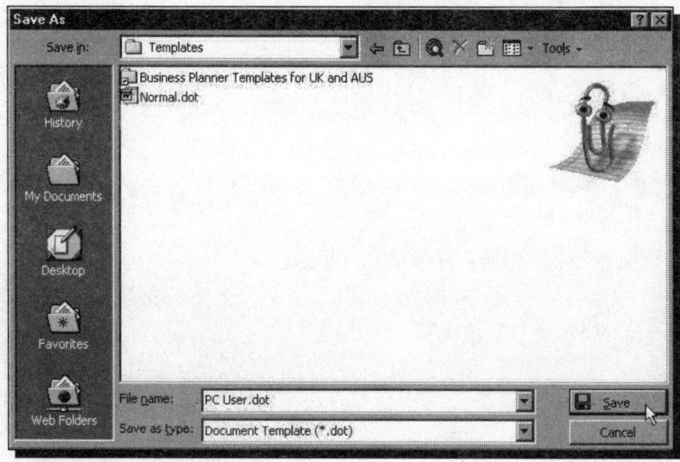

- In the **Save as type** box, select Document Template.
- In the **Save in** box, use the Templates folder which should have opened for you.
- In the **File name** box, type the name of the new template (PC User in our example).
- Press the **Save** button, which opens the template file **PC User.dot** in the Word working area.
- Add the text and graphics you want to appear in all new documents that you base on this template, and ***delete*** any items (including text) you do not want to appear. In our example, we deleted everything in the document, bar the heading, and added the words 'PC User Group' using **Insert, Picture, WordArt**, to obtain:

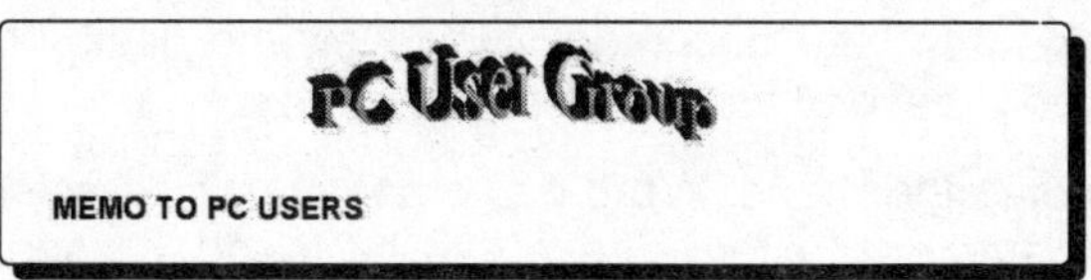

- Click the Save icon on the Toolbar, and close the document.

To use the new template, do the following:

- Use the **File**, **New** command which causes the New dialogue box to be displayed, as shown below.

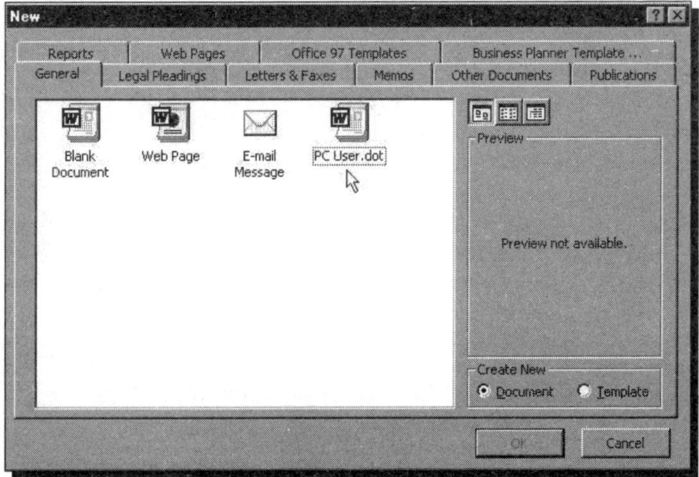

- Click the General tab and select the name of the template you want to use from the displayed list.
- Make sure that the radio button **Document** is selected, and click the **OK** button.

The new document will be using the selected template.

Templates can also contain Macros as well as AutoText; macros allow you to automate Word keystroke actions only, while AutoText speeds up the addition of boilerplate text and graphics into your document. However, the design of these features is beyond the scope of this book.

On the other hand, Word has a series of built-in templates to suit every occasion. These can be found, as seen in the above dialogue box, under the tabs of Letters & Faxes, Memos, Reports, etc. If you upgraded from Office 97, you even have its templates for your use. Try looking at some of these templates.

Special Formatting Features

Word has several special formatting features which force text to override style and style sheet formatting. In what follows, we discuss the most important amongst these.

Changing the Default Character Format

As we have seen, for all new documents Word uses the Times New Roman type font with a 12 points size as the default for the Normal style, which is contained in the Normal template. If the majority of your work demands some different font style or size, then you can change these defaults to suit yourself.

To change the default character formatting, use the **Format**, **Font** command, select the new defaults you want to use, and press the **Default** button, as shown below:

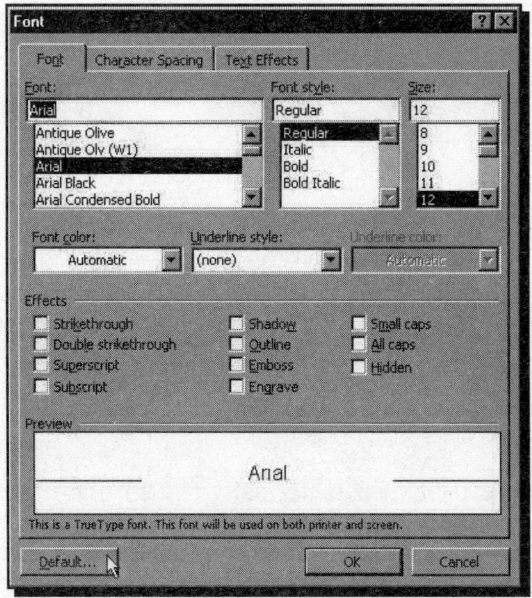

On pressing the **Default** button, the Help Assistant displays the following warning:

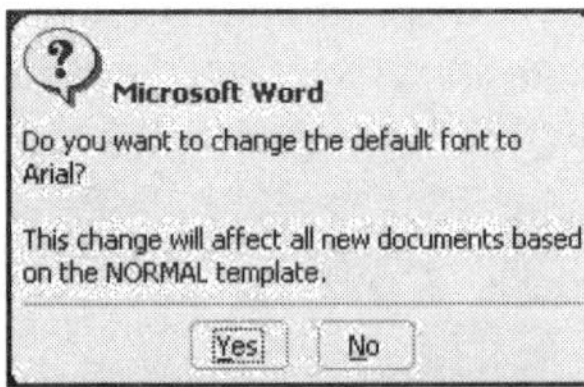

Pressing the **Yes** button, changes the default character settings for this and all subsequent new documents, but does not change already existing ones.

Inserting Special Characters and Symbols

Word has a collection of Symbol fonts, such as the characters produced by the Symbol, Webdings, and Wingdings character sets, from which you can select characters and insert them into your document using the **Insert, Symbol** command. When this command is executed, Word displays the following dialogue box:

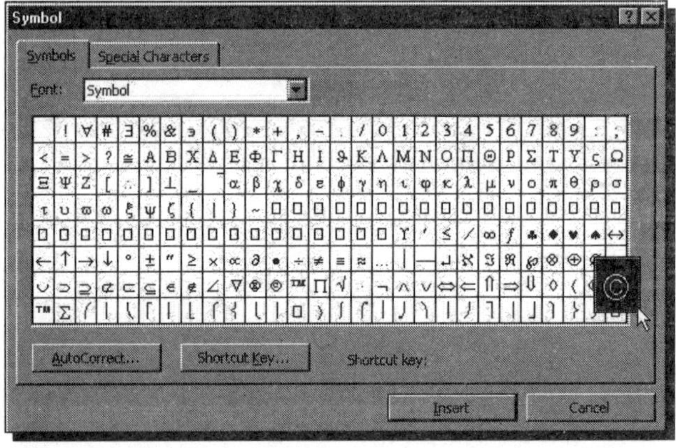

Pressing the down-arrow button next to the **Font** box, reveals the other available character sets. The set showing above is the Symbol set. If you point and click the left mouse button at a character within the set, it selects it and magnifies the selected character. If you double-click the left mouse button, it transfers the selected character to your document at the insertion point.

A Symbol character can be deleted with the <Del> key if you press it twice, or if you press the <BkSp> key once. The advantage of using Symbol is that Word embeds codes in your document which prevent you from changing the character by selecting it and changing to a different font. Thus, this type of formatting overrides any changes you might introduce with a new paragraph formatting.

Inserting Other Special Characters

You can include other special characters in a document, such as optional hyphens, which remain invisible until they are needed to hyphenate a word at the end of a line; non-breaking hyphens, which prevent unwanted hyphenation; non-breaking spaces, which prevent two words from splitting at the end of a line; or opening and closing single quotes.

There are two ways you could use to insert such special characters in your document. One is to click at the **Special Characters** tab of the Symbol dialogue box which reveals a long list of these special characters, as shown below, select one of them and click the **Insert** button. The other way is to use the default key combination (listed against the special characters of the Symbol dialogue box), which does not require you to open it in the first place.

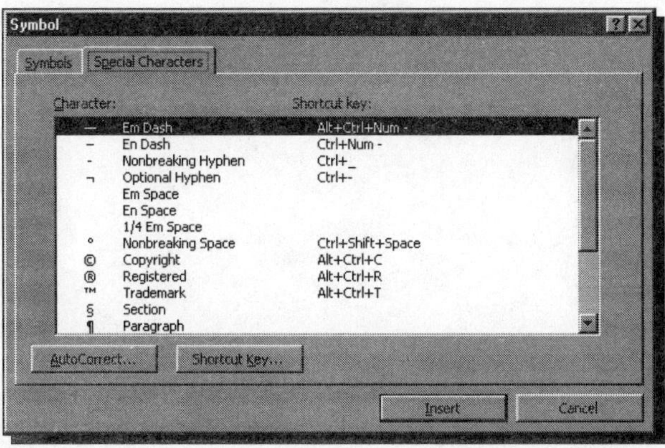

* * *

Word 2000 has many more features, far too numerous to mention in the space allocated to this book. What we have tried to do so far, is give you enough basic information so that you can have the confidence to forge ahead and explore the rest of Word's capabilities by yourself.

Perhaps, you might consider exploring page numbering, headers and footers, tables, frames, drawing, outlining, and Web pages in that order. We leave it to you. However, if you would prefer to be guided through these topics, then may we suggest you look up the later chapters of the book *Microsoft Word 2000 explained* (BP472), also published by BERNARD BABANI (publishing) Ltd.

* * *

8

The Works 2000 Spreadsheet

When you first enter the Works 2000 spreadsheet, the program sets up a huge electronic page, or worksheet, in your computer's memory, many times larger than the small part shown on the screen. Individual cells are identified by column and row location (in that order), with the present size extending to 256 columns by a massive 16,384 rows. The columns are labelled from A to Z, followed by AA to AZ, BA to BZ, and so on, to IV, while the rows are numbered from 1 to 16,384.

Clicking the **Programs** tab in the Task Launcher window, selecting **Works Spreadsheet**, and then clicking **Start a blank Spreadsheet** displays the following screen. The program can also be opened by selecting **Microsoft Works Spreadsheet** in the Windows **Start** menu system.

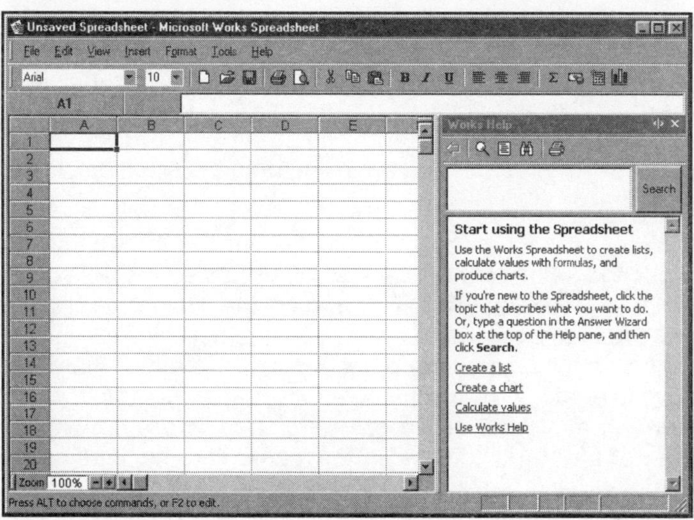

A spreadsheet can be thought of as a two-dimensional table made up of rows and columns. The point where a row and column intersect is called a cell, while the reference points of a cell are known as the cell address. The active cell (A1 when you first enter the program) is highlighted.

Worksheet Navigation

Navigation around the worksheet is achieved with the four arrow keys. Each time one of these keys is pressed, the active cell moves one position right, down, left or up, depending on which arrow key was pressed. The <PgDn> and <PgUp> keys can also be used to move vertically one full page at a time, while the <Ctrl+PgDn> and <Ctrl+PgUp> key combinations can be used to move horizontally one full page at a time. Pressing the arrow keys while holding down the <Ctrl> key causes the active cell to be moved to the extremities of the worksheet. For example, <Ctrl+→> moves the active cell to the IV column, while <Ctrl+↓> moves the active cell to the 16,384th row.

You can move the active cell with a mouse by moving the mouse pointer to the cell you want to activate and clicking the left mouse button. If the cell is not visible, then move the window by clicking on the scroll bar arrowhead that points in the direction you want to move, until the cell you want to activate is visible. To move a page at a time, click in the scroll bar itself, or for larger moves, drag the scroll box in the scroll bar.

When you have finished navigating around the worksheet, press the <Ctrl+Home> keys which will move the active cell to the A1 position. This is known as the 'Home' position. If you press the <Home> key by itself, the active cell is moved to the 1st column of the particular row. Note that there are several areas on your screen; the displayed area within which you can move the active cell is referred to as the working area of the worksheet, while the letters and numbers in the border around the displayed portion of the worksheet form the reference points.

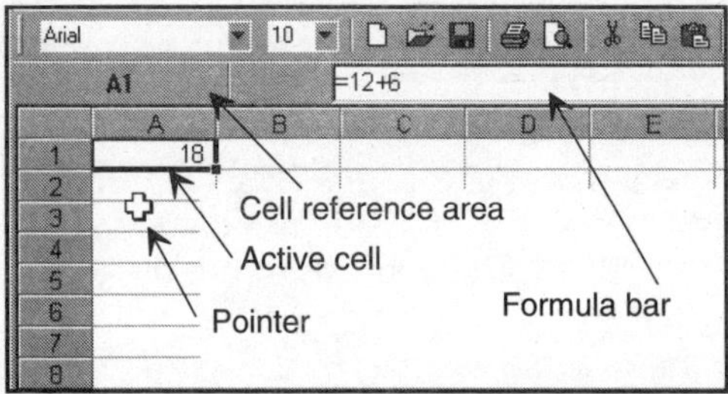

The location of the active cell is constantly monitored in the Cell Reference Area at the left end of the Formula Bar, below the Toolbar. If you type text in the active cell, what you type appears both in the formula bar and in the cell itself. Typing a formula which is preceded by the equals sign (=) to, say, add the contents of two cells, causes the actual formula to appear in the 'formula bar', while the result of the actual calculation appears in the active cell when the <Enter> key is pressed.

The GoTo Command

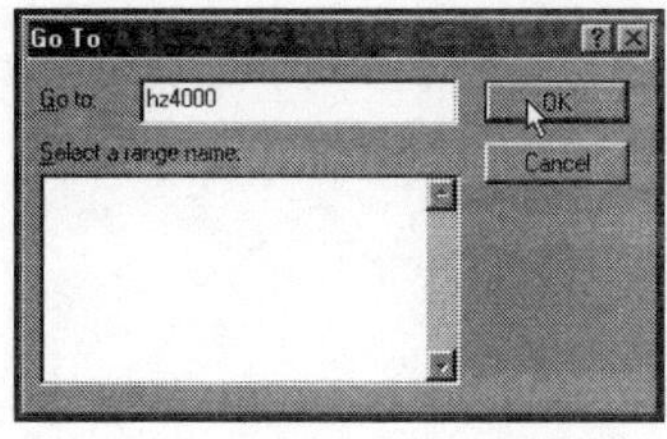

Sometimes it is necessary to move to a distant address in the worksheet when you can use the **F5** function key as a 'go to' command. For example, to jump to position HZ4000, press the **F5** key, and Works will ask for the address of the cell to which it is to jump.

Now, typing hz4000 (or HZ4000) and pressing **OK**, jumps the active cell to that address. To specify a cell address, you must always key one or two letters followed by a number. The letters can be in upper or lower case, and can range from A to IV corresponding to a column, while the numbers can range from 1 to 16,384 corresponding to a row. Specifying a column or row outside this range will cause an error message to be displayed which you have to clear by clicking on the **OK** button, before you can continue.

The Spreadsheet Toolbar

As with the word processor tool, mouse lovers have an advantage when using the spreadsheet, in that they can make use of the Toolbar. This occupies the third line down of the screen. If you prefer, you can turn it off by activating the **View**, **Toolbar** command. This is a toggle switch, when the '√' shows the Toolbar will display, otherwise it will not. The only advantage to be gained by not showing the Toolbar, is that you gain one line on your screen display. To use the Toolbar you simply click the mouse on one of the icon buttons shown below, and the command selected will be effected on worksheet cells that are highlighted.

The meanings of the Toolbar options are as follows:

Option	***Result***
Arial	Choose a font from the available list. Clicking the down arrow (▾) will open the list of fonts.
10	Choose from the available point sizes. Clicking the down arrow (▾) will open the list of sizes.
	Open new spreadsheet
	Open an existing file
	Save current document
	Print current document
	Print preview
	Cut to clipboard
	Copy to clipboard
	Paste from clipboard

B	Embolden selected text
I	Make selected text italic
U	Underline selected text
	Left align a paragraph
	Centre align a paragraph
	Right align a paragraph
Σ	Autosum a column, or row
	Format selected cells as currency, with 2 decimal places
	Use Easy Calc to enter functions
	Create a chart using the selected entry data

Entering Information

We will now investigate how information can be entered into the worksheet. But first, return to the Home (A1) position by pressing <Ctrl+Home>, then type in the words:

```
PROJECT ANALYSIS
```

As you type, the characters appear in both the 'formula bar' and the active cell window.

If you make a mistake, press the <BkSp> key to erase the previous letter or the <Esc> key to start again. When you have finished, press <Enter>. Note that what you have just typed in has been entered in cell A1, even though part of the word ANALYSIS appears to be in cell B1. If you use the right arrow key to move the active cell to B1 you will see that the cell is indeed empty.

Note that the text displayed in the 'formula bar' is prefixed by double quotation marks (") which were added automatically by the program to indicate that the entry is a 'label' and not a number, or a date. Thus, typing a letter at the beginning of an entry into a cell results in a 'label' being formed. If the length of a label is longer than the width of a cell, it will continue into the next cell to the right of the current active cell, provided that cell is empty, otherwise the displayed label will be truncated.

To edit information already in a cell, move the pointer to the appropriate cell and either press the **F2** function key, or click in the 'formula bar'. The cursor keys, the <Home> and <End> keys, as well as the <Ins> and <Del> keys can be used to move the cursor and/or edit the information displayed in the formula bar, as required. After such editing of information in the formula bar, you must either press the <Enter> key, or click the '√' button on the formula bar, to enter it in the active cell.

Now use the arrow keys to move the active cell to B3 and type

```
"Jan
```

Then press the right-arrow key, which will automatically enter the abbreviation 'Jan' into the cell, as a label, and will also move the active cell to position C3. Had we only typed Jan (without the double quotes prefix) on pressing either <Enter> or the right-arrow key, the word 'January' would have appeared automatically in the cell, as a date. In cell C3, type

```
"Feb
```

and again press the right-arrow key.

The looks of a worksheet can be enhanced considerably by placing lines, or cell borders, to separate information in different rows. Select the cells A4 to C4 (from the keyboard use the <Shift+→> keystroke; with the mouse drag the active cell) and choose the **Format, Border** menu command. This opens the Border tabbed section of the Format Cells dialogue box, from which you can place any combination of lines along the borders of selected cells. In our case, select

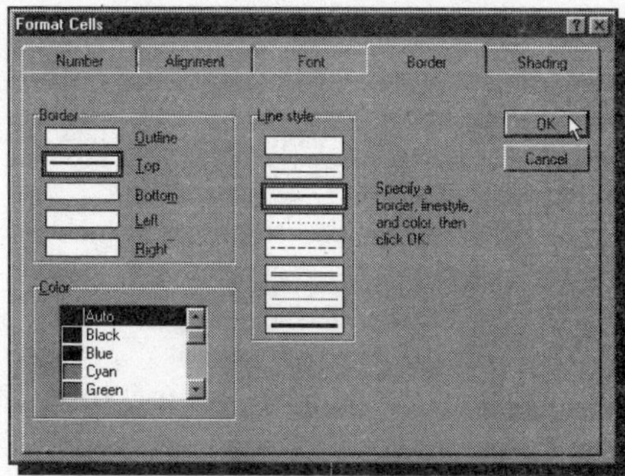

Top and the heavy **Line style** option, as shown above, and press **OK** to accept the settings.

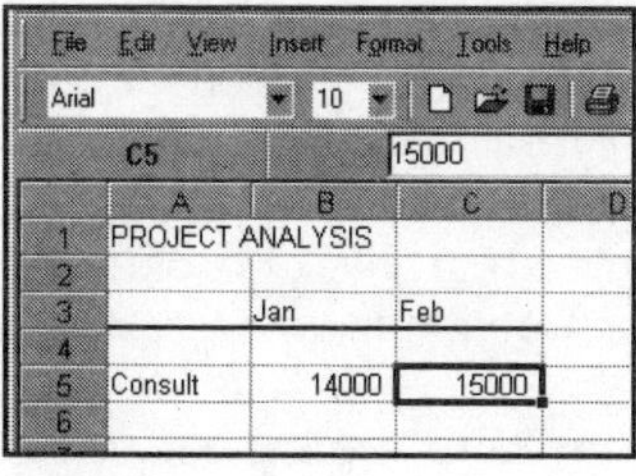

Finally, type in the label and amounts earned in columns A, B and C of row 5, as shown in the screen dump alongside.

Note how the labels 'Jan' and 'Feb' do not appear above the numbers 14000 and 15000. This is because by default, labels are left justified, while numbers are right justified.

Changing Text Alignment and Fonts

One way of improving the looks of this worksheet is to also right justify the labels 'Jan' and 'Feb' within their respective cells. To do this, move the active cell to B3 and mark the range B3 to C3 (from the keyboard use the <Shift+→> keystroke; with the mouse drag the active cell), choose the **Format, Alignment** command, then select the **Right** option listed in the Alignment tabbed section of the Format Cells dialogue box and press <Enter>. The labels should now appear right justified within their cells. An easier way to carry out this operation is to select the cells and click the Right Align Toolbar icon, shown here.

We could further improve the looks of the worksheet by choosing a different font for the heading 'Project Analysis'. To achieve this, move the active cell to A1, choose the **Format, Font and Style** command, then select Courier New, **Size** 8 and **Italic**, from the options listed in the displayed dialogue box, and press **OK**. The heading will now appear in Courier New 8, Italic font.

Once again the Toolbar gives a much quicker way of carrying out these operations. Simply click the down arrow alongside the Font Name or Font Size icons, shown above, and make your selection from the menus that drop down.

Finally, since the entered numbers in cells B5 to C5 represent money, it would be better if these were displayed with two digits after the decimal point and prefixed with the £ sign. To do this, move the active cell to B5 and select the cell block B5 to C5, then choose the **Format**, **Number, Currency** command and accept the default number of decimals, which is 2. This formatting operation can also be done by clicking the Currency Toolbar icon, shown here, which formats selected cells to currency with 2 decimal places. The numbers within the marked worksheet range should now be displayed in the new format. If the width of the relevant cells had not been large enough to accommodate all the digits of the new format, they would have been filled with the hash character (#) to indicate insufficient space. The columns would then need to be widened.

Changing Column Widths

To change the width of a given column or a number of columns, activate a cell in the relevant column, or block the number of required column cells, use the **Format** command and select the **Column Width** option from the pull-down sub-menu. This causes a dialogue box to be displayed with the **Standard** column width offered as 10 characters, or a **Best Fit** option which ensures all entries in the column fit. Typing 12 and pressing <Enter>, changes the width of the selected columns to 12 characters.

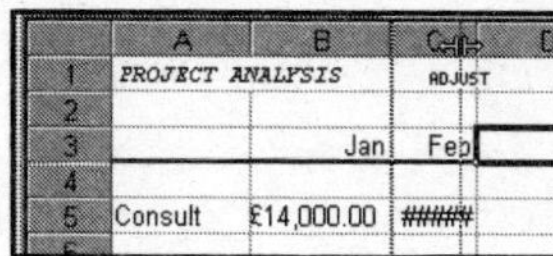

A quicker method of doing this, if you prefer, is to position the mouse pointer in the column headings at the top of the working area. It will change shape as you move it over the border of two columns. Dragging this new pointer right or left, will widen, or narrow, the column to the left.

If the currency symbol displays as a '$' don't panic, it just means your version of Windows is not set up for the UK. To remedy this open the Control Panel by clicking the **Start** button on the Windows TaskBar, followed by **Settings**, **Control Panel**. Double-click on the Regional Settings icon. Make sure that English (United Kingdom) is selected on the opening tabbed page. The Currency page settings should then be correct, as shown below, if not simply change them.

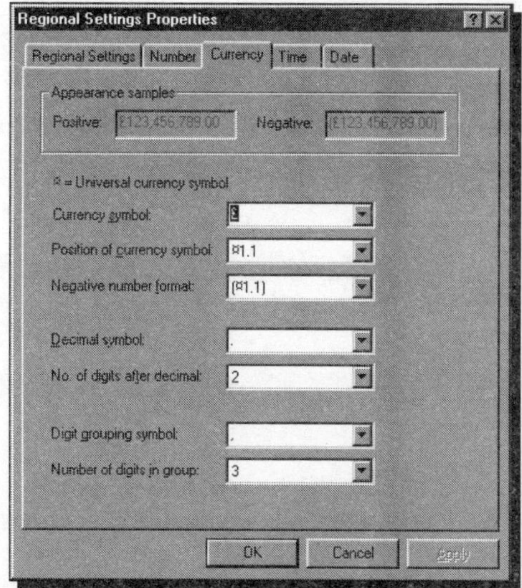

You can, of course, customise these Regional settings for wherever on the globe you happen to be.

Now change the contents of cell A5 from 'Consult' to 'Consultancy'.

Saving a Worksheet

At this point, you might like to stop entering information in your worksheet, and save the work so far carried out, before leaving the program. You can do this by choosing the **File, Save** command which, when used for the first time with a file, opens the Save As dialogue box.

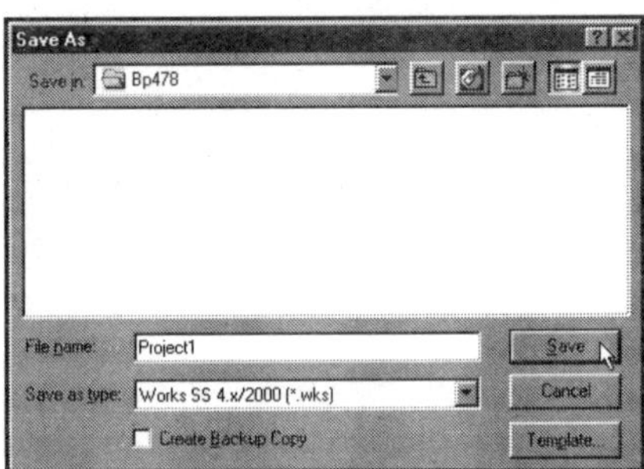

For our exercise, type the **File name** as **Project1** and press <Enter>, or click the **Save** button (the extension .wks will be added by Works). If you prefer to save your work on a floppy disc in, say, the A: drive, instead of in the default My Documents folder, you could make your selection in the **Save in** box.

What you should see displayed on your screen after the above commands have been issued, is shown below, at a zoom factor of 150% for clarity.

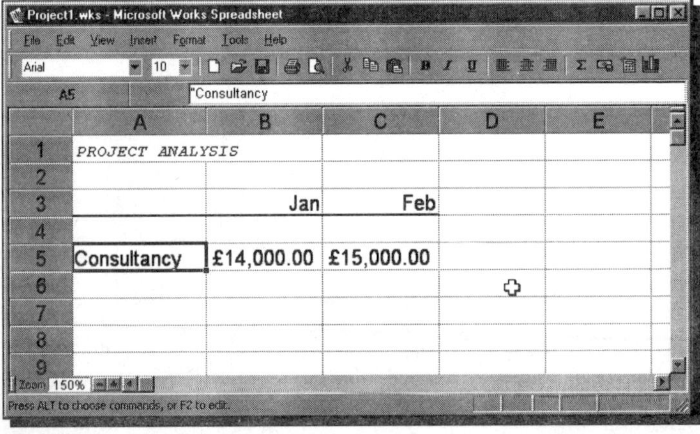

At this point you could exit Works 2000 and Windows and then switch off your computer, safe in the knowledge that your work is saved on disc and can be retrieved at any time.

Exiting a Spreadsheet

To exit Works, either click the Application 'X' Close button, use the **File, Exit** command, or the <Alt+**F4**> keys. If you have made any changes to your work since the last time you saved it, an alert box will be displayed on your screen to ask you if you would like to save the file before leaving the program.

Filling in a Worksheet

We will use, as an example of how a spreadsheet can be built up, the few entries on 'Project Analysis' which we used previously. If you haven't saved the **Project1** example, don't worry as you could just as easily start afresh.

Retrieving a Worksheet

There are two main ways of retrieving, or opening, existing files. Which you use depends on whether you have the Task Launcher or the Spreadsheet itself open.

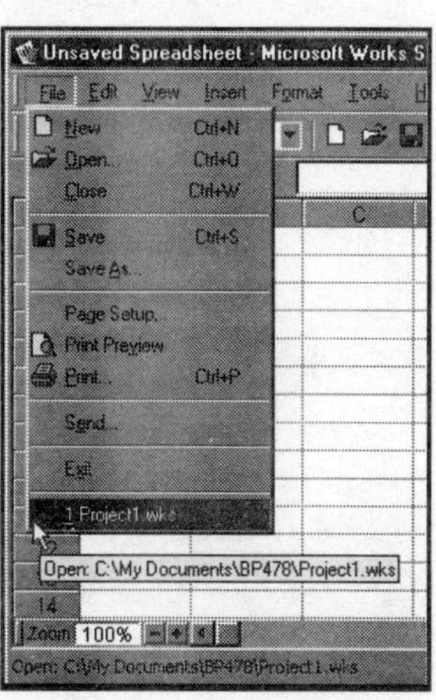

From the Spreadsheet itself:
Use the Open Toolbar button, or the **File**, **Open** command. A quick way to retrieve one of the last files used by Works is to open the **File** menu in a Spreadsheet window and click on the file's name at the bottom of the menu options, as shown here. As you highlight the files in this list their full path locations are shown on the status bar, and in a drop down banner.

From the Task Launcher:

Clicking the **History** tab in the Task Launcher opens a list of recently used files and documents, as shown below. Clicking one of these will open the file in the relevant application. In our case, this will be **Project1**, as shown.

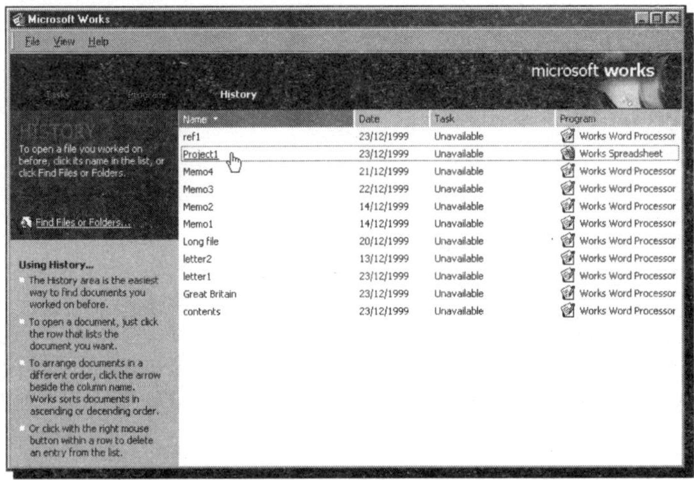

This list can get very untidy, often showing several references that are of no real use. To delete these from the history list, right-click a name, and select **Delete** on the shortcut menu. The entry in the history list is only a shortcut to a file, so when you delete an entry the file itself is not deleted from your computer's hard drive, only the shortcut.

If you don't know the document's actual location on your system, try using the **Find Files or Folders** link to search your whole hard disc system. When you have selected the file you want, in our case, **Project1**, just click to open it.

When the file is open, use the **F2** function key to 'Edit' the existing entries, or simply retype the contents of cells (see the next section for the formatting of the example) so that your worksheet looks like the one on the next page.

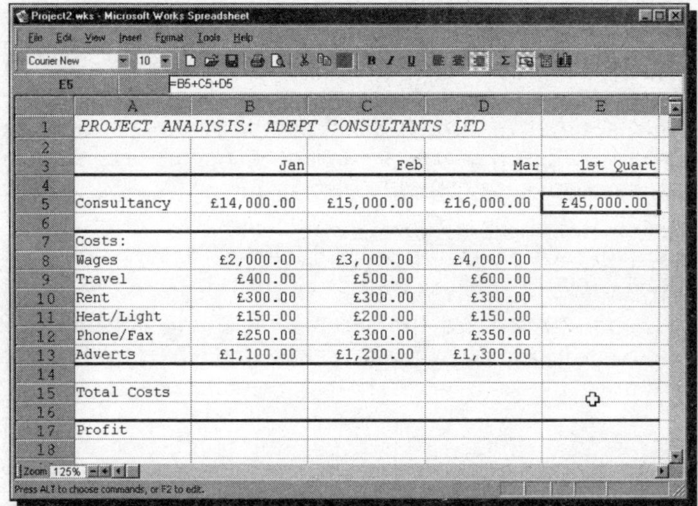

Formatting Entries

Because of the length of some of the labels used and the formatting of the numbers, the default widths of cells in our worksheet were changed from the existing 10, to 12. If you haven't done this already, mark the cell block A1:E1, and choose the **Format, Column Width** command, and type 12 for the new width of the cells. The information in cell A1

```
PROJECT ANALYSIS: ADEPT CONSULTANTS LTD
```

was entered left justified and formatted by choosing the Courier New, size 12, Italic Toolbar icons. The labels in the cell block B3-E3 were formatted with the Right Align icon, so they are displayed right justified.

The numbers within the cell block B5-E17 were formatted by clicking the Currency button. All the labels appearing in column A (apart from that in cell A1) were just typed in (left justified), as shown.

The lines in cells A4 to E4 and A14 to E14 were entered using the **Format**, **Border** command and selecting **Top**. Those in cells A6 to E6 and A16 to E16 were entered using **Format**, **Border** and selecting **Bottom**.

Entering Text, Numbers and Formulae

When text, numbers or formulae are entered into a cell, or reference is made to the contents of a cell by the cell address, or a Works function is entered into a cell, then the content of the message line changes from 'Press ALT to choose commands, or F2 to edit' to 'Press ENTER, or ESC to cancel'. This message can be changed back to the former one either by completing an entry and pressing <Enter> or one of the arrow keys, or by pressing the <Esc> key.

In our example, we can find the 1st quarter total income from consultancy, by activating cell E5 and typing the formula

```
=B5+C5+D5
```

followed by <Enter>. The total first quarter consultancy income is added, using this formula, and the result is placed in cell E5. Note, however, that when cell E5 is activated, the 'formula bar' displays the actual formula used to calculate the contents of the cell.

Complete the insertion into the spreadsheet of the various amounts under 'costs' and then choose the **File, Save As** command to save the resultant worksheet under the filename **Project2**, before going on any further. Remember that saving your work on disc often is a good policy to get used to, as even the shortest power cut can cause the loss of hours of hard work!

Using Functions

In our example, writing a formula that adds the contents of three columns is not too difficult or lengthy a task. But imagine having to add 20 columns the same way! For this reason Works, like all spreadsheets, has an in-built summation function (for the many others see the Appendix) in the form of =SUM( ) which can be used to add any number of columns (or rows).

To illustrate how this function can be used, activate cell E5 and type

```
=SUM(
```

then use the mouse pointer to highlight the cells in the summation range (B5 to D5 in this case). What appears against the cell indicator is the entry

```
SUM(B5:D5
```

which has to be completed by typing the closing parenthesis (round bracket) and pressing <Enter>.

The Autosum Function

Another clever feature in Works is the facility to automatically enter the above =SUM() function into the worksheet. To automatically sum a series of numbers in either a column, or a row, place the active cell below the column, or to the right of the row, and click the Autosum Toolbar button, shown here, or press the <Ctrl+M> quick key combination. Works enters the formula for you; all you have to do is press <Enter>, or click the Enter button (√) on the Formula bar, to accept it.

Easy Calc

The Easy Calc feature helps you add functions to your spreadsheets. To use it, place the active cell where you want to add a function (cell E8 in our example) and click the Easy Calc Toolbar button shown here. If you prefer, use the **Tools**, **Easy Calc** menu command. Both open the dialogue box shown here on the

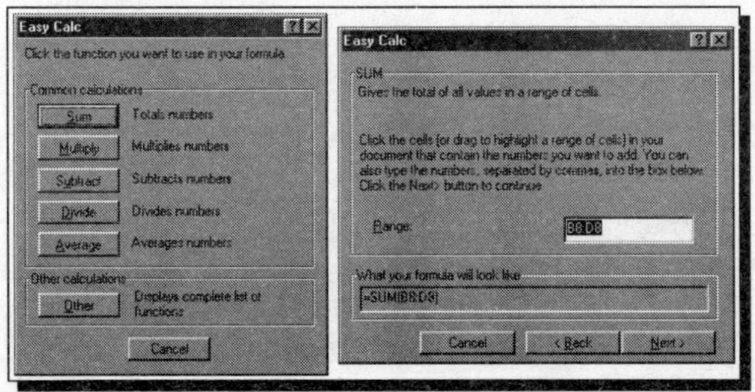

left, which should help to enter the correct function for your needs. Clicking **Sum** opens the box shown on the right.

Copying Cell Contents

To copy information into other cells we could repeat the above procedure (in this particular case entering the SUM() function in each cell within the cell range E8 through E13), or we could choose the **Edit**, **Copy** command, point to the cell we would like to copy information into and **Edit**, **Paste** it.

To illustrate the copy command, activate cell E5 and click the Copy icon, or choose the **Edit**, **Copy** command, or press <Ctrl+C>, which copies the cell contents to the Windows clipboard. Move the highlighted cell to E8 and click the Paste icon, or press **Edit**, **Paste**, or the <Ctrl+V> quick key. Then, block the cell range E8:E13 (by either using the <Shift+↓> keystroke or dragging the mouse) and choose the **Edit, Fill Down** command, or press <Ctrl+D>. This is a good shortcut to remember!

Immediately this command is chosen the actual sums of the 'relative' columns appear in the target area. Notice that when you activate cell E5, the function target range is B5:D5, while when you activate cell E8 the function target range changes to B8:D8 which indicates that copying formulae with this method causes the 'relative' target range to be copied. Had the 'absolute' target range been copied instead, the result of the various summations would have been wrong.

Now complete the insertion of functions and formulae in the rest of the worksheet, noting that 'Total Costs' is the summation of rows 8 through 13, 'Profit' is the subtraction of 'Total Costs' from 'Consultancy', and that 'Cumulative' in row 19 refers to cumulative profit.

Then add another column to your worksheet to calculate (and place in column F) the average monthly values of earnings, costs, and profit, using the =AVG( ) function.

The worksheet, up to this point, should look like the one on the next page. To make room on the screen for all 6 columns, we changed the Font to Courier 10 points, but we could have used the **View**, **Zoom** feature instead. We also emboldened all the column and row titles.

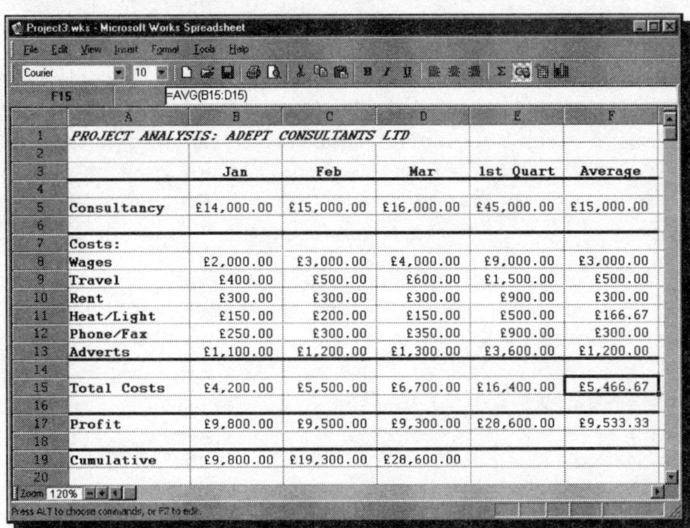

	A	B	C	D	E	F
1	*PROJECT ANALYSIS: ADEPT CONSULTANTS LTD*					
2						
3		**Jan**	**Feb**	**Mar**	**1st Quart**	**Average**
4						
5	**Consultancy**	£14,000.00	£15,000.00	£16,000.00	£45,000.00	£15,000.00
6						
7	**Costs:**					
8	**Wages**	£2,000.00	£3,000.00	£4,000.00	£9,000.00	£3,000.00
9	**Travel**	£400.00	£500.00	£600.00	£1,500.00	£500.00
10	**Rent**	£300.00	£300.00	£300.00	£900.00	£300.00
11	**Heat/Light**	£150.00	£200.00	£150.00	£500.00	£166.67
12	**Phone/Fax**	£250.00	£300.00	£350.00	£900.00	£300.00
13	**Adverts**	£1,100.00	£1,200.00	£1,300.00	£3,600.00	£1,200.00
14						
15	**Total Costs**	£4,200.00	£5,500.00	£6,700.00	£16,400.00	£5,466.67
16						
17	**Profit**	£9,800.00	£9,500.00	£9,300.00	£28,600.00	£9,533.33
18						
19	**Cumulative**	£9,800.00	£19,300.00	£28,600.00		
20						

Erasing Cell Contents

If you make any mistakes and copy information into cells you did not mean to, then choose the **Edit, Clear** command. To blank the contents within a range of adjacent cells, first select the cell block, then use the command.

There is also an **Edit**, **Undo...** menu option in the Works Spreadsheet, but unfortunately it is nowhere near as useful as that in the word processor.

Once you are satisfied that what appears on your screen is the same as our example, use the **File**, **Save As** command to save your worksheet under the filename **Project3**, as we shall be using this example in the next chapter.

Quick Key Combinations

We have already discussed how you can move around a worksheet, edit information in a cell, or mark a range of cells using the pull-down sub-menus, or the Toolbar.

Another method of achieving these and other operations (some of which will be discussed in the next chapter) is using quick key combinations, which do not require the menu bar to be activated. As you get used to the Works package, you might find it easier to use some of the quick key combinations which can save you a lot of time.

The following key combinations are some of those for use with the Works 2000 spreadsheet.

File Handling	
Open new file	Ctrl+N
Open an existing file	Ctrl+O
Close the current file	Ctrl+W
Save the current file	Ctrl+S
Print File	Ctrl+P

Moving and Selecting	
Go To	F5 or Ctrl+G
Move right one window	Ctrl+PgDn
Move left one window	Ctrl+PgUp
Move to next named range	Shift+F5
Move to next unlocked cell	Tab
Move to previous unlocked cell	Shift+Tab
Select worksheet row	Ctrl+F8
Select worksheet column	Shift+F8
Select whole worksheet	Ctrl+Shift+F8
Activate Autosum	Ctrl+M

Editing	
Undo / Redo last action	Ctrl+Z
Cut selection to the clipboard	Ctrl+X
Copy selection to the clipboard	Ctrl+C
Paste from the clipboard	Ctrl+V
Copy contents of cell above	Ctrl+' (apostrophe)

Re-calculate now	F9
Open object menu	Shift+F10
Activate menu bar	F10
Select all	Ctrl+A
Find	Ctrl+F
Replace	Ctrl+H
Fill cells to the right	Ctrl+R
Fill cells down	Ctrl+D
Check spelling	F7
Help	F1

Working in the Formula Bar

Activate/clear the formula bar	Backspace, or Del
Confirm information in a cell	Enter
Confirm a range of cells	Ctrl+Enter
Edit cell in formula bar	F2

Printing a Worksheet

When Windows was installed on your computer your printers should have been installed as well. Once a printer has been installed and selected, as described on Page 44, Works will happily print to that printer from all the tools.

To print a worksheet, choose the **File**, **Print** command, or use the <Ctrl+P> quick key combination, both of which when used for the first time open the dialogue box shown here.

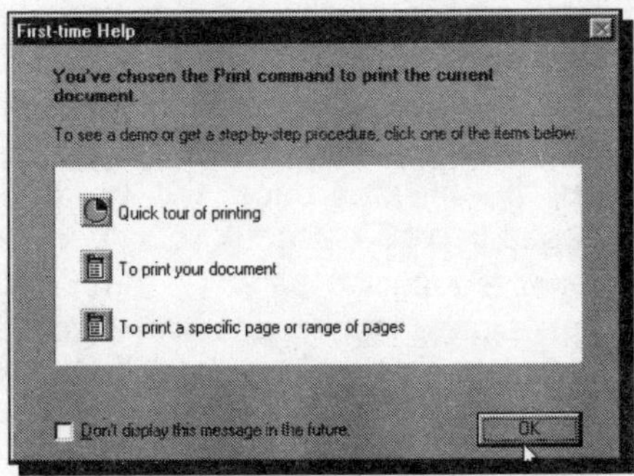

Have a look at the 'Quick tour of printing' offered, but then make sure you click the **Don't display this message in the future** option. The usual Print dialogue box to open is:

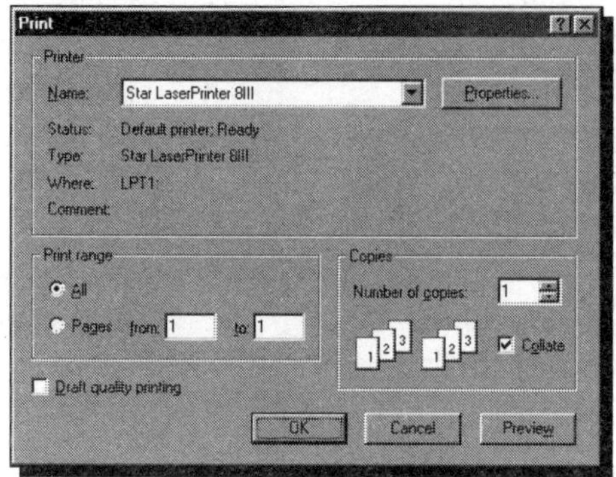

Note that the default print settings are 1 copy, **All** pages, and all text styles, etc. You can change any of the options by choosing to print a different **Number of copies**, selecting which pages to print, and setting **Draft quality printing** output, if you wish. You can also change which printer to use, as well as setting its **Properties**.

Note that clicking on the Print Toolbar icon will send your work straight to the printer without giving you a chance to check, or change, your settings.

Before printing to paper, select the **File**, **Print Preview** command, or click the Print Preview Toolbar icon, shown here, to see how much of your worksheet will fit on your selected paper size. This depends very much on the chosen font. If the **Print Preview** option displays only part of your worksheet, and you then direct output to the printer, what does not fit on one page will be printed out on subsequent pages. To fit more of your worksheet on one page, you should reduce the selected font. Thus, the **Print Preview** option allows you to see the layout of the final printed page, which can save a few trees and, equally important to you, a lot of frustration and wear and tear on your printer.

Setting a Print Area

To select a smaller print area than the current worksheet, first select the required area, then choose the **Format**, **Set Print Area** command and press **OK**. You can then either preview the selected area, or print it on paper.

To reset the print area to the entire worksheet, choose the **Edit**, **Select All** command, then **Format**, **Set Print Area** once more, before attempting to either preview your worksheet or send it to the printer.

Adding Headers and Footers

Headers and footers can be used in both the Works 2000 Spreadsheet and Database tools. These cannot be viewed in the actual spreadsheets, but appear on the print output.

To add them choose **View**, **Headers and Footers** and type the required text in the **Header** or **Footer** boxes.

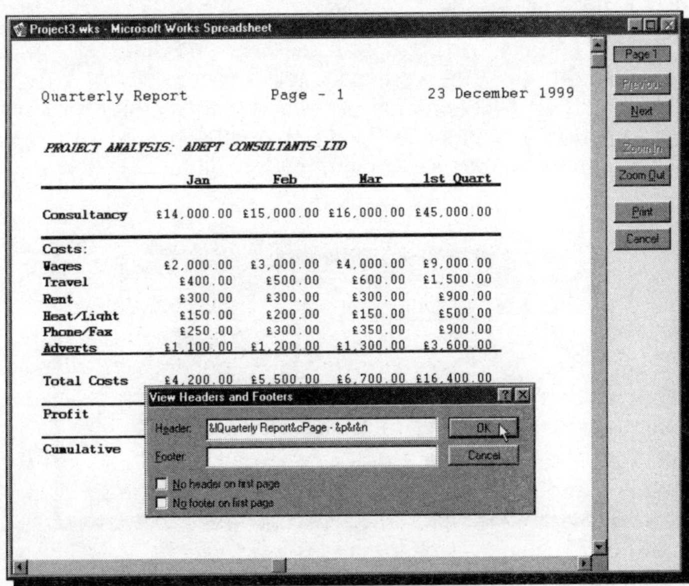

You can align parts of your headers or footers, and include other items automatically, by typing any of the special codes from the following list in with the text. Note that, unless you change the alignment, standard headers and footers are automatically centred.

Operation	*Special Code*
To align following text at left or right margin	&l or &r
To centre the following text	&c
To print page number	&p
To print filename	&f
To print date	&d
To print long date format	&n
To print time	&t
To print an ampersand	&&

As many of these codes, as required, can be placed on a single header or footer line. Our example, on the previous page, shows a line of **Header** codes entered and the resulting header in a print Preview of our example spreadsheet, **Project3**.

It can sometimes be useful to date and time stamp a spreadsheet so that you can tell exactly when it was produced. Our next example of using a footer shows how this can very easily be done in Works 2000. The code '&n' prints the long date and '&t' prints the time, as can be seen below.

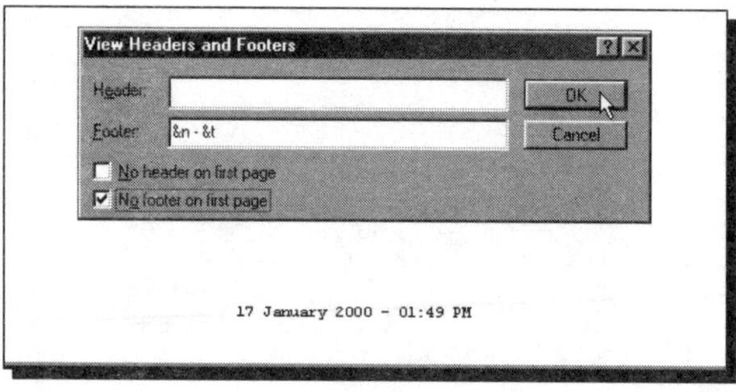

This example also shows how you can prevent a header or footer from appearing on the first page of your printout by selecting either **No header on first page** or **No footer on first page**. You might want to use this when adding page numbers to a printout, when you often don't want them to show on the first page.

To see the results of any header and footer codes you have added you only have to click the Print Preview button. It is then very easy to make changes until you get exactly the result you want without wasting yet more paper!

9

Spreadsheet Skills and Graphs

We will now use the worksheet saved under **Project3** in the previous chapter to show how we can add to it, rearrange information in it and freeze titles in order to make entries easier, before going on to discuss some more advanced topics. If you haven't saved **Project3** on disc, it will be necessary for you to enter the information into the Works spreadsheet so that you can benefit from what is to be introduced in this chapter.

Having done this, save your work before going on with the suggested alterations. If you have saved **Project3**, then click the Open File button on the Toolbar and select the file from those offered. The worksheet will be brought into the computer's memory and when displayed on screen should look like ours below.

Project3.wks - Microsoft Works Spreadsheet

F15 =AVG(B15:D15)

	A	B	C	D	E	F
1	*PROJECT ANALYSIS: ADEPT CONSULTANTS LTD*					
2						
3		Jan	Feb	Mar	1st Quart	Average
4						
5	Consultancy	£14,000.00	£15,000.00	£16,000.00	£45,000.00	£15,000.00
6						
7	Costs:					
8	Wages	£2,000.00	£3,000.00	£4,000.00	£9,000.00	£3,000.00
9	Travel	£400.00	£500.00	£600.00	£1,500.00	£500.00
10	Rent	£300.00	£300.00	£300.00	£900.00	£300.00
11	Heat/Light	£150.00	£200.00	£150.00	£500.00	£166.67
12	Phone/Fax	£250.00	£300.00	£350.00	£900.00	£300.00
13	Adverts	£1,100.00	£1,200.00	£1,300.00	£3,600.00	£1,200.00
14						
15	Total Costs	£4,200.00	£5,500.00	£6,700.00	£16,400.00	£5,466.67
16						
17	Profit	£9,800.00	£9,500.00	£9,300.00	£28,600.00	£9,533.33
18						
19	Cumulative	£9,800.00	£19,300.00	£28,600.00		
20						

Press ALT to choose commands, or F2 to edit.

Controlling Cell Contents

We will now add some more information to the worksheet with the insertion of another quarter's figures between columns E and F. In fact, we need to insert four columns altogether.

In general, you can insert or delete columns and rows in a worksheet, copy cell contents (including formulae) from one part of the worksheet to another and freeze titles in order to make entries into cells easier.

Inserting Rows and Columns

To insert columns into a worksheet, point to the column heading where a column is to be inserted, in our case F, and press the left mouse button, which highlights the whole column. Then choose the **Insert**, **Insert Column** command, or right-click with the mouse and select **Insert Column** from the opened object menu. Had you highlighted a specific cell, say F1, the **Insert** menu command would give you the options of inserting either columns, or rows.

Repeat the insertion command three more times so that the column headed 'Average' appears in column J. To insert three columns in one operation, select the three columns to the right of where you want the insertion before you use the **Insert Column** command. We could now start entering information into the empty columns, but if we did this we would then have to re-enter all the formulae used to calculate the various results for the first quarter.

An alternative, and much easier, way is to copy everything from the first quarter to the second and then only edit the actual numeric information within the various columns. We will choose this second method to achieve our goal. First, highlight the cell block B3:E19, move the highlighter to the top border of the block where it will change to a DRAG pointer. Hold down the <Ctrl> key and Drag copy the block four columns to the right, as shown on the next page.

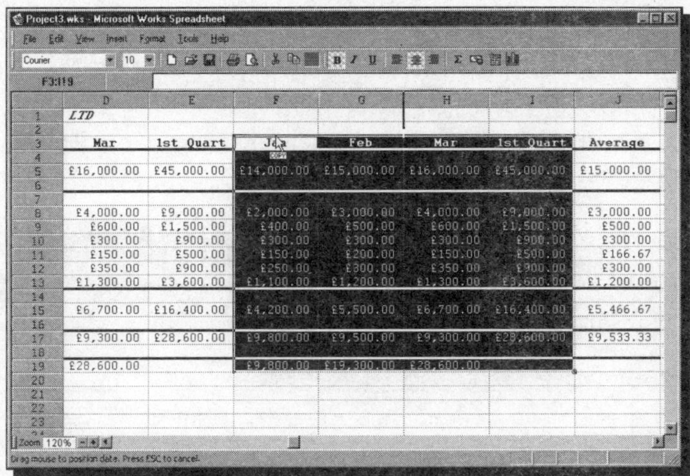

	D	E	F	G	H	I	J
1	LTD						
2							
3	Mar	1st Quart	Jan	Feb	Mar	1st Quart	Average
4							
5	£16,000.00	£45,000.00	£14,000.00	£15,000.00	£16,000.00	£45,000.00	£15,000.00
6							
7							
8	£4,000.00	£9,000.00	£2,000.00	£3,000.00	£4,000.00	£9,000.00	£3,000.00
9	£600.00	£1,500.00	£400.00	£500.00	£600.00	£1,500.00	£500.00
10	£300.00	£900.00	£300.00	£300.00	£300.00	£900.00	£300.00
11	£150.00	£500.00	£150.00	£200.00	£150.00	£500.00	£166.67
12	£350.00	£900.00	£250.00	£300.00	£350.00	£900.00	£300.00
13	£1,300.00	£3,600.00	£1,100.00	£1,200.00	£1,300.00	£3,600.00	£1,200.00
14							
15	£6,700.00	£16,400.00	£4,200.00	£5,500.00	£6,700.00	£16,400.00	£5,466.67
16							
17	£9,300.00	£28,600.00	£9,800.00	£9,500.00	£9,300.00	£28,600.00	£9,533.33
18							
19	£28,600.00		£9,800.00	£19,300.00	£28,600.00		

If necessary, use the **Format, Column Width** command, to change the width of any cells from 10 characters to 12. Now the widths of the highlighted columns are suitably adjusted, edit the copied headings 'Jan', 'Feb', 'Mar', and '1st Quart' to 'Apr', 'May', 'Jun', and '2nd Quart'. Save the resultant work under the filename **Project4** (don't forget to use the **Save As** command)!

Freezing Titles

Note that by the time the highlighted bar is moved to column J, the 'titles' in column A have scrolled to the left and are outside the viewing area of the screen. This will make editing of numeric information very difficult if we can't see what refers to what. Therefore, before we attempt any further editing, it would be a good idea to use the 'Titles' command to freeze the titles in column A and rows 1 to 3.

To freeze row (or column) headings on a worksheet, move the highlighted bar to the cell below the row (or to the right of the column) you wish to freeze on the screen (in our case B4), and select the **Format, Freeze Titles** toggle command.

On execution, the headings on the chosen column (and row) are frozen but the highlighter can still be moved into the frozen area. Moving around the worksheet, leaves the headings in these rows (and/or columns) frozen on the screen. Carry this out and change the numbers in the worksheet cells F5 to H13 to those below.

Save the file again, but this time use the Save Toolbar icon, to keep the name **Project4**.

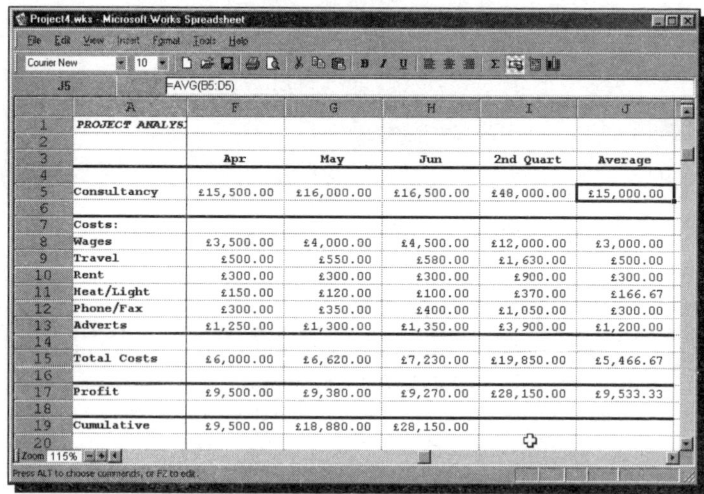

Project4.wks - Microsoft Works Spreadsheet

J5 =AVG(B5:D5)

	A	F	G	H	I	J
1	PROJECT ANALYSI					
2						
3		Apr	May	Jun	2nd Quart	Average
4						
5	Consultancy	£15,500.00	£16,000.00	£16,500.00	£48,000.00	£15,000.00
6						
7	Costs:					
8	Wages	£3,500.00	£4,000.00	£4,500.00	£12,000.00	£3,000.00
9	Travel	£500.00	£550.00	£580.00	£1,630.00	£500.00
10	Rent	£300.00	£300.00	£300.00	£900.00	£300.00
11	Heat/Light	£150.00	£120.00	£100.00	£370.00	£166.67
12	Phone/Fax	£300.00	£350.00	£400.00	£1,050.00	£300.00
13	Adverts	£1,250.00	£1,300.00	£1,350.00	£3,900.00	£1,200.00
14						
15	Total Costs	£6,000.00	£6,620.00	£7,230.00	£19,850.00	£5,466.67
16						
17	Profit	£9,500.00	£9,380.00	£9,270.00	£28,150.00	£9,533.33
18						
19	Cumulative	£9,500.00	£18,880.00	£28,150.00		
20						

Note: If you examine this worksheet carefully, you will notice that two errors have occurred; one of these has to do with the average calculations in column J, while the other has to do with the accumulated values in the second quarter.

Non-Contiguous Address Range

The calculations of average values in column J of the above worksheet are wrong because the range values in the formula are still those entered for the first quarter only.

To correct these, highlight cell J5 and press **F2** to edit the formula displayed in the formula bar from =AVG(B5:D5) to

```
=AVG(B5:D5,F5:H5)
```

which on pressing <Enter> changes the value shown in cell J5. Note the way the argument of the function is written when non-contiguous address ranges are involved. Here we have two such address ranges, B5:D5 and F5:H5, which we separate with a comma.

Now replicate the formula to the J8:J13 cell range by highlighting cell J5, choosing the **Edit, Copy** command, or <Ctrl+C>, move the highlight to cell J8 and use **Edit, Paste**. Then drag the highlight from J8 to J13 (to select the range) and choose the **Edit, Fill Down** command. Finally, repeat the **Paste** operation for the target cells J15 and J17.

You could also do all these actions with the Copy and Paste icons. The choice is yours!

Relative and Absolute Cell Addresses

Entering a mathematical expression into Works, such as the formula in cell C19 which was

```
=B19+C17
```

causes Works to interpret it as 'add the contents of cell one column to the left of the current position, to the contents of cell two rows above the current position'. In this way, when the formula was later replicated into cell address D19, the contents of the cell relative to the left position of D19 (i.e. C19) and the contents of the cell two rows above it (i.e. D17) were used, instead of the original cell addresses entered in C19. This is relative addressing.

To see the effect of relative versus absolute addressing, type in cell E19 the formula

```
=E5-E15
```

which will be interpreted as relative addressing. Now, add another row to your worksheet, namely 'Profit/Quart' in row 21, and copy the formula in cell E19 to cell E21, using the **Edit Copy** command. The displayed calculated value in E21 is, of course, wrong (negative) because the cell references in the copied formula are now given as

```
=E7-E17
```

as the references were copied relatively.

Now change the formula in E19 by editing it to

```
=$E$5-$E$15
```

which is interpreted as absolute addressing. Copying this formula into cell E21 calculates the correct result. Highlight cell E21 and observe the cell references in its formula; they have not changed from those of cell E19.

The $ sign must prefix both the column reference and the row reference. Mixed cell addressing is permitted; as for example when a column address reference is needed to be taken as absolute, while a row address reference is needed to be taken as relative. In such a case, only the column letter is prefixed by the $ sign.

Finally, correct the formulae in cells I19 and I21 (they should both contain '=$E$19+$I$17') in order to obtain the results shown below.

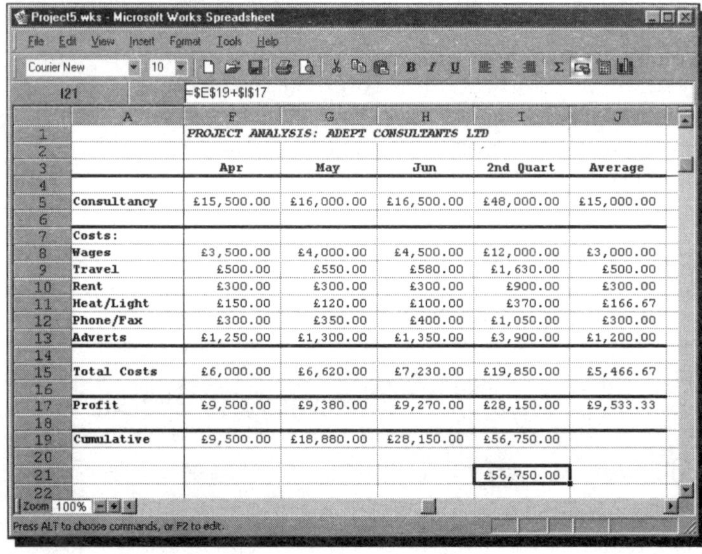

	A	E	G	H	I	J
1		*PROJECT ANALYSIS: ADEPT CONSULTANTS LTD*				
2						
3		**Apr**	**May**	**Jun**	**2nd Quart**	**Average**
4						
5	**Consultancy**	£15,500.00	£16,000.00	£16,500.00	£48,000.00	£15,000.00
6						
7	**Costs:**					
8	**Wages**	£3,500.00	£4,000.00	£4,500.00	£12,000.00	£3,000.00
9	**Travel**	£500.00	£550.00	£580.00	£1,630.00	£500.00
10	**Rent**	£300.00	£300.00	£300.00	£900.00	£300.00
11	**Heat/Light**	£150.00	£120.00	£100.00	£370.00	£166.67
12	**Phone/Fax**	£300.00	£350.00	£400.00	£1,050.00	£300.00
13	**Adverts**	£1,250.00	£1,300.00	£1,350.00	£3,900.00	£1,200.00
14						
15	**Total Costs**	£6,000.00	£6,620.00	£7,230.00	£19,850.00	£5,466.67
16						
17	**Profit**	£9,500.00	£9,380.00	£9,270.00	£28,150.00	£9,533.33
18						
19	**Cumulative**	£9,500.00	£18,880.00	£28,150.00	£56,750.00	
20						
21					£56,750.00	
22						

Moving Cell Contents

To improve the printed output of **Project4**, we could move the caption to somewhere in the middle of the worksheet. Since the cell whose contents we propose to move is frozen, the move command could be preceded by additional keystrokes. From the keyboard, first unfreeze the title with the **Format**, **Freeze Titles** command. Now, highlight cell A1 and choose the **Edit, Cut** command (or <Ctrl+X>), which removes the cell contents from the worksheet and places them on the Windows clipboard, then highlight cell F1 and **Paste** the clipboard's contents. Save the resultant worksheet under the filename **Project5**.

Other Useful Features

Works 2000 includes several other spreadsheet features worth mentioning briefly.

Alignment

Another method of carrying out the title formatting in the last example would be to use the ability to centre a cell's contents within a selected range with the **Format**, **Alignment**, **Center across selection** command.

Some other features to note in this dialogue box are the vertical alignment options and the ability to **Wrap text** (but not numbers or formulae) within a cell. You can now have several lines of text in the same cell.

Automatic Column Widths

Choosing the **Best Fit** check box in the **Format**, **Column Width** dialogue box lets Works determine the best column width to accommodate all the entries in selected columns, or parts of columns. You could use this after selecting the whole sheet and not have to worry about cell widths again.

Inserting Functions

You can automatically choose a function with the **Insert**, **Function** command and Works inserts it, including its arguments, into the formula bar. This feature saves you having to remember all the available function names, and from looking up the argument details every time. But remember they are all listed in the Appendix at the back of this book.

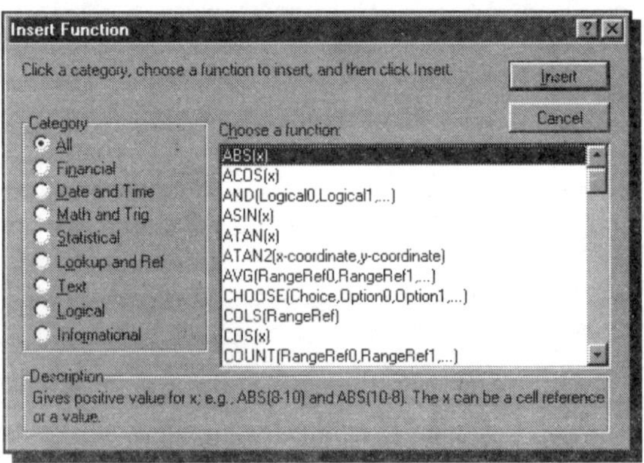

The Undo Command

The **Edit**, **Undo..** command reverses certain commands, or deletes the last entry you typed, but only if it is used straight away. Immediately after you undo an action, this command changes to **Redo..**, which allows you to reverse the action.

Automatic Cell Fill

A useful feature which could save you much typing is the **Edit**, **Fill Series** command, which fills highlighted cells with a series of numbers or dates. You type the first entry, highlight the cells to fill and use this command to quickly enter the rest of a series of consecutive dates or numbers in the column or row.

Try typing 'Jan' in a heading cell, highlight the next eleven cells to the right, use the **Edit**, **Fill Series** command, select

Month, and see what happens. Computers are supposed to make things easier after all!

Cell Formatting Options

The **Format**, **Shading** command gives you control over the pattern and colour of the background of highlighted cells. To change the foreground colour of a cell's contents you must use the **Format**, **Font and Style**, **Color** option.

The **Format**, **AutoFormat** option gives a series of built-in formats you can apply to any highlighted range to give it a more professional appearance.

Adding Spreadsheet Charts

Works 2000 allows you to represent information in graphical form which makes data more accessible to non-expert users who might not be familiar with the spreadsheet format. In any case, the well known saying 'a picture is worth a thousand words', applies equally well to charts and figures.

You use the charting facility of Works by first selecting a data range to be charted on your worksheet, such as A8:D10 on our file **Project5**, and then choosing the **Tools**, **Create New Chart** command, or pressing the New Chart Toolbar icon. The first time this is used it opens another 'First time Help' box as shown here. Have a look at the 'Quick tour of charting' offered, but then make sure you click the **Don't display this message in the future** option.

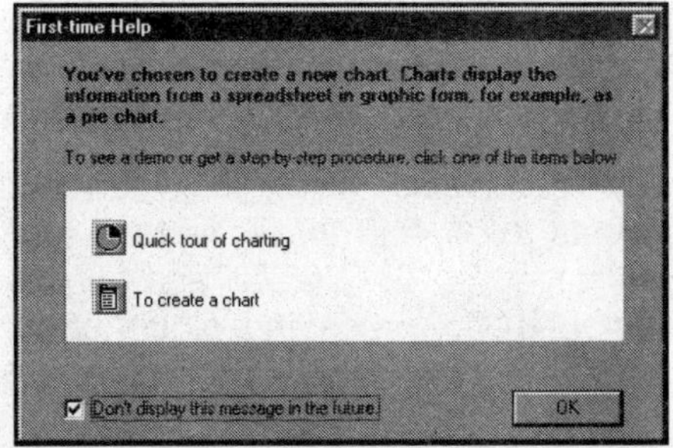

The **Tools**, **Create New Chart** command, or the New Chart Toolbar button will then open the New Chart box, shown below. To see what types of chart, or graphs, are available click the icons in the **What type of chart do you want?** section. An example of each, based on the selected spreadsheet data, is shown in the box.

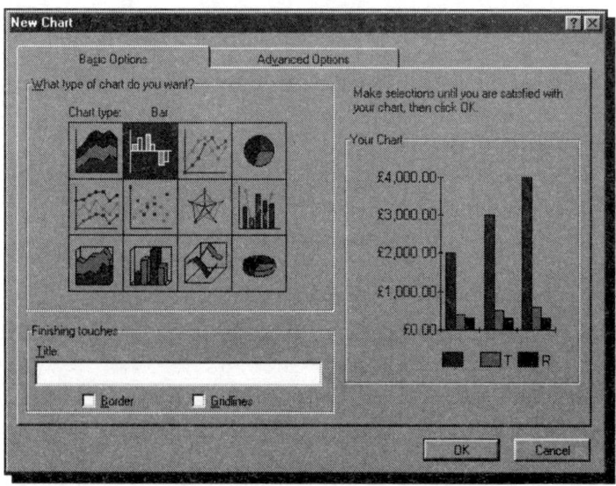

Although Works has eight main two-dimensional, and four three-dimensional, chart and graph types, there are many optional ways to view each type, and they can be grouped and overlapped, which allows you to add considerably to the list. All the different chart-types are selected from the box above, which is opened from the menu, or the Toolbar, when you are in a charting window.

To enhance your charts you can add titles, legends, labels, and can select grids, fill types, scaling, fonts, etc. These charts (you can have several per spreadsheet) can be displayed on the screen and can be sent to an appropriate output device, such as a plotter or printer.

The main graph types available are listed next, with their Charting Toolbar icons, where available. These chart types are normally used for the following relationships between data:

Area 	For comparing value changes to the total over a period of time; 2-D or 3-D options available.
Bar  	For comparing differences in data over a period of time. Displays the values of dependent variables as vertical columns. The stacked and 100% options, show relationships to the whole; with 2-D or 3-D options.
Line  	For representing data values with points joined by lines and appearing at equal intervals along the x-axis. For such charts, the x-axis could be intervals in time, such as labels representing months; 2-D or 3-D options.
Pie  	For comparing parts with the whole. Displays data blocks as slices of a pie. Can contain only one series; 2-D or 3-D options available.
Stacked Line	For representing the total in each category. A line chart in which the lines are stacked.
XY (Scatter) 	For showing the relationship, or degree of relationship, between numeric values in different groups of data; used for finding patterns or trends in data.
Radar	For showing changes in data relative to a centre point and to other data; useful for relative comparisons.
Combination 	For displaying related data measured in different units; used for comparing two different kinds of data or to show a correlation that might be difficult to recognise.

Charts can be displayed on the screen at the same time as the worksheet, but in a separate window. As charts are dynamic, any changes made to the data are automatically reflected on the defined charts.

Preparing for a Bar Chart

In order to illustrate some of the graphing capabilities of Works 2000 we will now plot an income from consultancies graph of the **Project5** file.

First we need to define what we want to chart. The specified range of data to be charted should be contiguous for each chart. But, in our example, the range of data is split into two areas; Jan-Mar (occupying cell positions B3:D3), and Apr-Jun (occupying cell positions F3:H3), with the corresponding income values in cells B5:D5 and F5:H5. Thus, to create an appropriate contiguous data range, we must first replicate the labels and values of these two range areas in another area of the spreadsheet (say, beginning in cell B23 for the actual month labels and B24 for the values of the corresponding income), as shown on the next page.

To do this, use the **Edit, Copy** and **Paste** commands, or buttons, to copy the labels in the above two cell-ranges into the target area. However, before you replicate the cells containing numeric values, consider what might happen if these cells contain formulae, and you used the **Edit, Paste** command to replicate them. Using this command would cause the relative cell addresses to adjust to the new locations and each formula will then recalculate a new value for each cell which will give wrong results.

The Paste Special Command

The **Edit, Paste Special** command allows you to copy only cell references without adjusting to the new location. To do this, mark the cell range to be copied (in this case B5:D5) and choose the **Edit, Copy** command, move the highlighter to cell B24 and press **Edit**, **Paste Special**, select the **Values only** option from the displayed dialogue box and press <Enter>, or select **OK**. Now repeat the same procedure for the values under Apr-Jun, but copy them into E24 to form a contiguous data range.

Finally, add labels for 'Months' and 'Income' in cells A23 and A24, respectively, as shown below, and save the resulting spreadsheet as **Project6**.

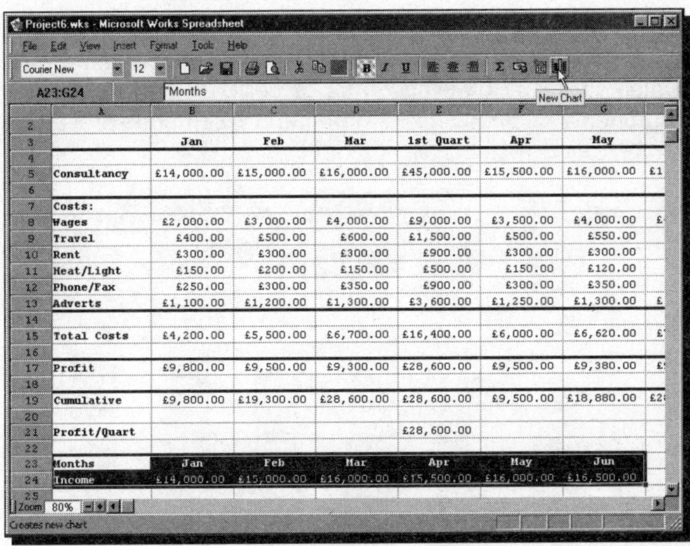

Note - The above way of copying cells is fine for our example where the data will not change. If you have data that changes, however, you would want your graphs to reflect these changes. This is easy to do; you set the graphing cells to 'mirror' the main sheet cells holding the variable data, by entering a formula consisting of a '+' sign followed by the cell address to be 'mirrored'. In our case, for example, cell B24 would contain the formula

```
+B5
```

It would then always show the contents of that cell.

The Chart Editor

To obtain a chart of 'Income' versus 'Months', block cell range A23:G24 and choose the **Tools**, **Create New Chart** command, or the New Chart Toolbar icon and type a **Title**, such as 'ADEPT MONTHLY INCOME'.

Select **OK** to accept the default Bar chart type and Works clears the screen and draws a bar chart of the information contained in the blocked range of cells. This places you in Charting mode with a new set of menu commands and a new Toolbar, as shown below.

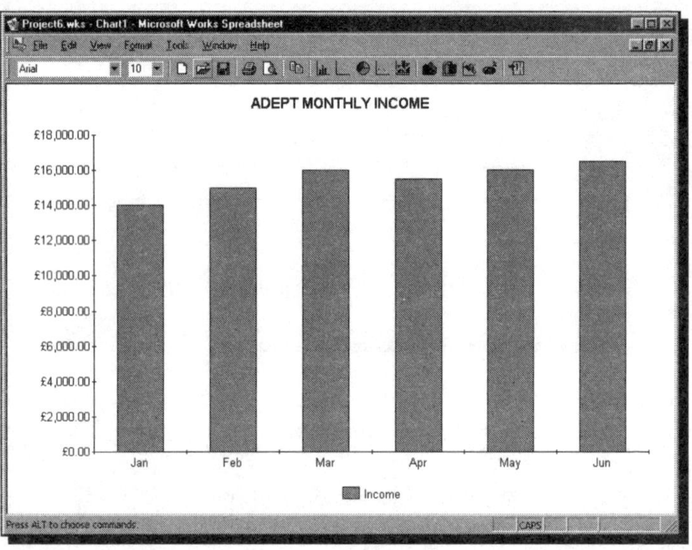

The chart is displayed in its own window, so to return to the worksheet you click the Go To 1st Series Toolbar button shown here, or you can press the <Ctrl+F6> keys, or use the **Window**, or **View** menu options. Choosing **View**, **Chart**, reveals that the chart just displayed on screen has been given the name **Chart1** in the list box. To select a different type chart, you must return to Chart mode by selecting a Chart window. You can then choose the **Format**, **Chart Type** menu command to open the Chart Type box again, but with some extra options. You could select another type from the displayed list, but if you do your Bar chart will not be saved.

To select another type of chart, but still retain the first one, activate the **Tools**, **Create New Chart** command, which opens a new chart as **Chart2**. Choosing the Line option and selecting **OK** will produce a line chart similar to the one below.

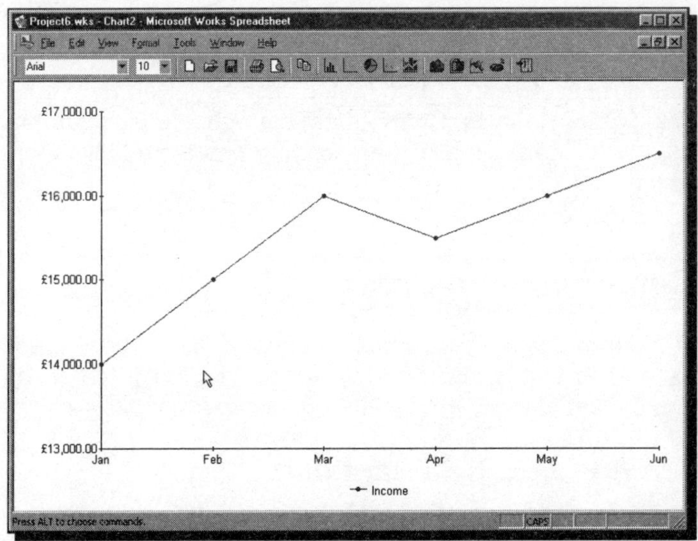

The shape of this line chart was improved by choosing the **Format**, **Vertical (Y) Axis** command and typing

```
13000
```

in the **Minimum** box.

There are a lot of other options that you can specify when creating a chart. Some of these are self evident, like titles, legends, data labels, and the inclusion of axis labels and grid lines. These will be discussed only if needed in the examples that follow.

Saving Charts

Charts are saved with a spreadsheet when you save the spreadsheet to disc. Thus, saving the spreadsheet under the filename **Project7**, will ensure that your charts are also saved under the same name. Since each chart is linked to the spreadsheet from which it was derived, if information on the spreadsheet changes, the charts associated with it will also change automatically.

Naming Charts

You can give your charts more meaningful names than the default ones 'Chart1, Chart2, etc.,' that are given by Works. The **Tools, Rename Chart** command opens a dialogue box from which you can select any of your charts and give them new names.

Customising a Chart

In order to customise a chart, you need to know how to add extra titles and labels, how to change text fonts, the colour and pattern of the chart, and how to incorporate grid lines.

Drawing a Multiple Bar Chart

As an exercise, open **Project7**, if it is not already in memory, so we can build a new bar-type chart which deals with the monthly 'Costs' of Adept Consultants. As there are six different non-contiguous sets of costs, first copy them (including the cost description labels) using the **Edit, Paste Special** command, into a contiguous range below the 'Income' range (starting, say, at cell A27), as shown on the next page.

Having done this, copy the 'Months' labels from row 23 to row 26 and save the resultant worksheet under the filename **Project8**.

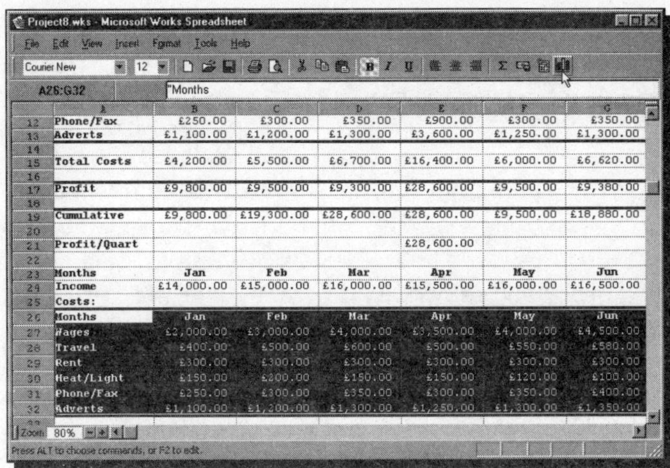

	A	B	C	D	E	F	G
12	Phone/Fax	£250.00	£300.00	£350.00	£900.00	£300.00	£350.00
13	Adverts	£1,100.00	£1,200.00	£1,300.00	£3,600.00	£1,250.00	£1,300.00
14							
15	Total Costs	£4,200.00	£5,500.00	£6,700.00	£16,400.00	£6,000.00	£6,620.00
16							
17	Profit	£9,800.00	£9,500.00	£9,300.00	£28,600.00	£9,500.00	£9,380.00
18							
19	Cumulative	£9,800.00	£19,300.00	£28,600.00	£28,600.00	£9,500.00	£18,880.00
20							
21	Profit/Quart				£28,600.00		
22							
23	Months	Jan	Feb	Mar	Apr	May	Jun
24	Income	£14,000.00	£15,000.00	£16,000.00	£15,500.00	£16,000.00	£16,500.00
25	Costs:						
26	Months	Jan	Feb	Mar	Apr	May	Jun
27	Wages	£2,000.00	£3,000.00	£4,000.00	£3,500.00	£4,000.00	£4,500.00
28	Travel	£400.00	£500.00	£600.00	£500.00	£550.00	£580.00
29	Rent	£300.00	£300.00	£300.00	£300.00	£300.00	£300.00
30	Heat/Light	£150.00	£200.00	£150.00	£150.00	£120.00	£100.00
31	Phone/Fax	£250.00	£300.00	£350.00	£300.00	£350.00	£400.00
32	Adverts	£1,100.00	£1,200.00	£1,300.00	£1,250.00	£1,300.00	£1,350.00

Now block the cell range A26:G32, as shown, click the New Chart Toolbar icon, type 'ADEPT CONSULTANTS' in the **Title** field and press **OK**.

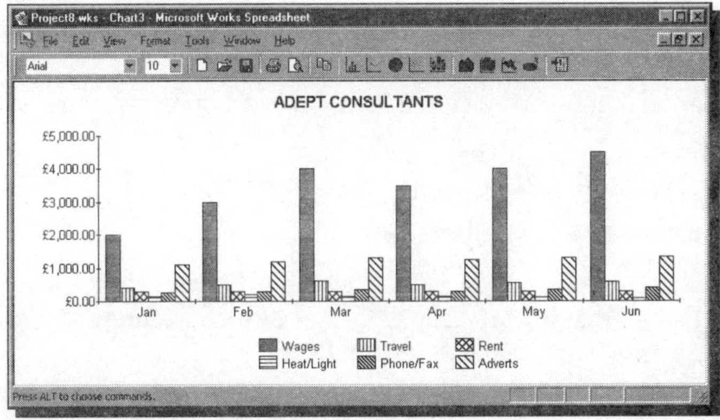

Immediately this is done, the bar chart of the 6 different monthly costs is drawn automatically with each month in a different colour. The diagram above shows the result, after using the **View**, **Display as Printed** command. As you can see, the colours have been replaced by shading patterns, as our default printer did not handle colours.

Chart Titles, Fonts and Sizes

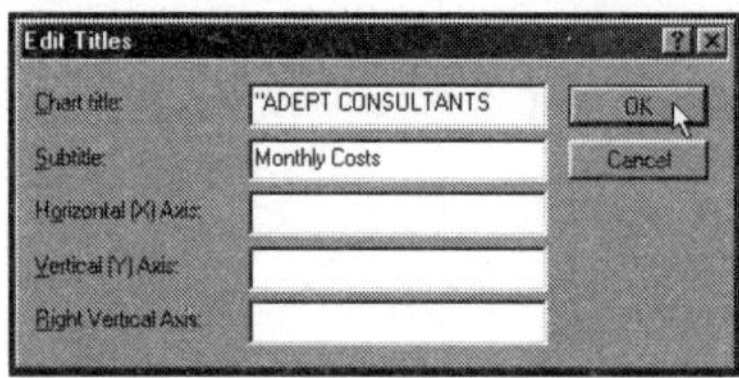

To edit a chart title, choose the **Edit**, **Titles** command which causes this dialogue box to be displayed on your screen.

Type 'Monthly Costs' in the **Subtitle** field of the dialogue box and select **OK,** to complete the addition.

You can change the font and size of any contained text on a chart. For example, click the title, to select it, and then choose **Format**, **Font and Style** to display the Font and Style - Title dialogue box. From this you can choose any of the fonts available to Windows, or set a new size by selecting from the list of sizes (given in points), or change the colour and set other attributes.

To change the font of **all** the other text and numbers in a chart, choose **Format**, **Font and Style** without first selecting an item.

The fonts and sizes of the text in the chart on the facing page were set as follows:

Chart title: Bodini Book, bold and italic, size 16

Other text & numbers: Bodini Book, size 10

Grid lines were added by selecting the **Format**, **Vertical (Y) Axis** command and activating the **Show gridlines** option. We then saved the file as **Project9**.

Note that you can, to a certain extent, control the vertical scaling of the final chart, by dragging the bottom edge of the Works window up or down. This works for the screen display, but not when the chart is printed.

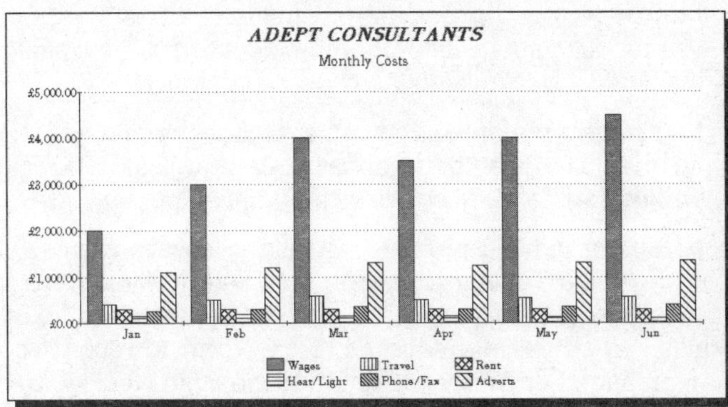

Printing a Chart

Before printing, or previewing a chart, you should check your page settings with the **File**, **Page Setup** command. This opens the dialogue box shown below with the **Other Options** section active. You use these to control how a chart will be printed on the page.

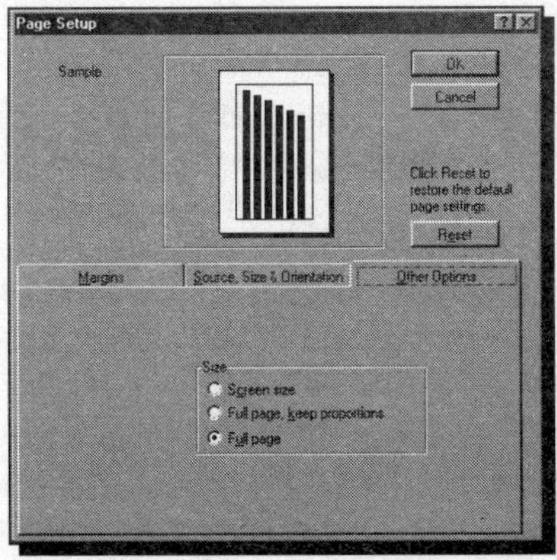

Screen size - prints the chart the same size as it appears on the screen - about a quarter page size.

Full page, keep proportions - prints charts so that they use the full paper width (between the margins), but scales the vertical size to keep the chart in proportion.

Full page - the default option, stretches the chart to take up the full page (between all four margins). This can produce some weird charts with portrait paper setting.

Before printing a chart it is wise to always Preview it, from the Toolbar icon. You may find that you have to adjust your text font settings to get all the chart text to display. When you are satisfied, press **Print** to record your chart on paper, or **Cancel**, to return to the chart window.

Drawing a Pie Chart

As a second example in chart drawing, use the 'Average' values of the costs from the worksheet of **Project9** to plot a pie chart. Select the range J8:J13 and again, click the New Chart icon, select Pie as the chart type followed by **OK**.

Next, click the Pie icon on the Charting Toolbar followed by the **Variations** tab, and select the last of the six pie chart type options (in the bottom right-hand corner) and press **OK**. Your range should now be displayed in a colourful pie chart.

The labels on each segment are not very self explanatory though. To remedy this, use the **Edit**, **Data labels** command, type A8:A13 in the **Cell Range** text box, as shown here, and select **OK** to leave the box and return to your chart.

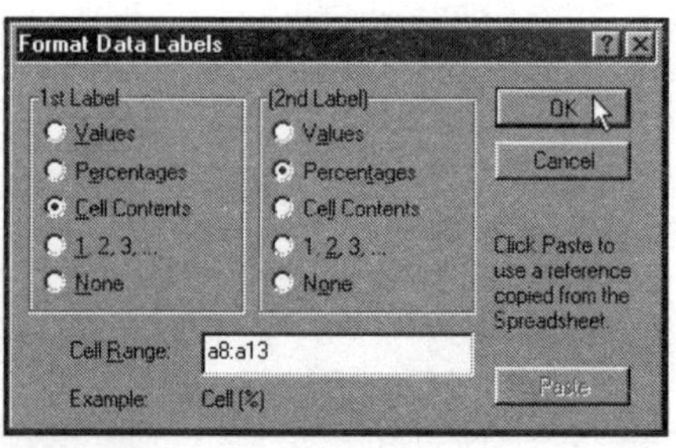

Add an appropriate title to the chart and allocate a font and size to it as described previously.

Your chart should now look something like that shown on the next page.

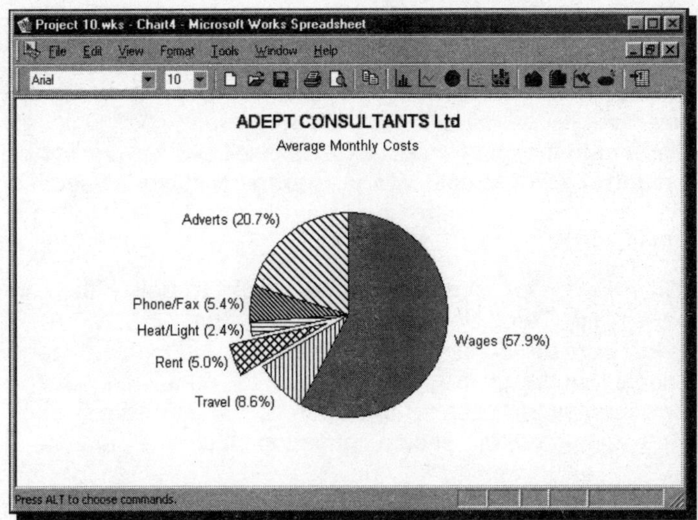

To explode one of the segments of the pie chart, choose the **Format**, **Shading and Color** command and select the number of the slice you would like to appear detached, from the displayed dialogue box. Slices, in this case, are numbered from 1 to 6 and are allocated to the pie chart in a clockwise direction. Thus, to explode the 'Rent' slice, select **3** in the **Slices** box, then activate the **Explode slice** option and press the **Format** and **Close** buttons. In this way, you can emphasise one or more portions of the chart.

Finally, save the file as **Project 10**. Yes, with Windows 95/98 or higher you can give all your files long names (up to 255 characters), which can include spaces and capitals.

To cancel an exploded selection, use the **Format**, **Patterns and Colors** command and press the **Format All** and **Close** buttons. Selecting other slices for exploding, without first cancelling previous selections, adds to the selection.

Mixing Chart Types

To illustrate a combination of a bar and line chart, we will consider the variable monthly costs of Adept Consultants. This requires us to delete row 29 (the 'Rent' cost, which is fixed) from the worksheet. Just as well, since Works for Windows can only deal with a maximum of six categories and we would like to introduce average monthly costs as our sixth category.

Use the **Insert**, **Delete Row** command to delete the row dealing with 'Rent' from your worksheet, then create a new category in the renumbered row 32, to hold the average variable monthly costs. We will leave it to you to work out and place the cell formulae for this operation. If you have worked your way to here, this should not be too much of a problem.

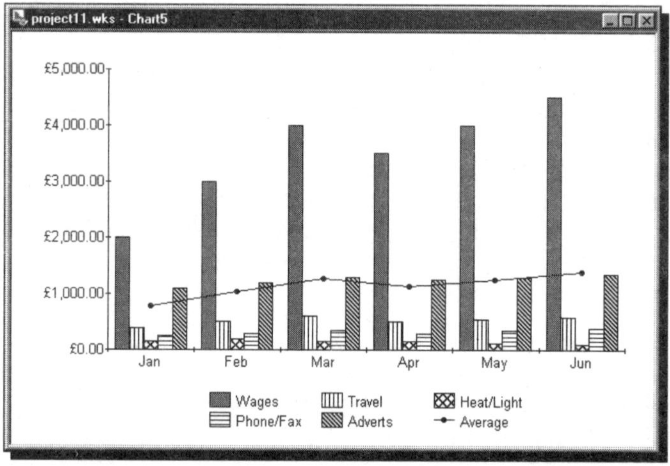

To create a mixed chart, like the one above, first mark the A26:G32 cell block and use the New Chart icon, select Combination and press **OK**. The chart may be a little mixed up, so use the **Format**, **Mixed Line and Bar** command, select the **Line L** option for the **6th Value Y-Series** from the revealed dialogue box, and **Bar** options for the other series, then press the **OK** button. Good luck.

10

The Works 2000 Database

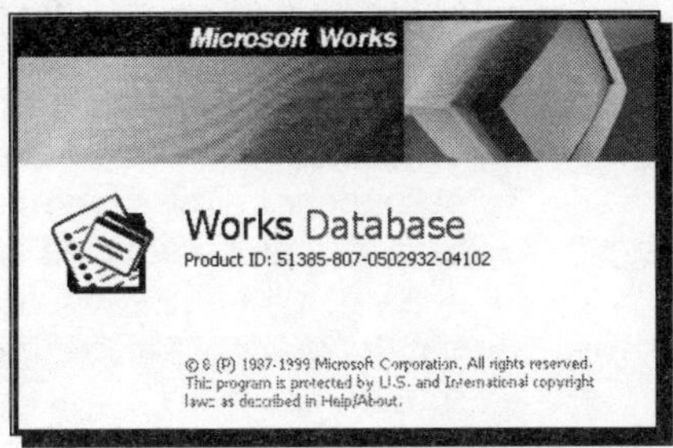

A Works database is a file which contains related information, such as 'Customers' Names', 'Consultancy Details', 'Invoice No.', etc. A phone book is a simple database, stored on paper. In Works, each record is entered as a worksheet row, with the fields of each record occupying corresponding columns.

The next section deals with the basic concepts of using a simple database, along with the database 'jargon' that is used in this book. If you are not familiar with database terminology then you should read this section first.

A database is a collection of data that exists, and is organised around a specific theme, or requirement. A database is used for storing information, so that it is quickly accessible. In the case of Works, data is stored in **data-files** which are specially structured files kept on disc like other disc-files. To make accessing the data easier, each row or **record** of data within a database is structured in the same fashion, i.e., each record will have the same number of columns, or **fields**.

We define a database and its various elements as follows:

Database	A collection of data organised for a specific theme.
Data-file	Disc-file in which data is stored.
Record	A row of information relating to a single entry and comprising one or more fields.
Field	A single column of information of the same type, such as people's names.
Form	A screen in which one record of data can be entered, displayed, or edited.
List	The whole database displayed in a spreadsheet-like format. Multiple records can be entered and edited.
Filter	A set of instructions to search the database for records with specific properties.

A good example of a database is a telephone directory. To cover the whole country many directories are needed, just as a database can comprise a number of data-files. The following shows how data is presented in such a directory.

Prowse H.B., 91 Cabot Close	Truro 76455
Pruce T.A., 15 Woodburn Road	Plymouth 223248
Pryce C.W., 42 North Gate Road	St Austell 851662
Pryor A., 38 Western Approach	Plymouth 238742
Pryor B.E., 79 Trevithick Road	Truro 742310
Queen S.R., 4 Ruskin Crescent	Camborne 712212
Regan R.B., 1 Woodland Avenue	Bodmin 78236

Information is structured in fields which are identified below, for a single record, as follows:

Name	**Address**	**Town**	**Tel No.**
Pryor B.E.	79 Trevithick Road	Truro	742310

Creating a Database

A database file, in Works 2000, is created either using a Template, or manually. Several useful templates to help you rapidly design specific databases are provided with the package and are briefly described in a later Chapter.

Here, we are going to step you through the process of manually designing and building a simple database, suitable for keeping track of the invoices issued by a small engineering consulting company.

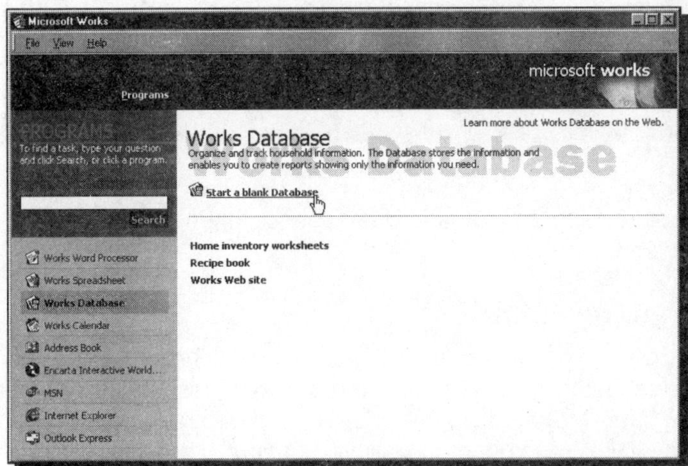

Clicking the **Programs** tab in the Task Launcher window, selecting **Works Database**, and then clicking **Start a blank Database** as shown above, displays the screen shown on the next page.

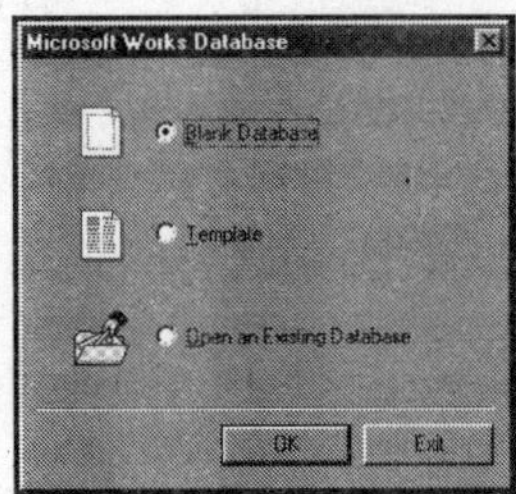

The program can also be opened by selecting **Microsoft Works Database** in the Windows **Start** menu system and selecting **Blank Database**, as shown here.

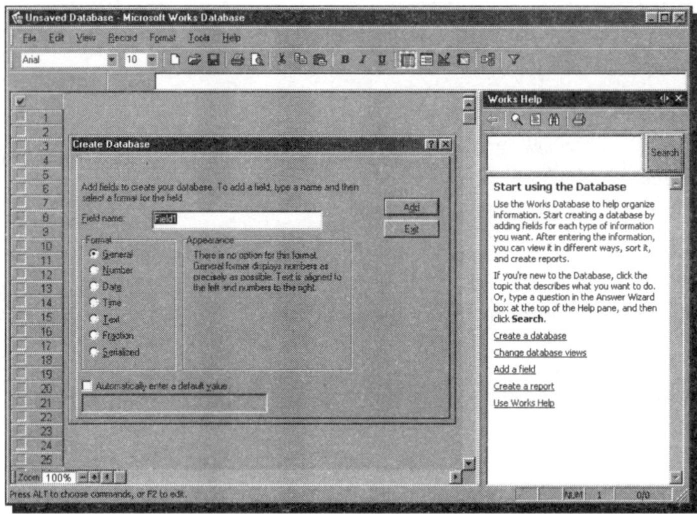

As shown, the Database window has its own menu and Toolbar, and the Create Database dialogue box is opened automatically waiting for you to enter your database fields.

Entering Fields

Type 'Customer Name' as Field 1 in the highlighted **Field name** text box and click the **Add** button to accept **General** as the format for the field data. The format determines how your data will be stored and displayed in your database. Clicking each format type in the list will show its description.

Enter the remaining fields as shown in the table below.

Field Name	***Width***	***Format***	
Details	25	**General**	
Inv.No	7	**Number**	(01235 - but 4 digits)
Issued	12	**Date**	(28/12/99)
Paid	10	**Number**	(True/False)
O/D	5	**Number**	(01235 - but 1 digit)
Total	10	**Number**	(£1,234.56 - 2 dec's)

The format examples shown above are those to select from the list of options given to you.

There are no more fields to enter so press **Done**. You should now have a basic, but empty, database in List View form (see below) which looks like the one shown below.

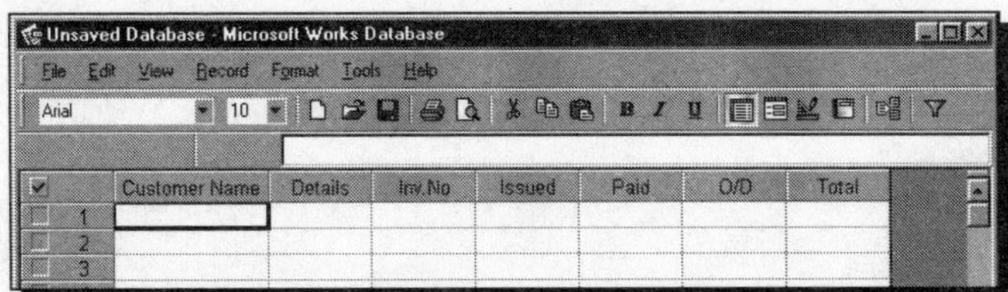

This List screen now has a row of field titles along the top, above an empty 'spreadsheet' working area. The default column width for a List screen is 9, and we want some of our fields to be different from that, so click the cursor in the title of the 'Inv.No' field, to select the column and choose the **Format, Field Width** command. Type **7** as the **Column width**, as shown here, and press **OK**.

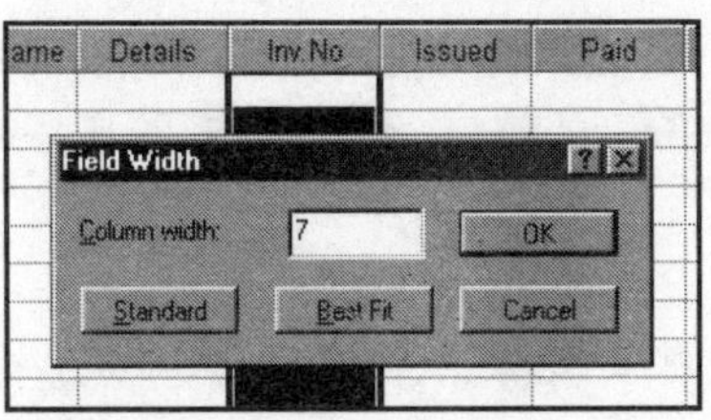

Database Screens

As we have seen, the opening screen of a Works database is a 'List View' window, which gives a spreadsheet type view of the database, with the numbers down the left-hand side referring to individual records, and the column headings referring to the database fields. The status line shows which record the cursor is in, how many records are currently displayed, and how many are in the database.

The other way of looking at, and accessing, a Works database is through a 'Form' window, as shown next, which is a 'front end' to easily enter, and access, data. You use the **F9** key, or the Form View Toolbar icon shown, or the **View**, **Form** menu command, to change to the Form window.

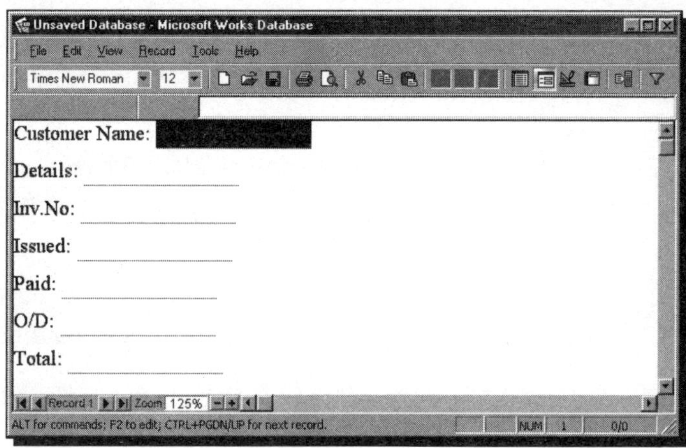

Pressing <Ctrl+F9>, or the Form Design Toolbar icon, or choosing **View, Form Design** will open a window in which you can customise the 'basic' form produced by Works, as shown in our example below.

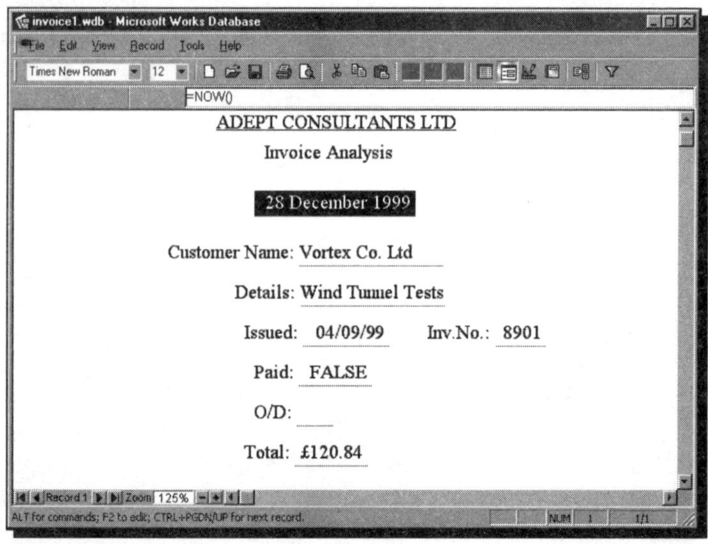

Pressing <Shift+F9>, or the List View Toolbar icon, or choosing **View, List,** will return you to the List screen.

Form Editing

We suggest you click the Form Design Toolbar icon, shown here, and use the Form Design window to alter the entry form for your database to something a little nearer ours at the bottom of the previous page.

As it is a multi-page window, the co-ordinate information on the line below the Toolbar could be needed to keep track of the current cursor position. This gives X and Y co-ordinates in the current system dimension units, (measured from the top left-hand corner of each printed page). The page number of the current cursor position is shown on the Status Bar, as shown below. The overall maximum form dimensions can be 3 pages long by 3 screens wide. A form can contain up to 256 database fields, as well as titles, labels and other text. Each field can hold up to 256 characters. A database can contain up to 32,000 records, which should be enough for most people!

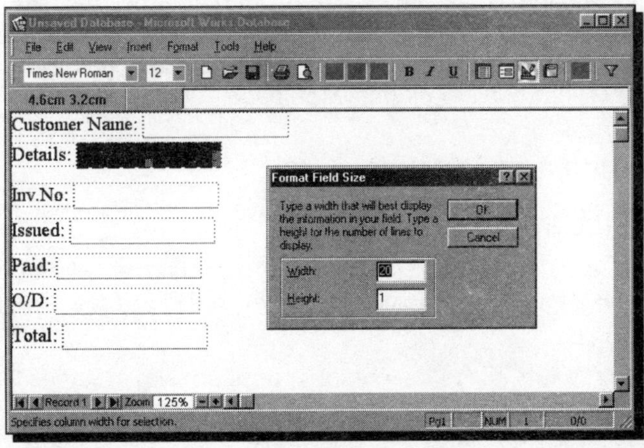

Before entering any records, the entry form would benefit from some cosmetic attention. The List screen field widths are in fact independent of those of the Form screen. In our example, we want them to be the same, so place the cursor in the 'Details' field, click to select it and choose the **Format**, **Field Size** command. This opens the box shown above, in which you can set the **Width** or **Height** of form fields. Type **25** as the width and press **OK**. Then alter the other form widths to those given in our table on page 196.

When a field is selected in the Design window the mouse pointer changes and lets you drag an outline of the field around the screen, as shown here. You could move the fields so that all the colons are in one vertical line, or until you have a layout you prefer. With the Drag and Drop function you simply select a field with your mouse pointer and drag it to a new position.

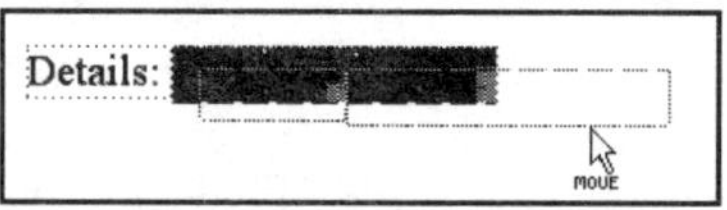

To place a label on your form, click the cursor where you want it to start and type the label text. In our example, type the database title 'ADEPT CONSULTANTS LTD' and drag it until you are happy with its position. Labels can be placed in any unused space on the form screen. With the title still highlighted it is a good time to carry out any enhancements. Click on the Underline Toolbar icon and then enter the other labels shown in our example (on page 198).

Hiding a Field Name

The 'date' cell, shown in our example as 28 December 1999, is not a label. It actually has a dotted line below it and is, in fact, a database field (called Date:), containing a formula to generate the current date, but with its field name switched off.

To do this, place the cursor in position, and create a 'Date' field with the **Insert**, **Field** command. For the moment we will leave this cell empty. To hide it, highlight its field name, and choose the **Format, Show Field Name** command. The field name 'Date:' should now be turned off. If you wanted, you could now place a different label on top of it. This technique is useful if you want to keep actual field names short, but need longer descriptive ones on the database form, as could have been used with the 'O/D:' field (Overdue), shown in our example.

Entering Data in a Form

Now change to the Form view and enter the first record into the database. If your form is the same as ours, your cursor should be in the date cell. Press <Tab> to move to the 'Customer Name:' field, and type the following:

Vortex Co. Ltd	press <Tab> and type,
Wind Tunnel Tests	press <Tab> and type,
4/9/99	press <Tab> and type,
8901	press <Tab> and type,
0	press <Tab> twice, and type,
120.84	press <Tab>

Nothing should have been entered in the 'O/D' field. The last <Tab> should have completed the entry of record 1, and brought up an empty form for the next record. Press <Ctrl+PgUp>, to move back one record, to the date cell of record 1.

When moving about a form, <Tab> and <Shift+Tab>, move the cursor between fields, whereas <Ctrl+PgUp> and <Ctrl+PgDn>, move between adjacent records.

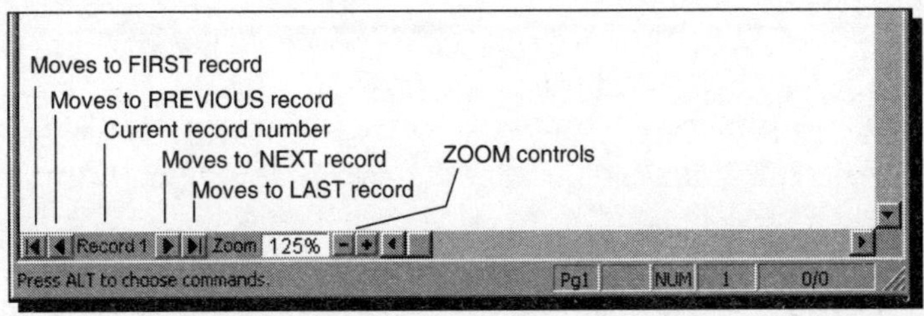

The arrow buttons at the bottom of a form window can also be used to step through the records of a database, as shown above.

Using Formulae in a Field

Database formulae have two main applications; to automatically force the same entry in each similar field of every record in the database, or to calculate the contents of one field based on those of another. Each database field can only contain one formula. Once it is entered in the field of one record, it is automatically entered into all the other records. As in the spreadsheet, a formula is preceded by an equal sign (=).

In our database example we will enter formulae in two fields, the date formula next, and one that calculates the contents of a field, a little later on. Change to List view and with the cursor in the date cell, type:

```
=NOW()
```

As with the spreadsheet, this formula is shown on the screen, both in the cell and in the formula bar at the top of the screen.

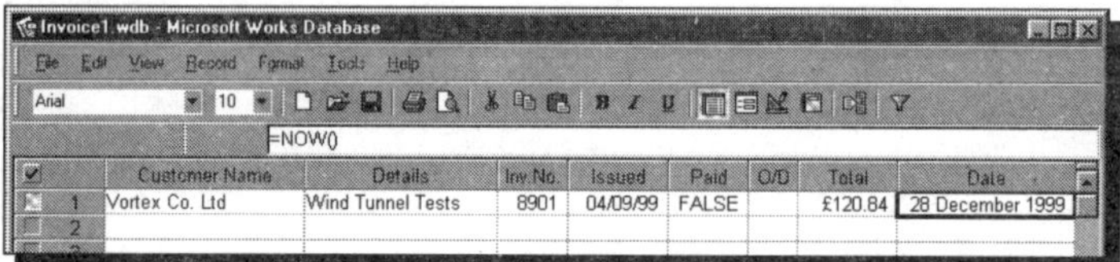

When you press <Enter>, the cell may fill with the hash character (#). Do not panic, it only means the date is too long for the cell width. Simply alter the cell width with the **Format, Field Size** command, or re-size it with the pointer.

Protecting Fields

You can 'lock' fields in your database to prevent their contents being accidentally changed, or to force the <Tab> key to ignore the cell when you are moving around the form, or entering data. To demonstrate this, highlight the Date field in List View and use the **Format**, **Protection** command, click the **Protect field** option and press the **OK** button. The date field should now be fully protected. In fact, it is now inaccessible until the field's protection is toggled off again.

Now complete the data entry by typing in the remaining 14 records shown in the screen dump below. You can do this in either Form or List view, but you may find it easier in Form view. In the 'Paid' field, enter 1 (TRUE) if the invoice has been paid, or 0 (FALSE) if not. When you have saved the database as **Invoice1**, a List view should then be similar to our printout.

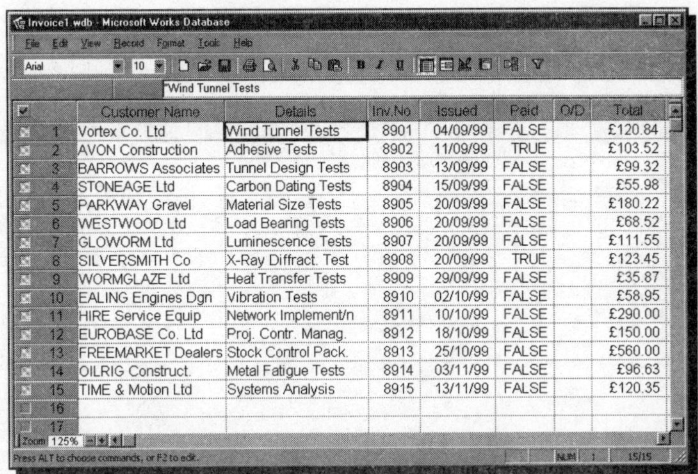

	Customer Name	Details	Inv.No	Issued	Paid	O/D	Total
1	Vortex Co. Ltd	Wind Tunnel Tests	8901	04/09/99	FALSE		£120.84
2	AVON Construction	Adhesive Tests	8902	11/09/99	TRUE		£103.52
3	BARROWS Associates	Tunnel Design Tests	8903	13/09/99	FALSE		£99.32
4	STONEAGE Ltd	Carbon Dating Tests	8904	15/09/99	FALSE		£55.98
5	PARKWAY Gravel	Material Size Tests	8905	20/09/99	FALSE		£180.22
6	WESTWOOD Ltd	Load Bearing Tests	8906	20/09/99	FALSE		£68.52
7	GLOWORM Ltd	Luminescence Tests	8907	20/09/99	FALSE		£111.55
8	SILVERSMITH Co	X-Ray Diffract. Test	8908	20/09/99	TRUE		£123.45
9	WORMGLAZE Ltd	Heat Transfer Tests	8909	29/09/99	FALSE		£35.87
10	EALING Engines Dgn	Vibration Tests	8910	02/10/99	FALSE		£58.95
11	HIRE Service Equip	Network Implement/n	8911	10/10/99	FALSE		£290.00
12	EUROBASE Co. Ltd	Proj. Contr. Manag.	8912	18/10/99	FALSE		£150.00
13	FREEMARKET Dealers	Stock Control Pack.	8913	25/10/99	FALSE		£560.00
14	OILRIG Construct.	Metal Fatigue Tests	8914	03/11/99	FALSE		£96.63
15	TIME & Motion Ltd	Systems Analysis	8915	13/11/99	FALSE		£120.35
16							
17							

Sorting a Database

The records in our database are in the order in which they were entered, with the invoice numbers, in the 'Inv.No' field, shown in ascending order. However, once records have been entered, you might find it easier to browse through the database if it were sorted in a different way, say, in alphabetical order of 'Customer Name'. This might also make it easier to use the database for other operations, such as a mail merge. The Works database has an easy to use sort function, which can be accessed from either the Form or List screen.

With the cursor in any location, choose the **Record**, **Sort Records** command. Click the arrow in the **Sort by** drop-down list, select 'Customer Name', make sure **Ascending** is selected, and press **OK** to sort the database.

This sorts the field in an ascending order, from A - Z, and from 0 - 9. A descending sort order is the reverse. If you decide to have a secondary sort field (say you want invoices for the same company to appear in ascending order of invoice number), it is a simple matter to define a secondary sort range in the **Then by** box, before sorting. The three sort ranges available should be enough for most purposes.

Issuing these commands should produce the display shown below.

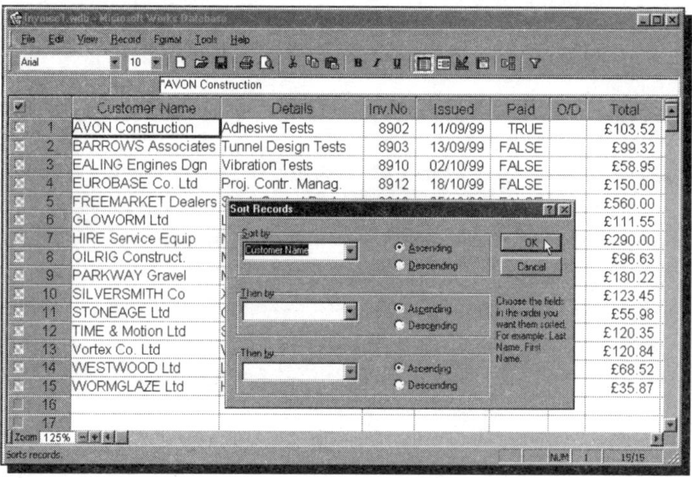

Now re-sort the database, in ascending order on the 'Inv.No' field, to return it to the original format.

Date Arithmetic

There are several date functions which can be used in Works to carry out date calculations. For example, typing the function =DATE(99,12,28) - that is 28/12/99 backwards - works out the number of days between 31 December 1899 and that date. These functions are included to make Works more compatible with older versions, but Works 2000 has an easier, and quicker, way of dealing with date arithmetic. Just typing a date into a cell, in one of the accepted date formats, allows Works to use the date number in any calculations. When a date is typed in a field, or a spreadsheet cell, what actually shows in that cell depends on the cell format. If '30/10/66', (a date in short date format), is typed into a cell, it will be shown as 30 October 1966 in long date format, or 24410, in any of the number formats.

The function

```
=NOW()-30/10/66
```

gives the difference in days (if the appropriate cell is formatted for integer numbers) between now and the mentioned date.

We will use this function to work out the number of overdue days for the unpaid invoices in our example, by typing the following formula into an O/D field cell in List View:

```
=NOW()-Issued
```

However, before we go any further, we should take into consideration the fact that, normally, such information would not be necessary if an invoice has already been paid. Therefore, we need to edit the formula to make the result conditional on non-payment of the issued invoice.

The IF Function

The =IF function allows comparison between two values with the use of special 'logical' operators. The logical operators we can use are listed below.

Logical operators

=	Equal to
<	Less than
>	Greater than
<=	Less than or Equal to
>=	Greater than or Equal to
<>	Not Equal to

The general format of the IF function is as follows:

=IF(Comparison, Outcome-if-true, Outcome-if-false)

which contains three arguments separated by commas. The first argument is the logical comparison, the second is what should happen if the outcome of the logical comparison is 'true', while the third is what should happen if the outcome of the logical comparison is 'false'.

Thus, we can incorporate an =IF function in the formula we entered in the O/D cell, to calculate the days overdue, only if the invoice has not been paid, otherwise '0' should be written into that cell. The test will be on the contents of the corresponding 'Paid' field of a record, and will look for anything else but '0', or FALSE.

To edit the formula in the O/D cell, highlight any cell in that field and press the Edit key <F2>. Then press the <Home> cursor key, followed by →, to place the cursor after the '=' of the existing formula in the formula line at the top of the screen and change the formula to:

```
=IF(Paid=0,NOW()-Issued,0)
```

The edited formula should now correspond to that shown in the screen printout below.

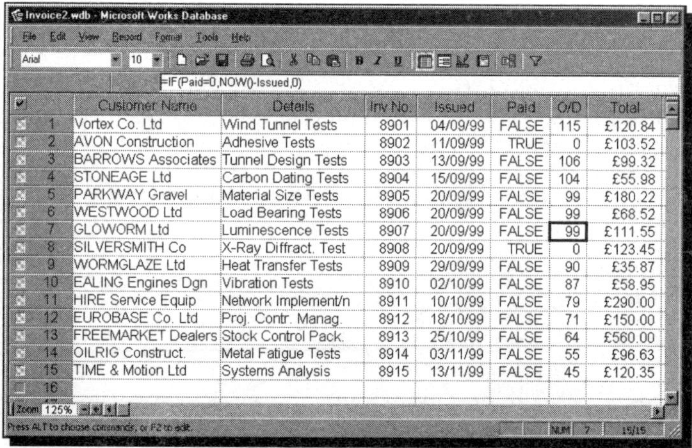

	Customer Name	Details	Inv No.	Issued	Paid	O/D	Total
1	Vortex Co. Ltd	Wind Tunnel Tests	8901	04/09/99	FALSE	115	£120.84
2	AVON Construction	Adhesive Tests	8902	11/09/99	TRUE	0	£103.52
3	BARROWS Associates	Tunnel Design Tests	8903	13/09/99	FALSE	106	£99.32
4	STONEAGE Ltd	Carbon Dating Tests	8904	15/09/99	FALSE	104	£55.98
5	PARKWAY Gravel	Material Size Tests	8905	20/09/99	FALSE	99	£180.22
6	WESTWOOD Ltd	Load Bearing Tests	8906	20/09/99	FALSE	99	£68.52
7	GLOWORM Ltd	Luminescence Tests	8907	20/09/99	FALSE	99	£111.55
8	SILVERSMITH Co	X-Ray Diffract. Test	8908	20/09/99	TRUE	0	£123.45
9	WORMGLAZE Ltd	Heat Transfer Tests	8909	29/09/99	FALSE	90	£35.87
10	EALING Engines Dgn	Vibration Tests	8910	02/10/99	FALSE	87	£58.95
11	HIRE Service Equip	Network Implement/n	8911	10/10/99	FALSE	79	£290.00
12	EUROBASE Co. Ltd	Proj. Contr. Manag.	8912	18/10/99	FALSE	71	£150.00
13	FREEMARKET Dealers	Stock Control Pack.	8913	25/10/99	FALSE	64	£560.00
14	OILRIG Construct.	Metal Fatigue Tests	8914	03/11/99	FALSE	55	£96.63
15	TIME & Motion Ltd	Systems Analysis	8915	13/11/99	FALSE	45	£120.35
16							

Note that once a formula is entered into any one field cell it is automatically copied to all the other cells in that field of the database. Save the file under the name **Invoice2**, but make sure you use the **Save As** command.

Your results will almost certainly differ from those above. The reason for this is, of course, that the NOW() function returns different numerical values when used on different dates. To get the same results as those shown, you could reset your computer clock to that used in our example. This is easily done from the Windows Control Panel.

Save your work and Exit the Works program. Open the Control Panel, double-click the Date/Time icon, reset the **Date** to '28/12/99' and press **OK**. Close the Control Panel and the new date will be operational when you re-enter Works.

WARNING - Make sure you have saved your work before doing this, and when you have finished this section remember to reset the date.

Searching a Database

A database can be searched for specific records, that meet several complex criteria, with the **Tools, Filters** command, once a filter has been set as described below. Or, more simply, by clicking the Toolbar Filters icon, shown here. For a simple search, on one field only, the **Edit, Find** command is, however, both quicker and easier.

We will use the previously saved database **Invoice2** to illustrate both these methods.

Let us assume we needed to find a record, from our database, containing the text 'x-ray'. In the List View window, choose **Edit**, **Find**, type **x-ray** in the **Find what** box, and select the option, **All records**. The record for 'SILVERSMITH Co' is brought to the screen, and the status line (1/15) indicates that this is the only record that meets the search criterion. Only the one record is shown, and all the others are hidden. The command, **Record**, **Show**, **1 All Records** will display the complete database again.

Database Filtering

Sometimes it is necessary to find records in a database that satisfy a variety of conditions. For example, in a warehouse stock database, you may need to find all the items that were purchased between May and July of last year, that were ordered by a specific person, cost between £5.00 and £100.00, and that remained in stock for more than 60 days. In Works this kind of search is called a filter.

When a filter operation is carried out in Works, all the records that match the filter criteria are extracted. In List View these are all displayed, whereas in Form view you see one matching record at a time. Every time a filter is applied the program searches the complete database for matches. A database can have up to 8 filters saved with it.

If necessary, retrieve the file **Invoice2**, and select the List View. Clicking the Filters icon presents the Filter box, as shown below. The first time you can step through a Quick Tour on filtering, but make sure you turn this off.

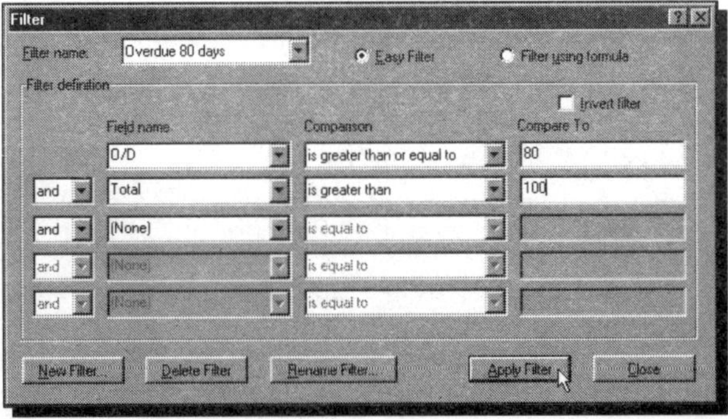

First type a name for the new filter if you want to. The above box is completed assuming that we would like to search the database for all the details of our customers whose invoices are overdue by 80 or more days, and who owe more than £100.

This intuitive approach to filters is very much easier than having to develop long logical expressions yourself. In fact what is actually created, in the above case, is the expression

```
='O/D'>=VALUE("80")#AND#Total>VALUE("100")
```

which is placed in the 'O/D' field cell of the filter.

When all the required criteria have been entered, select the **Apply Filter** button to action the filter. Unless you have renamed it, this first filter in your database will be **Filter1**.

You are then returned to List view, where only the records which meet the search requirements will be listed. In our case this should be three only. The screen should now look similar to that shown here.

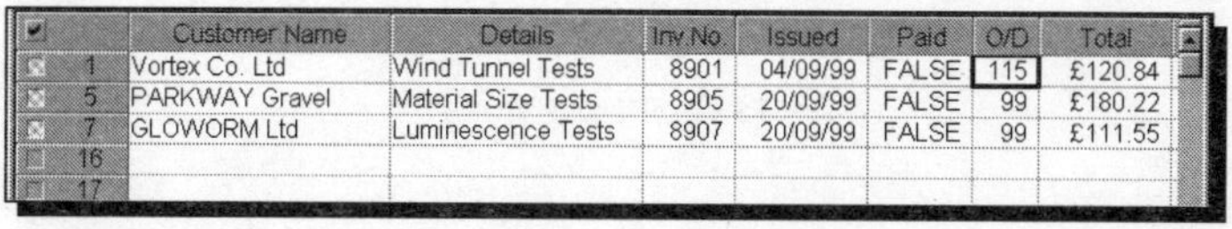

		Customer Name	Details	Inv.No.	Issued	Paid	O/D	Total
	1	Vortex Co. Ltd	Wind Tunnel Tests	8901	04/09/99	FALSE	115	£120.84
	5	PARKWAY Gravel	Material Size Tests	8905	20/09/99	FALSE	99	£180.22
	7	GLOWORM Ltd	Luminescence Tests	8907	20/09/99	FALSE	99	£111.55
	16							
	17							

To view all the records again, choose **Record**, **Show**, **1 All Records**. The filter criteria will remain intact until next edited.

Save the file with the name **Invoice3**, but again make sure you use the **Save As** command.

Marking Records

You can also manually mark records that do not easily filter, by clicking in the box to the left of their row number, as can be seen above.

Using the **Record**, **Show**, **2 Marked Records** will separate them for processing, or inclusion in a report.

The Database Toolbar

Most of the database Toolbar icons are common to the other Toolbars already described, but there are six icons on this bar specific to the database tool, whose meanings are as follows:

Option	*Result*
	Change to List view
	Change to Form view
	Change to Form Design view
	Change to Report view
	Insert new record
	Carry out a filter

Once you get used to all of these buttons, you will find that designing and manipulating databases becomes very much easier!

11

Database Applications

Once a database has been created, the data sorted in the required order, and specific records have been searched for, the retrieved data can be browsed on the screen, either one record at a time, or in the list format, one full screen at a time. Some form of hard copy will almost certainly be required at some stage, by printing part, or all, of the database to paper.

Printing from a Database

There are three main ways of printing information from a database. In the 'Form' view, selected records are printed out in the same format as the screen form. Printing from a 'List' view will produce rows and columns just as they appear on the screen; little manipulation of the printed result is possible. To obtain a customised print-out, possibly containing selected fields only, but with report and page titles, totals and sub-totals, a 'Report' must first be defined. Data can then be printed from the Report screen. To see what will actually print use the Print Preview Toolbar icon.

What is printed from the List and Form windows is controlled by the settings in the **File**, **Page Setup**, **Other Options** dialogue box, as shown overleaf. Printing from List view, will produce a spreadsheet like layout, which will only be of use if your database has only a few fields per record.

Printing from the Form view could probably be best used with a diary type appointment database, or with a simple database designed to hold, say, personnel lists or parts inventories. Space could maybe be built into each form to hold a scanned photograph, for example.

To demonstrate the process, load the database **Invoice3**, which was created in the last chapter. From the Form view choose **File**, **Page Setup**, **Other Options** to display the dialogue box shown here.

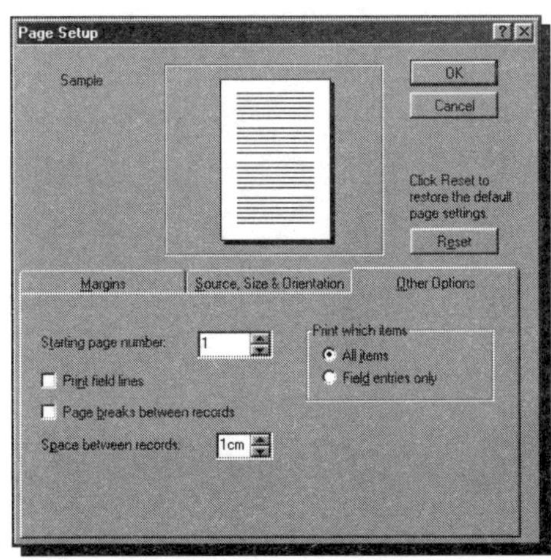

Switch off **Page breaks between records**, type '1' as the **Space between records**, and select **All items** as in our example. When you accept these settings a print preview should show two or three neatly spaced records on the page, depending on how you laid out your form, and what font size was chosen.

Creating a Report

A report can present records sorted and grouped, with summaries, totals, and with explanatory text. Once a report format has been set up, producing a report is a quick, almost automatic process. The current records 'displayed' in a database are those used to make the body of a report. The initial process is to create a report definition, which indicates what information will be in a report, and where it will be placed. Works 2000 has a 'semi-automatic front end' to make the production of simple report formats much easier.

ADEPT CONSULTANTS LTD
Invoice Analysis Report

Summary of Overdue Invoices

Customer Name	Invoice Number	Days Overdue	Total Amount
TIME & Motion Ltd	8915	46	£120.35
OILRIG Construct.	8914	56	£96.63
1 - 2 Months Overdue	2	51	£216.98
FREEMARKET Dealers	8913	65	£560.00
EUROBASE Co. Ltd	8912	72	£150.00
HIRE Service Equip	8911	80	£290.00
EALING Engines Dgn	8910	88	£58.95
2 - 3 Months Overdue	4	76	£1,058.95
WORMGLAZE Ltd	8909	91	£35.87
PARKWAY Gravel	8905	100	£180.22
WESTWOOD Ltd	8906	100	£68.52
GLOWORM Ltd	8907	100	£111.55
STONEAGE Ltd	8904	105	£55.98
BARROWS Associates	8903	107	£99.32
Vortex Co. Ltd	8901	116	£120.84
3 - 4 Months Overdue	7	102	£672.30
Overall Totals and Averages	13	86	£1,948.23

Using the database we built up in the last chapter, we will step through the process of setting up a report definition. If necessary, retrieve the file saved as **Invoice3**, which was a database to store details of the invoices sent out by a small company. It would be very useful, for both the accountant and the company management of Adept, if a report like that above could be 'instantly' produced, and printed out. This summarises all the unpaid invoices and ranks them in groups depending on the number of months they have been overdue. Once we have defined the format of this report, it will only take a few keystrokes, at any time in the future, to produce a similar but updated report.

To start the process, change to the Form Design screen of **Invoice3**, as we must first add an extra field to the form. This will show the number of months an invoice is overdue. We will need it, to provide the basis for sorting the database records, and breaking them up into groups.

Create a new field called 'Months' with the **Insert**, **Field** command, placed wherever you like on the form, but give it the integer **Number** format with **1** digit. Now change to Form View, highlight the empty cell, type the formula

```
=Int(O/D/30)
```

and press <Enter>. Note that Works places single inverted commas around the field name O/D, to show it as a label; this is because it contains the slash character '/'. The formula produces the integer part of the number of days overdue, divided by thirty. In other words, approximately the whole number of months overdue.

We are now ready to create the report definition. Choose the **Tools**, **ReportCreator** command, or click the Toolbar Report View button. Ignore the initial Report Name box, but type ADEPT CONSULTANTS LTD into the **Report title** box of the main ReportCreator dialogue box, which is shown below.

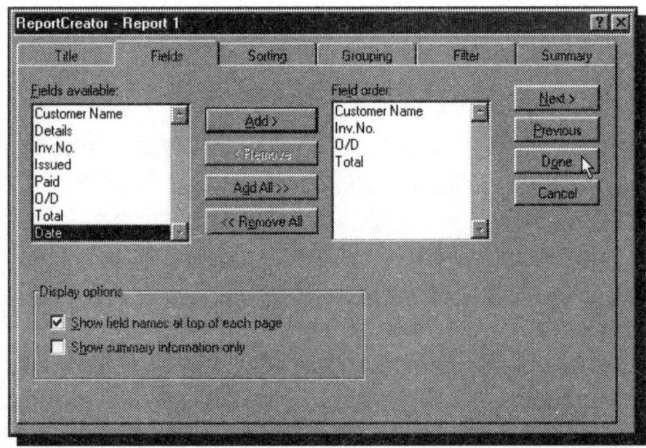

Click the **Next** button to move to the **Fields** tabbed section, select the field 'Customer Name' in the **Fields available** list box and press **Add>**, or <Alt+A>, to add the field to the **Field order** list. In the same way add the fields 'Inv.No', 'O/D' and 'Total' as shown above.

The other tabbed sections provide a quick way of entering instructions and formulae into the report definition, to carry out calculations and produce totals or averages, for example. In the future you may find this an easier way to generate rapid reports, but at this stage we will not use this method, so press **Done** to move to the report definition screen, shown below.

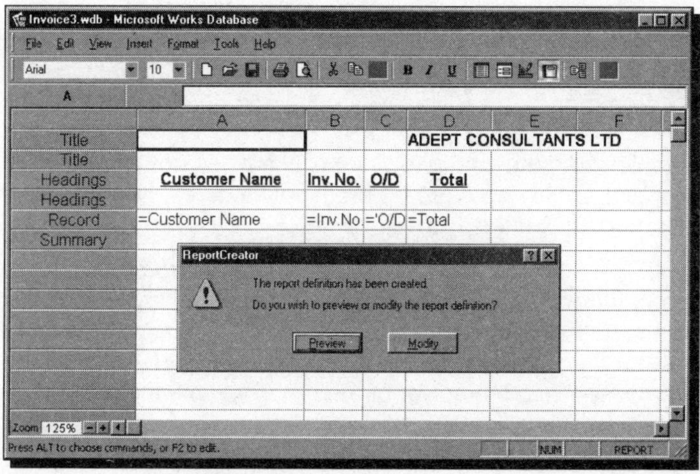

The message in the pop-up box suggests you use the Print Preview to see what your report will look like when printed, at this stage there is not much point, so select **Modify** which places you in Modify Report mode.

The working area of the screen contains columns and rows which intersect, as in the spreadsheet, to form cells. The row types, shown on the left part of the screen, determine the order the rows will be printed in the report, and what action will be taken in that row.

Row type	*Prints*
Title	At the beginning of a report.
Headings	At the top of each page.
Intr *1st breakfield*	At the beginning of each group created by the 1st breakfield.
Intr *2nd breakfield*	At the beginning of each group created by the 2nd breakfield.
Intr *3rd breakfield*	At the beginning of each group created by the 3rd breakfield.
Record	Each displayed record.
Summ *3rd breakfield*	At the end of each group created by the 3rd breakfield.
Summ *2nd breakfield*	At the end of each group created by the 2nd breakfield.
Summ *1st breakfield*	At the end of each group created by the 1st breakfield.
Summary	At the end of a report.

At this stage the 'Intr' and 'Summ' line types do not appear on our screen, as there are no breakpoints defined for the report (more on this later!).

If you printed the report generated from this initial procedure we don't think you would be overly impressed with the results. As long as you can persevere, though, and follow us to the end of the chapter, we are sure you will be impressed with the power of the report generating facility.

Naming a Report

If you open the **View** sub-menu you will see that a '√' has been placed against the **Report** option, which when selected opens a box showing the option **Report1.** Works 2000 gives any reports generated a series of names, numbered 1, 2, 3, etc. To change this report name, choose T**ools**, **Rename Report**, type 'Overdue' in the text box and select **Rename** followed by **OK**. The **View**, **Report** box should now contain the option Overdue. When a database is saved, any report definitions generated are saved with it, including sorting instructions. Obtaining a similar report in the future is simply a matter of selecting it from the **View**, **Report** box.

Defining a Report

The definition to automatically produce the report on page 213 is shown in the next screen dump example. This was designed to print on an A4 sheet of paper.

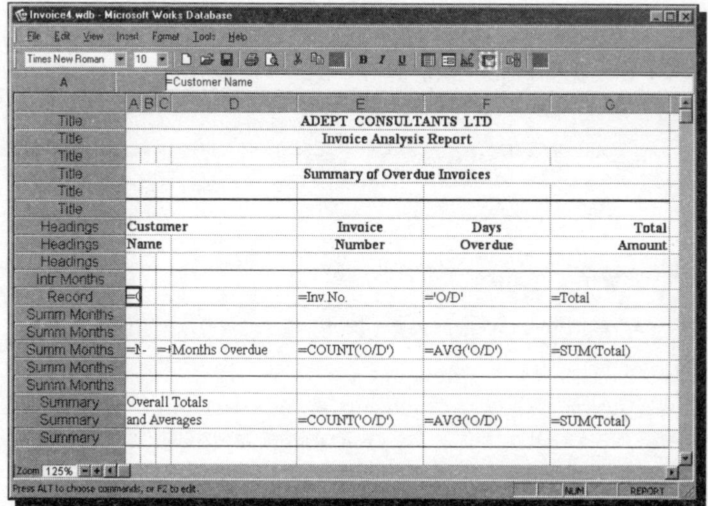

As an example we will step through the procedure of producing this report. Most of the reporting features should become apparent during the operation. You may also find it useful to spend a few minutes with the Works Help sections.

This report definition will be easier to prepare from an empty work area, so choose **Edit**, **Select All** and then **Edit, Clear** to clear the working area cells.

The first operation is to reset the column widths. Set columns A, B and C to a width of 2, by selecting these columns, choosing **Format, Column Width** and typing 2, followed by <Enter>. In the same way, alter the other columns as follows: D, E and F to 17 and G to 16.

Adding a Report Title

The 'Title' rows hold any text that is to appear at the top of the first printed page of the report. In our example we will need six rows of this type, so we must insert four more. Press <Ctrl+Home> to move the cursor to the Home cell, highlight the top four rows by selecting their headers and choose **Insert**, **Insert Row**. The next box asks what type of rows are to be inserted; we want 'Title', which is highlighted, so press <Enter> to complete the operation.

To position the main report title in the centre of the printed page, move the cursor to column A of the top row, type

```
ADEPT CONSULTANTS LTD
```

and press <Enter>. We will leave it to you to add the other two title lines in column A of rows 2 and 4. Now highlight the first four rows of columns A to G and use the **Format**, **Alignment**, **Center across selection** command.

To place the horizontal line across the page, select the cells A5 to G5 and place a **Bottom** line with the **Format**, **Border** command. There are several line options to choose from.

Adding Page Titles

Page titles are placed in 'Headings' type rows, and appear below the report title on the first page of a report, and at the top of all subsequent pages. We will need three of this type of rows, so insert one more, as described earlier. The top two of these rows will hold the four report column titles, as shown on page 213. To enter these, place:

Customer and **Name** -	left aligned -	in column A
Invoice and **Number** -	centre aligned -	in column E
Days and **Overdue** -	centre aligned -	in column F
Total and **Amount** -	right aligned -	in column G

The way to select the above alignments is from the **Format**, **Alignment** box. Produce any lines with the **Format**, **Border** command, as described previously.

Using Formulae in a Cell

The body of the report will be produced by the contents of the 'Record' row. If we type a field name, preceded by an equal sign, in a 'Record' cell, Works places the contents of that field for each record into the report.

There are also a series of statistical operators that can be included in cell formulae. These are mainly used in 'Summ' type rows, to produce totals, averages, etc. When placed in a 'Summ fieldname' row they give field statistics for the previous group printed. In a 'Summary' row the statistics refer to that field for the whole report.

Statistic	*Calculates*
SUM	Total of the group.
AVG	Average of the group.
COUNT	Number of items in the group.
MAX	Largest number in the group.
MIN	Smallest number in the group.
STD	Standard deviation of the group.
VAR	Variance of the group.

There are several ways to enter formulae in a cell. If you can remember all your database fields, you could simply type the formulae in.

If not, the **Insert**, **Field Name** command places the selected field name in a cell, **Insert**, **Field Entry** places an '=' followed by the name; both dialogue boxes list all the fields of the database. The **Insert**, **Field Summary** box lists not only the database fields, but all the above functions, which you can select to place formulae in a 'Summ', or 'Summary', type row.

In our example, to complete the 'Record' row, enter the following formulae into the cells shown below and format the cells, in the **Format**, **Number** box as follows:

Cell	*Contents*	*Alignment*	*Format*
A	=Customer Name	Left justified	
E	=Inv.No.	Centre justified	Fixed (0)

F	=O/D	Centre justified	Fixed (0)
G	=Total	Right justified	Currency (2)

Sorting a Report

A report is sorted to arrange the database entries in a certain order, such as alphabetical (order) or by date. A sort order specified in a report stays with that report, until it is physically changed. The main sort field, in our case, is on the Months field. We must specify the sort parameters now, as 'Summ' type rows cannot be used without a breakpoint having been entered.

The **Tools**, **Report Sorting** command opens the Report Settings dialogue box. The selections shown on the next page, are those required for our example. To obtain them, select 'Months' in the **Sort by** box and an **Ascending** sort.

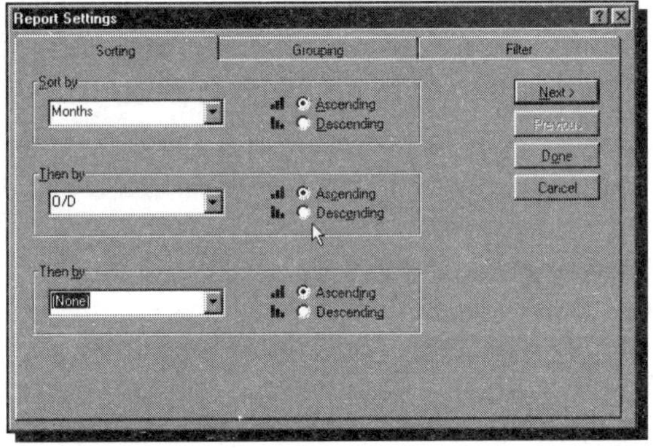

In our case, for neatness, we have also specified a **Then by** ascending sort on the 'O/D' field. If our database contained many hundreds of records, with several for each customer, we could also sort, and break, on the 'Customer Name' field. A summary for each customer would then be produced.

Click the **Grouping** tab and select the **When contents change** option, which will cause the report to split its output every time the value of the sorted field 'Months' changes.

Filtering a Report

For a report to show the correct records, the database must first be searched using the required retrieval criteria, as was described in the previous chapter.

In our case, the report should include all the invoices which have not been settled. Click the **Filter** tab and choose **Create New Filter**, giving it the name 'Overdue'. Select the field 'Paid' in the **Field name** box, the statement 'is equal to' in **Comparison** and type '0' in the **Compare to** section and press **OK**.

When the above settings are accepted, two extra rows, 'Intr Months' and 'Summ Months', are placed in the report definition.

An 'Intr' row is placed before a report break section and can contain headings to identify the following data. In our case we will leave this line blank, or if you prefer you could delete it. It is only by 'playing around' like this and checking the printed results with Print Preview that you can fully master the report generator.

Completing the Report Definition

Insert four more 'Summ Months' rows, and enter the following formulae in the middle row cells, with the formats and styles shown, as before.

Cell	*Contents*	*Alignment*	*Format*
A	=Months	Left justified	Fixed (0)
B	"–	Left justified	
C	=Months+1	Right justified	Fixed (0)
D	" Months Overdue	Left justified	
E	=COUNT('O/D')	Centre justified	Fixed (0)
F	=AVG('O/D')	Centre justified	Fixed (0)
G	=SUM(Total)	Left justified	Currency (2)

When you have completed this row, place horizontal lines, as described previously, above and below it.

Our report definition is almost complete now, only the 'Summary' rows remain to be done. If you have worked your way to this stage, entering these rows on your own should present no problems.

Insert two more 'Summary' type rows. Place a line in the bottom one, and type the following in the remaining two rows:

Cell	*Contents*	*Alignment*	*Format*
Row 17			
A	"Overall Totals	Left justified	
Row 18			
A	"and Averages	Left justified	
E	=COUNT(O/D)	Centre justified	Fixed (0)
F	=AVG(O/D)	Centre justified	Fixed (0)
G	=SUM(Total)	Right justified	Currency (2)

Printing a Report

Printing a report is similar to printing a word processor document, except that the facility to force column page breaks is included, as is the case with spreadsheets. From the Report screen choose **File**, **Page Setup** and make sure your page is set up with a 3.2cm left margin, and select Print Preview to see what your report will look like on paper. It should be similar to the screen dump shown on the next page. Press **Print** to start printing, or **Cancel** to return to the Report definition screen.

Our report definition is now complete. It probably took several hours to build, but an instant report can now be generated from it, no matter how big the database gets. Also you should by now be able to tackle any reports of your own design.

Save the file with the name **Invoice4**, but yet again make sure you use the **Save As** command.

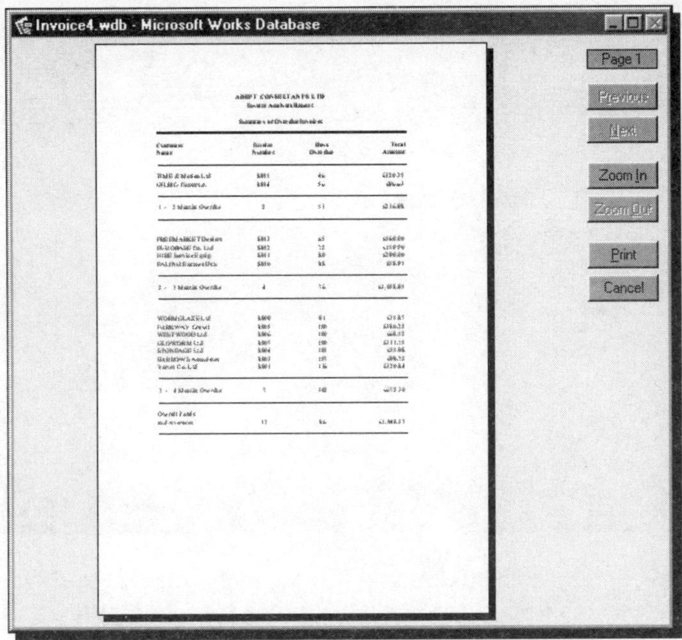

Form Letters

We are now in a position to use the mail merge capability of Works 2000 to create customised 'form letters', which make use of information stored in a database. As an example of this, you could create the simple database shown next, which contains the personal details of our potential customers. Save it as **Business address**.

Now type the letter shown below it, using the word processor. Note the way the various field names are enclosed by angled brackets. These 'field name markers' cannot be just typed in place. Move the cursor to where you want a field name marker and choose the **Insert**, **Database Field** command. Click the **Merge information from another type of file** option and select the file name of the database to

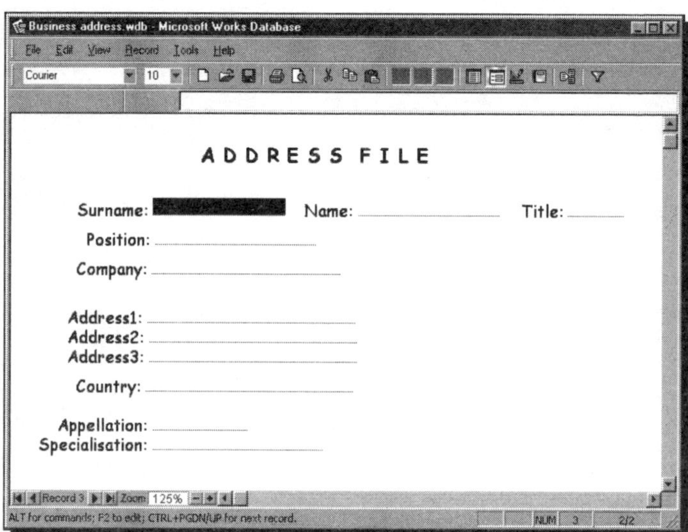

use, in our case **Business address**. In the **Insert Fields** box choose the field name you want, press **Insert** and Works will place the field name in the document.

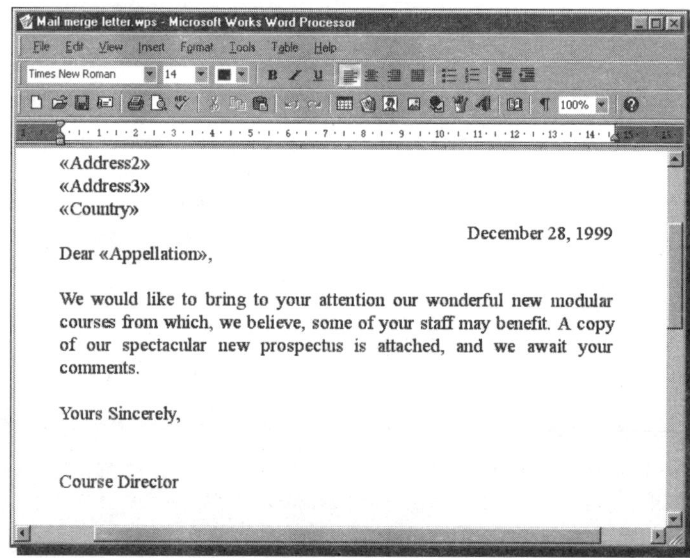

You can use the **View Results** button to get the word processor to substitute the database field information in your letter. This way you can make sure you have selected the correct field!

When the letter is completed close the **Insert Fields** box and save the document with the name of **Mail merge letter**.

Note the field 'Appellation' which could be 'Sir', if you didn't know the name of the recipient, 'Mr Brown', if you did or 'John', if he was a friend of yours.

The field 'Specialisation' is included so that your form letters are only sent to relevant people. You would use information in this field in a Filter to select records.

Printing Form Letters

Works 2000 will print one copy of the letter for each record displayed in the database, assuming of course that you have entered some records.

Open the word processor file holding the form letter, in our case **Mail merge letter**. Before continuing make sure the database has been searched and sorted to display the records you need. You now do this from the word processor, with the **Tools**, **Mail Merge**, **Filter and Sort** command.

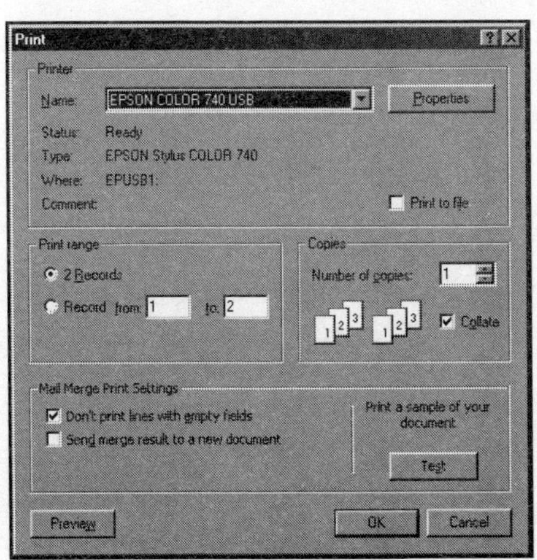

When your printer is set up correctly, choose **File**, **Print**, select what options you want from **Mail Merge Print Settings** and click the **Preview** button to see what will be printed.

Then complete the usual Print dialogue box options for **Number of copies**, etc., and finally press **OK** to start the print run. Obviously if you don't want to actually print the letters you would press **Cancel**.

That is all there is to it. As long as your printer does not run out of paper, Works will print as many letters as there are records selected.

This procedure is not, of course, restricted to producing letters. It can be used for any word processed document which extracts information from a database.

If you have all your important names and addresses stored in the Works 2000 Address Book, as described in the next chapter, you could use the Address Book in this procedure instead of the database.

12

The Works 2000 Address Book

As Works 2000 includes Outlook Express to handle its communications functions, it is not surprising to find that the Works Address Book is actually the one built into Outlook Express. It provides a convenient place to store information on your personal and business 'contacts', for easy retrieval by the other Works 2000 applications, or by Outlook Express itself.

Address Book Features

In the address book, you can easily store e-mail addresses, home and work addresses, phone and fax numbers, digital IDs, conferencing information, instant messaging addresses, as well as personal information such as birthdays, anniversaries, and details of a contact's family members. You can also store individual and business Internet addresses, and link directly to them from your address book. There is also a generous section for notes.

As long as you are connected, you can look up names and addresses on the Internet to find people using Lightweight Directory Access Protocol (LDAP) directory services.

You can create groups of contacts to make it easy to send e-mail to a set of people, such as relatives, or members of work groups. Any time you want to send an e-mail to everyone in the group, just use the group name instead of entering each contact individually. This is how junk e-mail starts!

You can send and receive electonic business cards. When you create a business card in the Address Book, your contact information is stored in vCard format, so it can be exchanged between different programs (such as e-mail, address books, and personal planners), and between different digital devices (such as desktop computers, laptops or portable computers, personal digital assistants, and telephony equipment).

You can print all or part of your address book and take it with you, maybe as part of your personal planner. There are three page styles to choose from, printing all contact information, only business information, or only phone numbers, for all or selected contacts.

Using the Address Book

You open the Address Book from the **Programs** page of the Task Launcher, the same way as the other Works 2000 applications, by clicking **Start the Address Book**, as pointed to below.

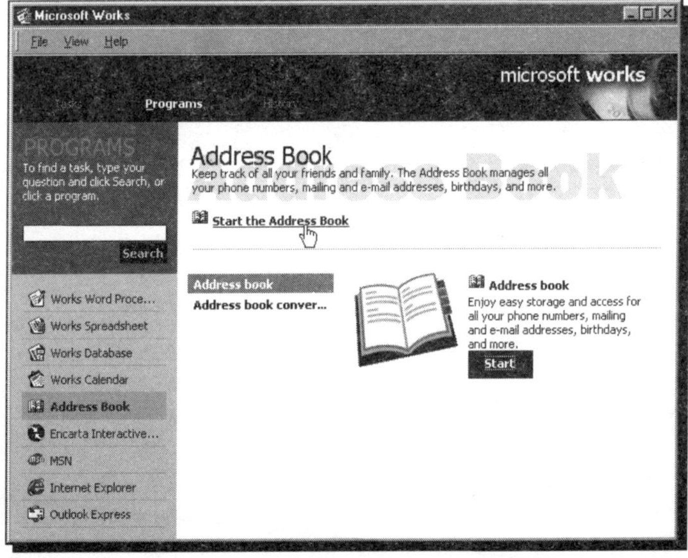

The program can also be opened by selecting **Address Book** in the Works section of the Windows **Start** menu.

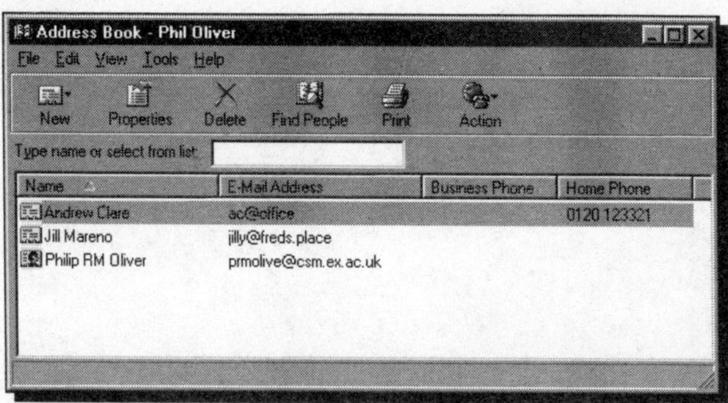

When open it looks like our example above which only shows a few entries, and for obvious reasons these are mostly fictitious! From the Address Book window you can manually add a person's full details and e-mail address, in the Properties box that opens when you click the New Toolbar icon and select **New Contact** from the drop down menu.

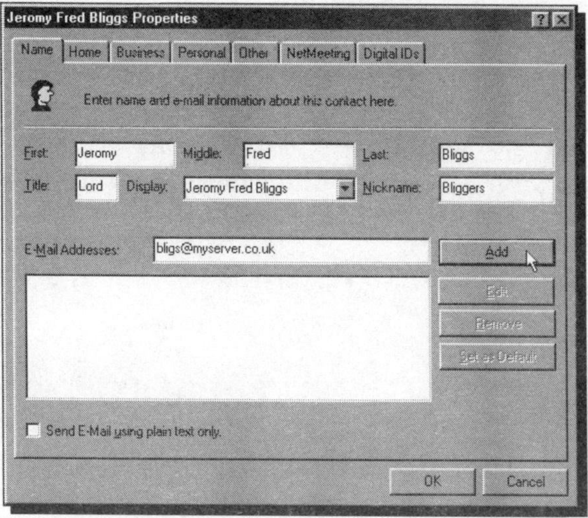

Once you have filled in all the details you want on the new contact, including those in the Home, Business, Personal, etc., tabbed sections, clicking the **Add** button pointed to above will save the new details for future use.

To edit these details in the future, you simply select the contact's name from the main list and click the Properties Toolbar button. This opens the same dialogue box as before, but with a Summary sheet on the front, as shown below.

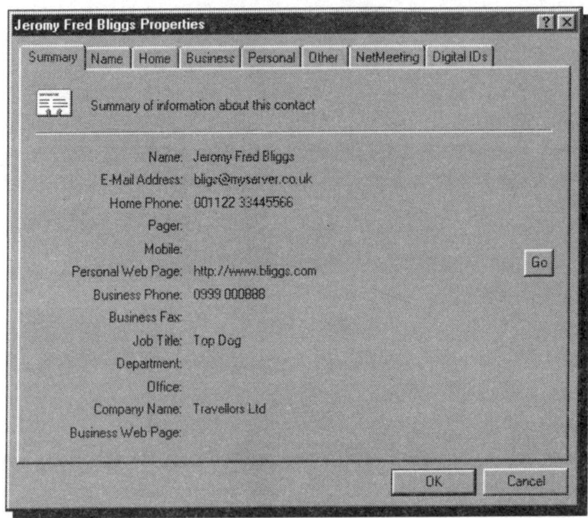

It is easy to add an individual name to your address book when reading e-mails in Outlook Express itself. From a message you are viewing or replying to, just right-click the person's name, and then click **Add to Address Book**. From the message list of any mail folder or the Inbox, right-click a message, and then click **Add Sender to Address Book**.

Using E-mail Groups

This feature lets you create a grouping of e-mail addresses, you can then send mail to everyone in the group with one operation.

To create a group, click the New button on the toolbar, and then click **New Group**. The Properties dialogue box, shown next, opens.

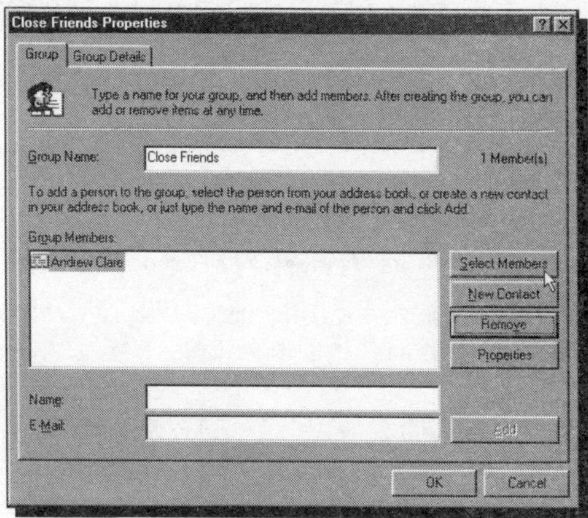

In the **Group Name** box, type the name of the group, which then forms part of the box title, as shown above. To add a person from your address book list, click **Select Members**, highlight their name in the address book list and then click the **Select** button, as shown below.

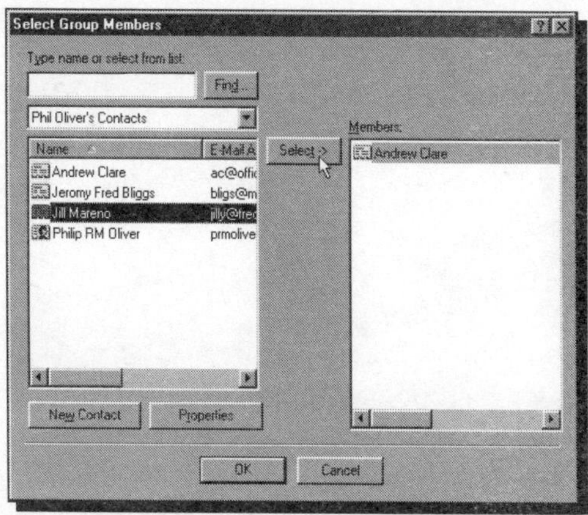

To add a person to both the group and your address book, click the **New Contact** button in either of the two boxes above and fill in their details.

To add a person directly to the group without adding them to your address book, type the person's **Name** and **E-Mail** address straight into the lower half of the Properties dialogue box, and then click the **Add** button.

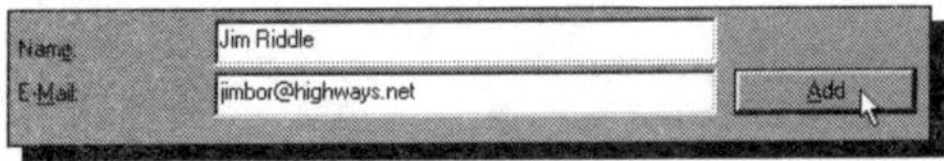

Click **OK** to get back to the Address Book and you will find a new item in the main list, as shown below.

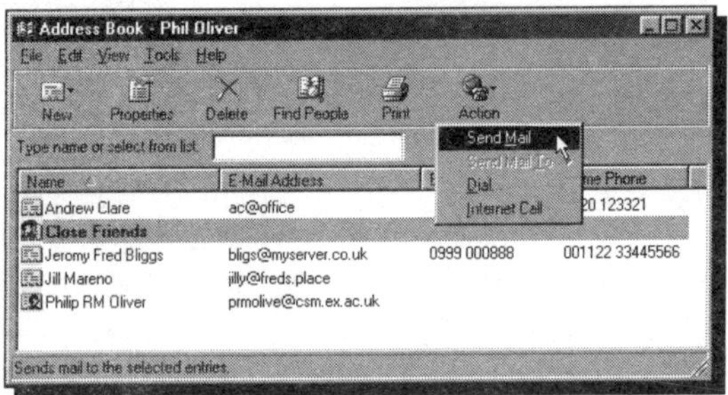

To send a new message to a person or group listed in your Address Book click the Action Toolbar button and select **Send Mail** from the drop-down menu, as above. As long as Outlook Express is set up properly its New Message window should be opened with the addressing details already completed.

Finding People

The Address Book gives you two main ways of finding people's details, both from the Find People Toolbar button. If your Address Book has hundreds of entries you can use this feature to find a particular person. But how many far-away friends do you have that you would love to contact, but whose e-mail address you have lost or never even known? No problem with the Address Book, if they have an e-mail address you should be able to find it, as it supports LDAP (Lightweight Directory Access Protocol) for accessing directory services, and has built-in access to several popular directory services. Directory services are powerful search tools that you use to find people and businesses around the world.

If the Address Book is open, click the Find People Toolbar button. If it is not, you can simply open the Windows **Start** menu and select **Find**, **People**. Both methods open the box shown here.

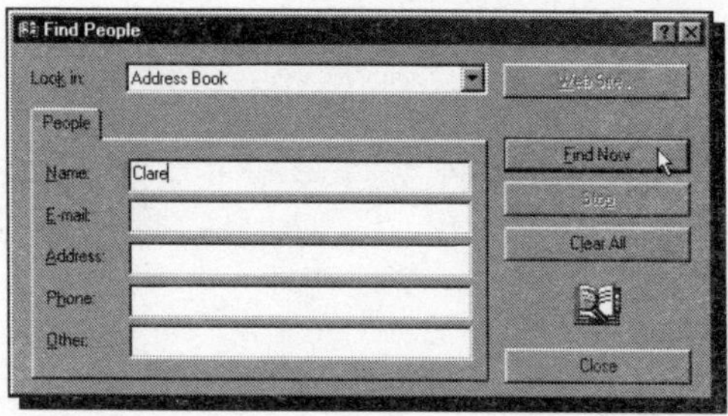

To search the Address Book itself, make sure it is selected in the **Look in** text box, type as many search details as you can remember in the **People** boxes, and click on **Find Now**.

To use a directory service, click the down arrow next to the **Look in** text box and select one of the options given, as shown on the left. The Find People dialogue box then changes to that shown below.

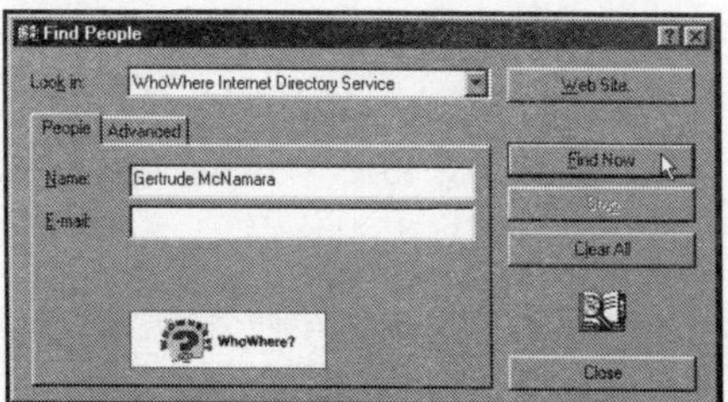

Type the **Name** or **E-mail** address of the person you want to look for on the **People** tab, and then click **Find Now**. The **Advanced** tab lets you define extra search criteria to use. Clicking the **Web Site** button lets you access the directory Web site itself. You must have an Internet connection though for any of this to work.

Electronic Business Cards

An easy way to exchange contact information with people over the Internet is by attaching a 'business card' to your e-mail messages. This gives all your Address Book information about yourself in vCard format, which can be used with a wide variety of digital devices and operating systems.

You may have wondered why we had our own information in the simple Address Book example we have used here. Of course, this is needed before you can create a business card. You should be careful to include only the information that you do actually want to give. We only include some of our business details. It depends, of course, to whom you are sending the card!

To create a Business Card, add an entry for yourself, and then select it from the Address Book list, and use the **File, Export**, **Business Card (vCard)** menu command. Choose a location in which to store the file, and then click **Save**.

To add your business card to an e-mail message in Outlook Express, use the **Insert**, **My Business Card**, menu command.

If you want to look at the contents of the card you have saved, use the **File, Import**, **Business Card (vCard)** menu command, select the file, which as shown here, is in '.vcf' form and click the **Open** button. You should see that it contains the same details as those saved.

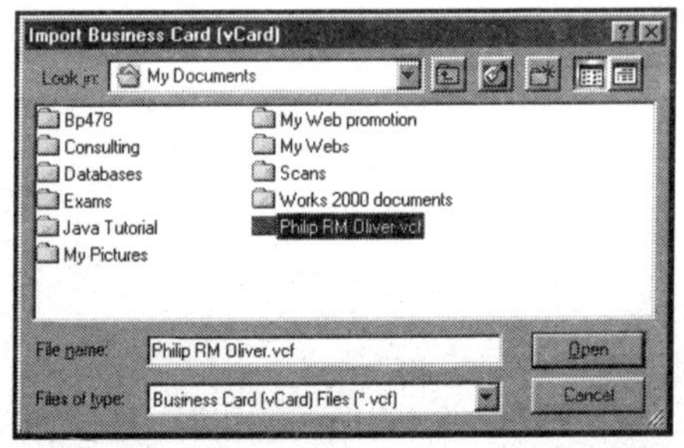

Printing Contact Details

To print details from your Address Book, select the contact, or contacts, you want to print in the usual Windows way. Click the Print button on the toolbar, and then in the **Print Style** area of the Print dialogue box, select a printing style, as follows:

Memo	Prints all address book information about the selected contact(s).
Business Card	Prints business-related information about the selected contact(s).
Phone List	Prints a list of phone numbers for the selected contact(s).

The following print information was obtained using the **Business Card** option for one of our entries.

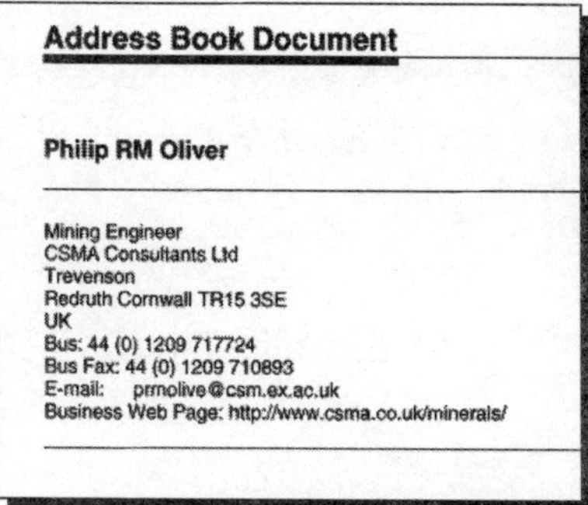
Address Book Document

Philip RM Oliver

Mining Engineer
CSMA Consultants Ltd
Trevenson
Redruth Cornwall TR15 3SE
UK
Bus: 44 (0) 1209 717724
Bus Fax: 44 (0) 1209 710893
E-mail: prmolive@csm.ex.ac.uk
Business Web Page: http://www.csma.co.uk/minerals/

It is very easy to print your contact information in these useful formats. With some trial and error you could print out pages that will fit into your diary or personal planner.

Depending on your printer, you should be able to customise the size and orientation of your printed Address Book pages. To view your printer's options, click the **Properties** button in the Print dialogue box. You will probably have a little more trouble punching the correct holes in the pages though!

Address Book Help

The Address Book comes with quite a detailed Help system built in that you can use with the **Help**, **Contents and Index** menu command, or the **F1** key. An example section is shown open below.

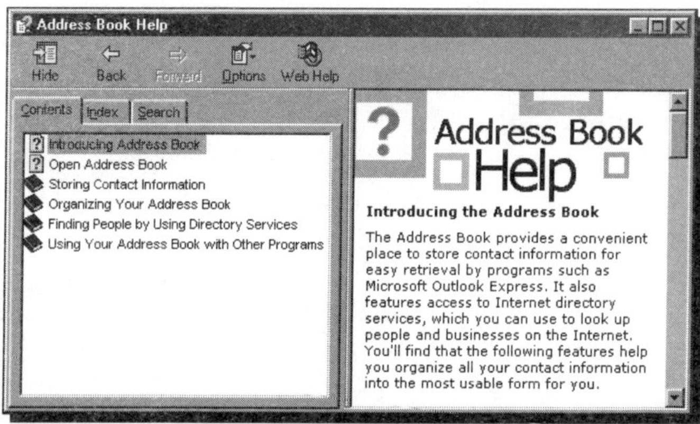

It is well worth working your way through all of the items on the **Contents** list. We have only covered the main ones here.

****

We find the Address Book to be a very useful feature of the package, but like all such things it is only of continual use if you keep it up to date!

13

The Works 2000 Calendar

The Works 2000 Calendar is exactly what its name suggests; an electronic calendar very similar to the one you have on your wall, or desk, but a lot more powerful. Not only can you use it to see what day it is, but to keep track of appointments, meetings and events such as holidays and birthdays, and to set reminders. As long as you keep it up to date, and check it every day, you need never get yourself in an embarrassing forgetful mess again!

Like the other Works 2000 applications you open the Calendar from the Task Launcher, by selecting **Works Calendar** in the **Programs** window list and then clicking on the **Start the Calendar** link, shown below.

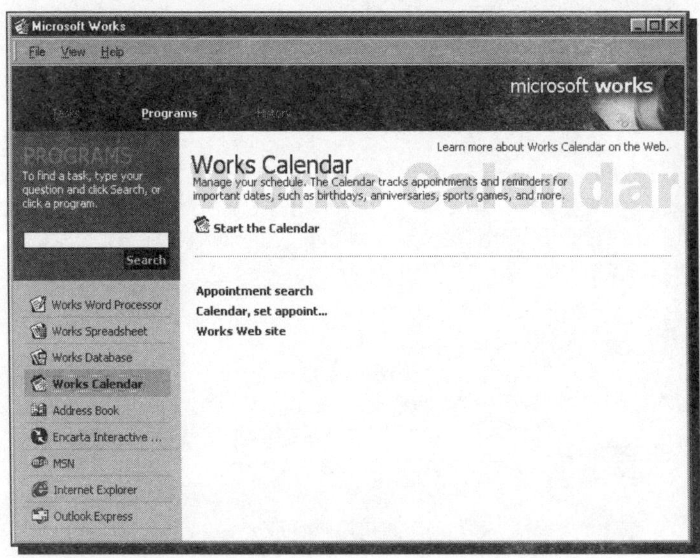

The Calendar Screen

Before we get too involved with entering dates and appointments in the calendar perhaps we should look at the parts that make up the screen.

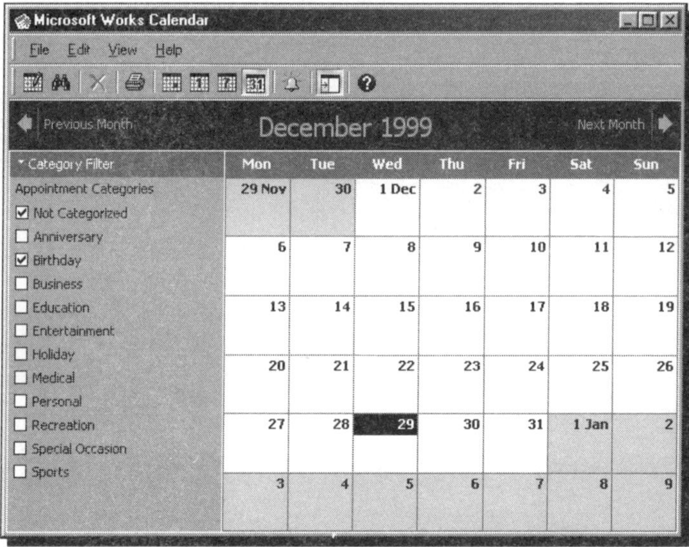

As shown above, it has its own menu and Toolbar and shows either the current month, week or day, depending on the setting. Also shown open above is the **Category Filter** bar on the left. This bar has its own toggle button on the Toolbar and will be discussed a little later on.

The Toolbar

Most of the Toolbar buttons are new to the Calendar so we will describe their operation before we go on.

Make a new appointment

Find a Calendar entry

Delete an entry

Print all, or selected, appointments

Go to today's date, but stay in same view

Change to one day view

Change to week day view

Change to one month view

View the current reminders

Toggle the Category Filter on and off

Open the Calendar Help pane.

The Toolbar can be switched on and off with the **View**, **Toolbar**, **Show Toolbar** menu command, and the same sub-menu gives you the option of using large icons on the bar.

Viewing Appointments

There are three main ways to view your calendar, one day, one week and one month at a time. In all these views you can see any diary entries that have been made, or you can click in a day's area to make a new appointment entry.

In any view, to look at the next day, week or month just left-click on the respective button on the right of the black Date bar, as shown here. The Previous day, week or month buttons on the left of the bar take you back one day, week or month.

To change between the views, simply click the appropriate button on the Toolbar as shown above, or use the **View**, **Day** command or <Alt+1>, the **View**, **Week** command or <Alt+->,or the **View**, **Month** command or <Alt+=>. The choice is yours, whichever method you use the result is the same.

Entering Appointments

To start with, let us type in a recurring appointment to, say, meet Section Managers, that takes place on Thursday every four weeks starting at 10:00 a.m. on 6 January and lasts for 2 hours.

To do so, go to Month View, select January 2000 and double-click the 6 January on the calendar. This opens the New Appointment dialogue box shown below in which you can type 'Managers' meeting' in the **Title** box, and 'My Office' in the **Location** box, and de-select the **All-day event** option. This allows you to enter the **When Appointment starts** as 10.00 and **When Appointment ends** as 12.00, as shown.

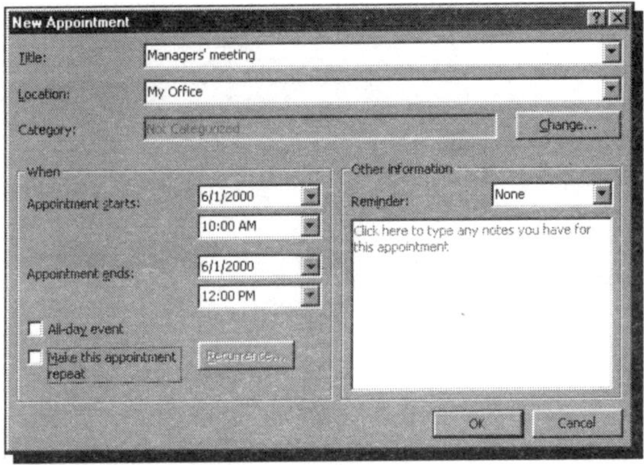

If you then select to **Make this appointment repeat**, part of the dialogue box changes once more to that shown below.

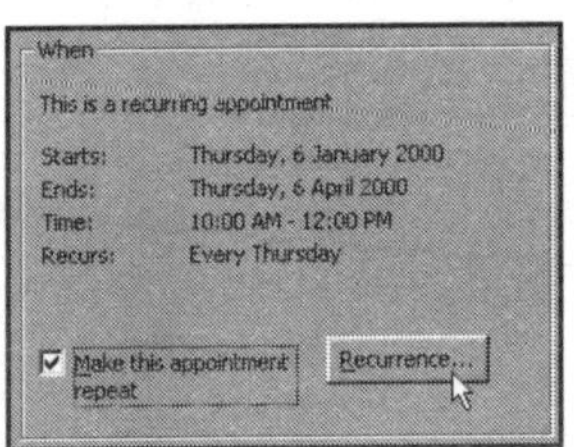

Click the **Recurrence** button and in the Recurrence Options dialogue box, click the **Monthly** radio button and select **Every first Thursday**. You could place notes about the meetings if you wanted to. Finally click **OK** twice to return to the Calendar.

Your Calendar now shows the series of entries on the correct days. Below is the Day View of the 6 January.

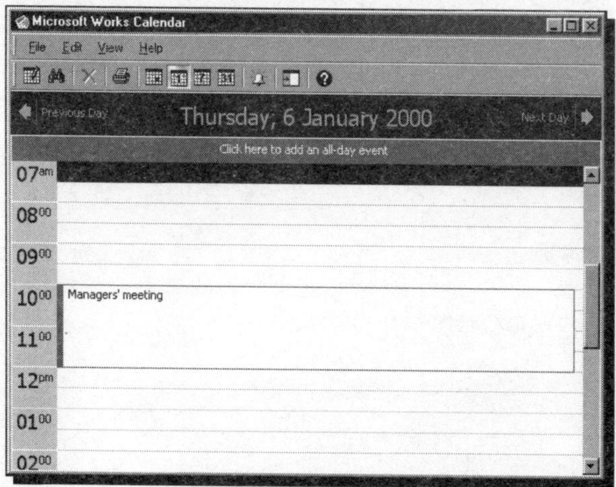

If you want to make any changes to the newly created appointment, double-click on it. Select **Open this occurrence**, from the menu box that opens, to make changes that only affect it on that date, or select **Open the Series** to open the Recurring Options dialogue box where you can make changes that will affect all future appointments.

To delete an appointment, select it and either click the Delete Toolbar icon, or right-click and select **Delete Item**. Both methods will open a warning box to give you a chance to 'change your mind'.

Category Filters

A category is an assigned name that can help you define and organise the appointments in your calendar. You associate an appointment with a category to help you remember what type of appointment it is.

You can also view appointments based on the categories assigned to them. For example, you can view only those appointments that have the Entertainment category assigned.

To add a category, click and select an appointment in the calendar and action the **File**, **Open Appointment** menu command. Click the Change button followed by the category you want to assign to the appointment, as shown below.

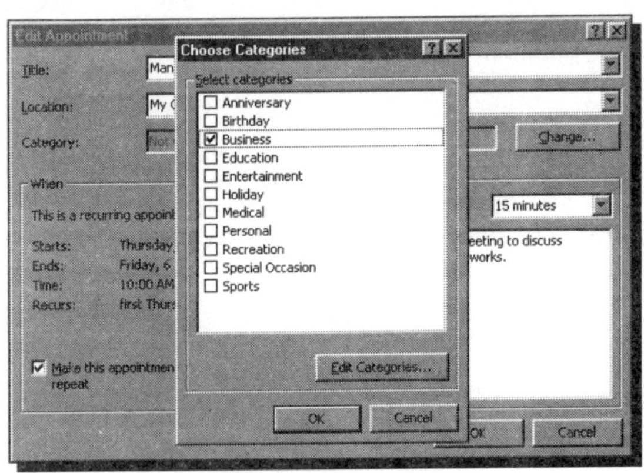

Clicking on **OK** will complete the operation. The Choose Categories box above shows all the default categories built into the calendar. You can change any of these by clicking the **Edit Categories** button, maybe by adding new ones and deleting those that you will never use.

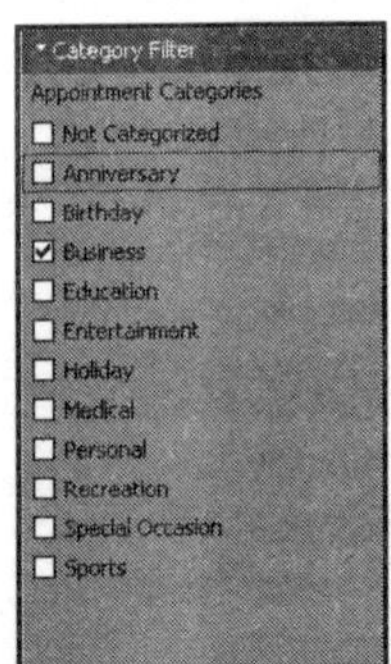

Once you have added categories to your appointments, you can use the Category Filter button to open the filter, shown to the left. This lets you control which appointments are displayed at any one time.

If **Not Categorized** is selected in the filter, only appointments with no categories will show on the calendar. If you select another category from the filter list and de-select **Not Categorized**, then only entries with that category will be displayed. In our example here only **Business** appointments will be visible.

Adding Holidays

When you first open the Works 2000 calendar it is empty and has no appointments or other entries. You can soon change this by adding what holidays you want to show, such as the national holidays of your country (and others if you like), or religious holidays, such as Christian, Jewish or Islamic.

To do this, use the **Edit**, **Add Holidays** menu command, or <Ctrl+H>, and select the holidays you want to add to your calendar, as shown below.

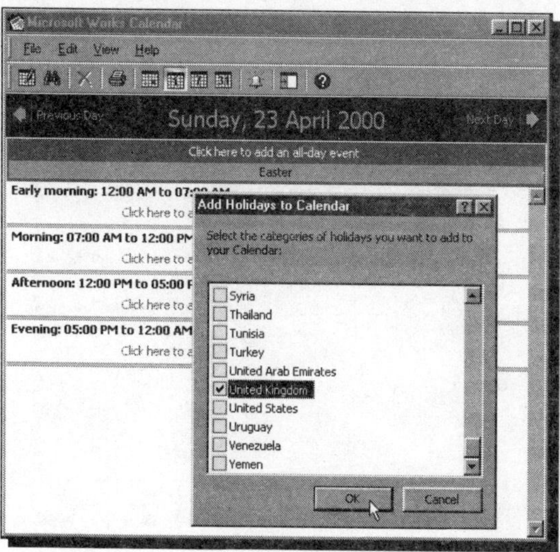

We suggest you don't go too mad here, the calendar screen can get very easily cluttered with duplicate holiday entries which are not always easy to get rid of. Be warned. If you need to, you can delete holiday entries the same as other appointments, as described earlier.

Adding Birthdays

If you have already entered birthdays and anniversaries in the Address Book, you can add them to your calendar automatically with the **Edit**, **Birthdays** menu command.

To add birthdays manually is a little more time consuming. You add them in the Month View the same as any other appointments, but give them the Birthday category, as described earlier. Remember to make them recur yearly in the New Appointment dialogue box, or they will only show for the day you enter them, not every year from then on.

Calendar Printing

Your calendar information can be printed on paper. Simply use the **File, Print** command to open the dialogue box below.

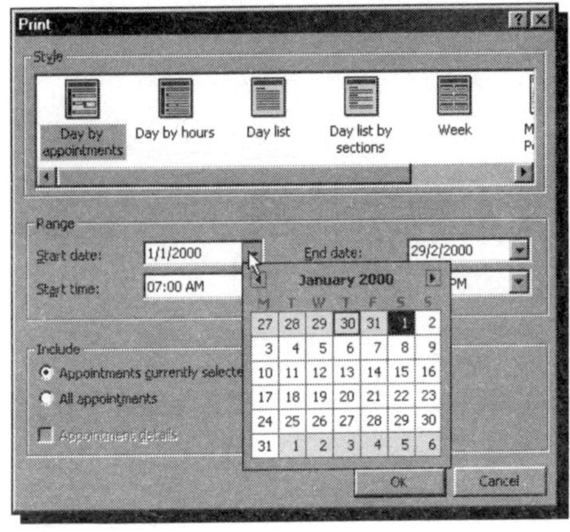

As you can see, this gives you plenty of control on what parts of the calendar to print and what style to use. Note the drop-down 'calendar views' to help you select the start and end dates of your printout. You will need to experiment a little here to find the settings that suit you best.

When you click on **OK** to accept the settings selected, the 'normal' Print box is opened so that you can control your printer and paper settings, etc. It's a pity there is no Preview option to save a few trees!

14

Outlook Express

When Works 2000 was installed on your system both Microsoft's Explorer 5 Web browser and Outlook Express 5 should also have been installed, if they were not already there. In this book we will not bother with Explorer itself, but Outlook Express being an e-mail package is the way Works communicates electronically with the rest of the world and certainly merits a chapter.

There are several ways to start the Outlook Express program, you can click the Desktop icon shown here, or the small icon on the left of the Windows Taskbar. Also like the other Works 2000 applications you can use the Task Launcher, by selecting **Outlook Express** in the **Programs** window list and then clicking the **Start Outlook Express** link. In all these cases a window something like ours below should be opened.

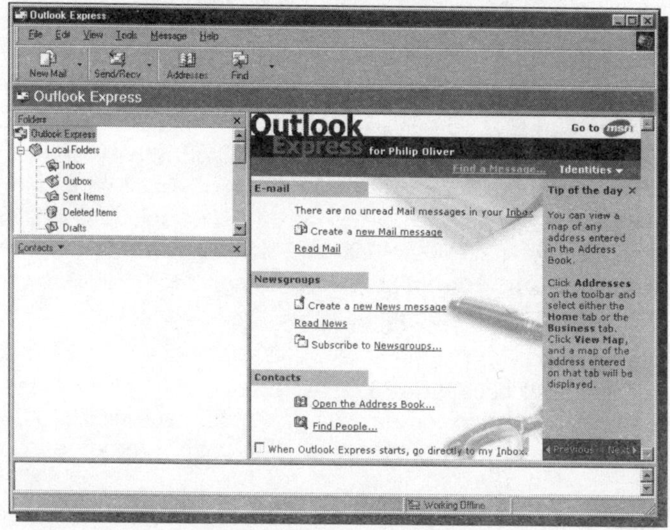

Connecting to your Server

Before you can use Outlook Express to send, or receive, mail you have to tell the program how to connect to your server's facilities. You do this by completing your personal e-mail connection details in the Internet Connection Wizard shown here, which opens when you first attempt to use the Read Mail facility.

The other way to enter this Wizard, if it does not open, or if you want to change your connection details, is to use the **Tools**, **Accounts** menu command, select the mail tab and click **Add**, followed by **Mail**.

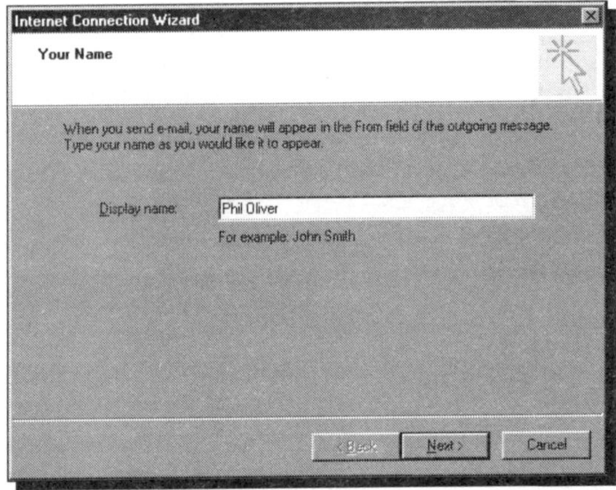

Type your name in the first box, as shown above, and click the **Next** button to open the second box. Enter your e-mail address in this box, if you have not organised one yet you could always check the **I'd like to sign up for a new account from Hotmail** option. Hotmail is a free browser based e-mail service now owned by Microsoft. Hence its inclusion!

In the third dialogue box enter your e-mail server details, as shown for us, on the next page. To complete some of the details here you may need to ask your Internet service provider, or system administrator, for help.

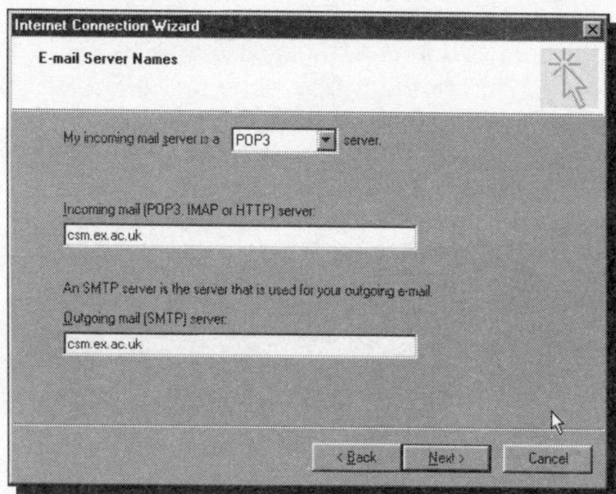

The details shown above will obviously only work for the writer, so please don't try them! In the next box enter your log-in name and password. Details of these should have been given to you by your Internet service provider or system administrator when you opened your 'service account'. You have now completed the Wizard so press **Finish** to return you to the Internet Accounts box, with your new account set up as shown below for us.

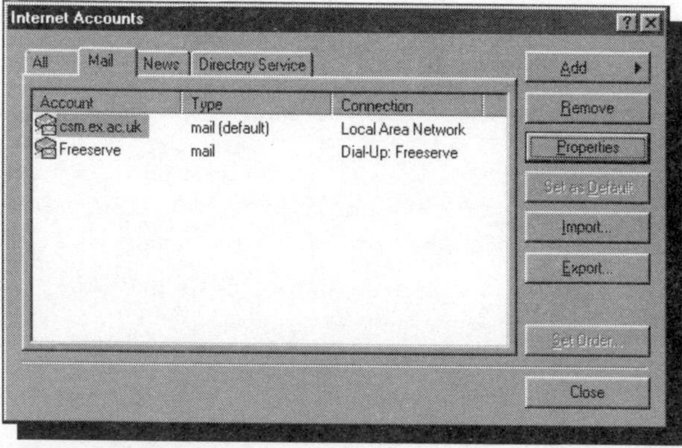

In the future, selecting the account in this box and clicking the **Properties** button will give you access to the settings sheets to check, or change, your details. We changed the Connection settings here to LAN (local area network).

Once your connection is established, you can click the Read Mail coloured link, or the **Inbox** entry in the Folder List on the left side of the Outlook Express opening window. Both of these actions open the Inbox, which the first time opened, will probably contain a message from Microsoft, as shown below.

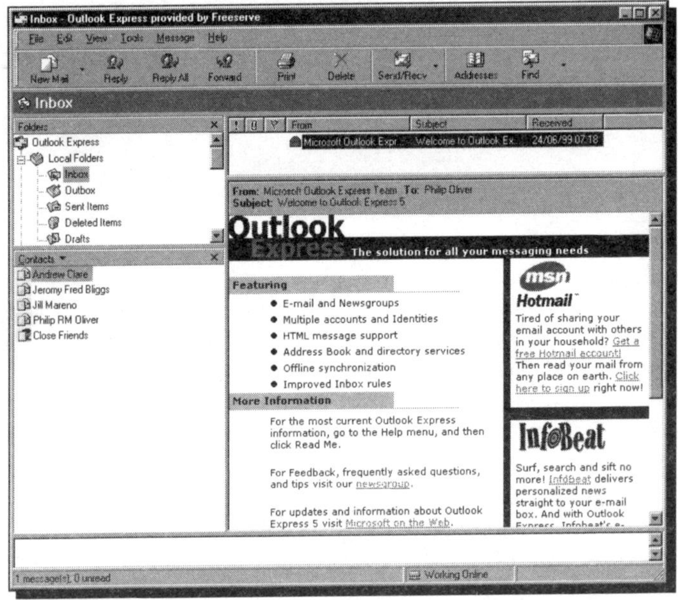

This message is well worth reading as it demonstrates some of the features of Outlook Express and also shows how decorative your e-mails can be.

The illustration above shows the default Outlook Express Main window layout, which consists of a Folder List to the left with a Contacts list from the Address Book below it, a Message List to the right and a Preview Pane below that. The Folder List contains all the active mail folders, news servers and newsgroups. Clicking on one of these places its contents in the Message List, and clicking on a message opens a Preview of it below for you to see. Double-clicking on a message opens the message in its own window.

To check your mail, click the Send/Recv Toolbar icon which will download any new messages from your mailbox to your hard disc. You can then read and process your mail at your leisure without necessarily being still connected to the Internet.

With the default set-up, Outlook Express will only check your mailbox when you click the Send/Recv Toolbar icon. We suggest you make a change in the **Tools**, **Options**, **General** tab settings sheet. Selecting the **Check for new messages every** 10 **minute(s)** option will make the program check your mail box when it starts and at regular intervals while it is open.

A Trial Run

Before explaining in more detail the main features of Outlook Express we will step through the procedure of sending a very simple e-mail message. The best way to test out any unfamiliar e-mail features is to send a test message to your own e-mail address. This saves wasting somebody else's time, and the message can be very quickly checked to see the results.

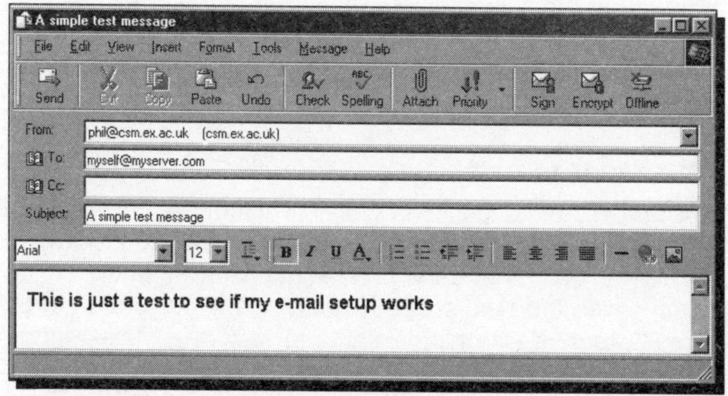

Click the New Mail icon and select **No Stationery** to open the New Message window, shown above.

Type your own e-mail address in the **To:** field, and a title for the message in the **Subject:** field. The text in this subject field will form a header for the message when it is received, so it helps to show in a few words what the message is about. Type your message and when you are happy with it, click the Send toolbar icon.

By default, your message is stored in an Outbox folder, and pressing the Send/Recv Toolbar icon will send it, hopefully straight into your mailbox. When Outlook Express next checks for mail, it will find the message and download it into the Inbox folder, for you to read and enjoy!

After the initial opening window, Outlook Express uses three other main windows, which we will refer to as; the Main window which opens next, the Read Message window for reading your mail; and the New Message window, to compose your outgoing mail messages.

The Main Window

The Main window consists of a Toolbar, a menu, and five panes with the default display shown in our example on page 248. You can choose different pane layouts, and customise the Toolbar, with the **View**, **Layout** menu command, but we will let you try these for yourself.

The Folders List

The folders pane contains a list of your mail folders, your news servers and any newsgroups you have subscribed to. There are always at least five mail folders, as shown in our example on the next page. You can add your own with the **File**, **Folder**, **New** menu command from the Main window. We added 'My new folder' like this. You can delete them again with the **File**, **Folder**, **Delete** command. These operations can also be carried out after right-clicking a folder in the list.

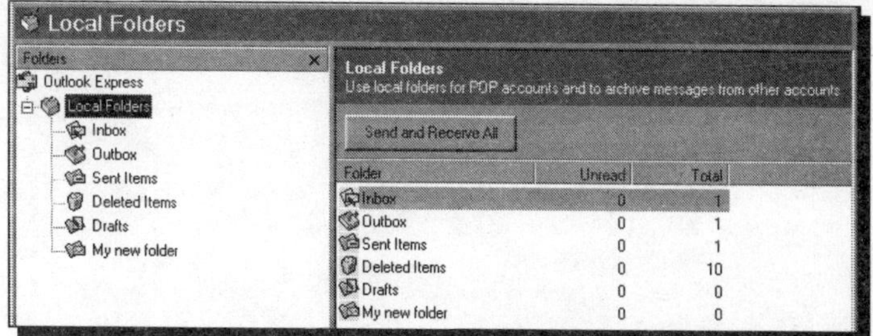

Note the icons shown above, any new folders you add will have the same icon as that of our added one above.

The Contacts Pane

This pane simply lists the contacts held in your Address Book. Double-clicking on an entry in this list opens a New Message window with the message already addressed to that person.

The Message List

When you select a folder, by clicking it in the Folders list, the Message list shows the contents of that folder. Brief details of each message are displayed on one line.

The first column shows the message priority, if any, the second shows whether the message has an attachment, and the third shows whether the message has been 'flagged'. All of these are indicated by icons on the message line, like our example to the left. The 'From' column shows the message status icon (listed on the next page) and the name of the sender; 'Subject' shows the title of each mail message, and 'Received' shows the date it reached you. You can control what columns display in this pane with the **View**, **Columns** menu command.

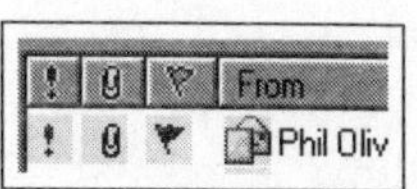

To sort a list of messages, you can click the mouse pointer in the title of the column you want the list sorted on, clicking it again will sort it in reverse order. The sorted column is shown with a triangle mark.

Message Status Icons

This icon	Indicates this
	The message has one or more files attached.
!	The message has been marked high priority by the sender.
↓	The message has been marked low priority by the sender.
	The message has been read. The message heading appears in light type.
	The message has not been read. The message heading appears in bold type.
	The message has been replied to.
	The message has been forwarded.
	The message is in progress in the Drafts folder.
	The message is digitally signed and unopened.
	The message is encrypted and unopened.
	The message is digitally signed, encrypted and unopened.
	The message is digitally signed and has been opened.
	The message is encrypted and has been opened.
	The message is digitally signed and encrypted, and has been opened.
⊞	The message has responses that are collapsed. Click the icon to show all the responses (expand the conversation).
⊟	The message and all of its responses are expanded. Click the icon to hide all the responses (collapse the conversation).
	The unread message header is on an IMAP server.
	The opened message is marked for deletion on an IMAP server.
	The message is flagged.
	The IMAP message is marked to be downloaded.
	The IMAP message and all conversations are marked to be downloaded.
	The individual IMAP message (without conversations) is marked to be downloaded.

The Preview Pane

When you select a message in the Message list, by clicking it once, it is displayed in the Preview pane, which takes up the rest of the window. This lets you read the first few lines to see if the message is worth bothering with. If so, double clicking the header, in the Message list, will open the message in the Read Message window, as shown later in the chapter.

You could use the Preview pane to read all your mail, especially if your messages are all on the short side, but it is easier to process them from the Read Message window.

The Main Window Toolbar

Opens the New Message window for creating a new mail message, with the To: field blank.

Opens the New Message window for replying to the current mail message, with the To: field pre-addressed to the original sender. The original Subject field is prefixed with Re:.

Opens the New Message window for replying to the current mail message, with the To: field pre-addressed to all that received copies of the original message. The original Subject field is prefixed with Re:.

Opens the New Message window for forwarding the current mail message. The To: field is blank. The original Subject field is prefixed with Fw:.

Prints the selected message.

Deletes the currently selected message and places it in the Deleted Items folder.

Connects to the mailbox server and downloads waiting messages, which it places in the Inbox folder. Sends any messages waiting in the Outbox folder.

Opens the Address Book.

Finds a message or an e-mail address using Find People facilities of the Address Book.

The Read Message Window

If you double-click a message in the Message list of the Main window the Read Message window is opened, as shown below.

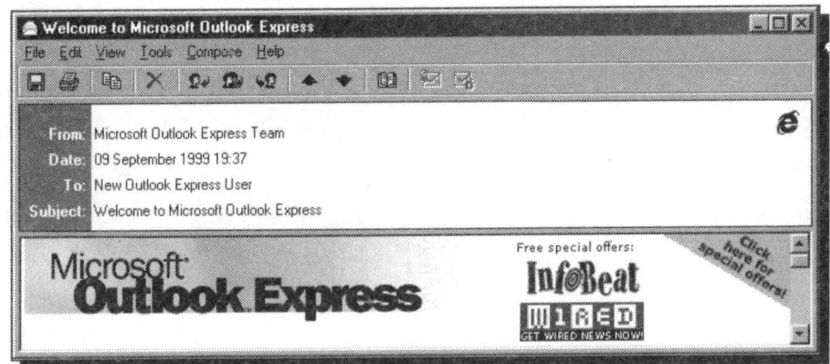

This is the best window to read your mail in. It has its own menu system and Toolbar, which lets you rapidly process and move between the messages in a folder.

The Read Message Toolbar

This window has its own Toolbar, but only two icons are different from those in the Main window.

Previous - Displays the previous mail message in the Read Message window. The button appears depressed if there are no previous messages.

Next - Displays the next mail message in the Read Message window. The button appears depressed if there are no more messages.

Viewing File Attachments

Until fairly recently, e-mail on the Internet was good only for short text notes. You couldn't send attachments like formatted document or graphic files with your messages. That changed with the advent of MIME, which stands for Multipurpose Internet Mail Extension. With Outlook Express you can send Web pages, other formatted documents, photos, sound and video files as attachments to your main e-mail message, and some of them as part of the actual message itself.

One thing to be careful of though, is to make sure that the person you are sending your message to has e-mail software capable of decoding them. In our experience many people seem to stick to their tried and trusted 'old' e-mail software that does not.

A file attachment appears at the bottom of the message in the Read Message window. To save the attachment, use the **File**, **Save Attachments** menu command, or right-click the attachment and select the **Save As** option.

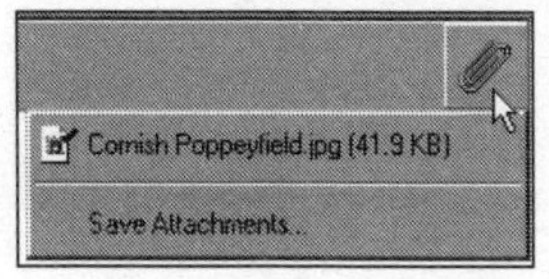

To display, or run, an attachment from the preview pane, click the paper clip file attachment icon in the preview pane header, and then click the file name. You may get a virus warning here, but if you are happy about the document source just carry on. To save the attachment click the **Save Attachments** button that is opened, as shown above.

The New Message Window

We briefly looked into the New Message window earlier in the chapter. This is the window, shown next, that you will use to create any messages you want to send electronically from Outlook Express. It is important to understand its features, so that you can get the most out of it.

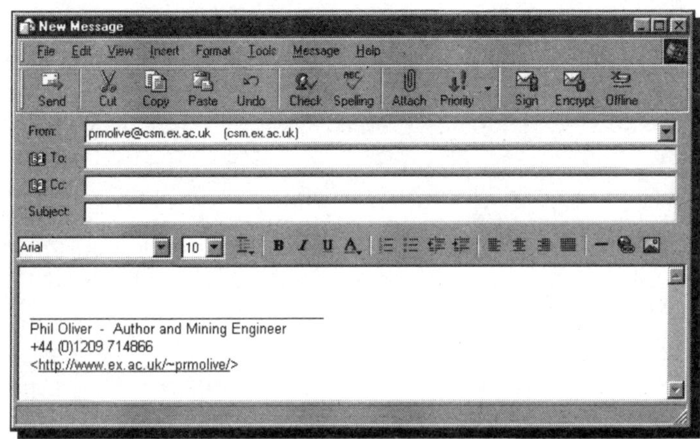

As we saw, this window can be opened by using the New Mail Toolbar icon from the Main window, as well as the **Message**, **New Message** menu command. From other windows you can also use the **Message**, **New** command, or the <Ctrl+N> keyboard shortcut. The New Message window has its own menu system and Toolbar, which let you rapidly prepare and send your new e-mail messages.

Message Stationery

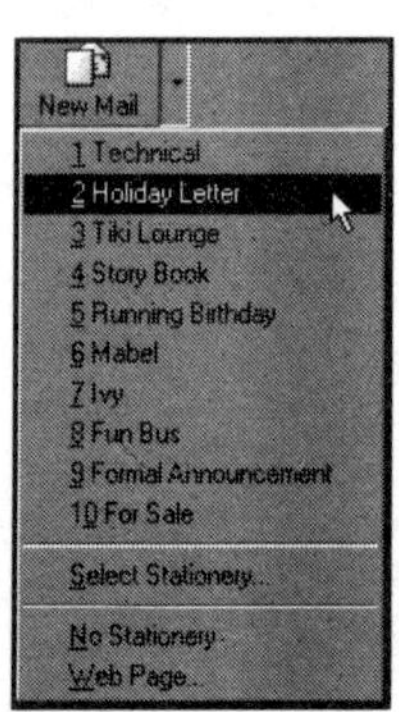

Another Outlook Express feature is that it lets you send your messages on pre-formatted stationery for added effect, as in our example on the facing page.

To access these, click the down arrow next to the New Mail button in the Main window and either select from the **1** to **10** list, as shown here, or use the **Select Stationery** command to open a box with many more stationery types on offer.

To send a plain message, with no 'fancy' effects, use the **No Stationery** option.

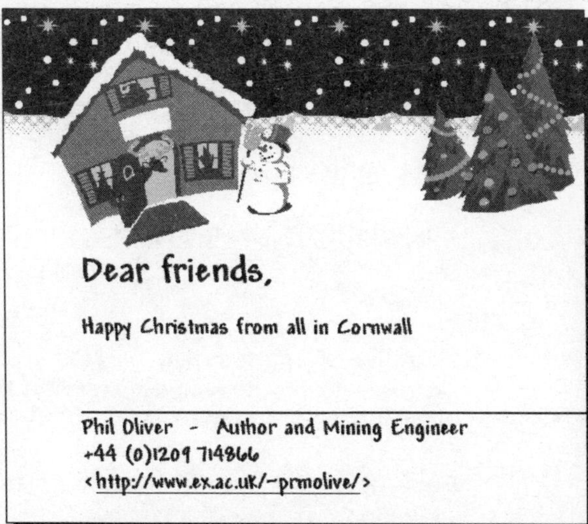

The New Message Toolbar

Send Message - Sends message, either to the recipient, or to the Outbox folder.

Cut - Cuts selected text to the Windows clipboard.

Copy - Copies selected text to the Windows clipboard.

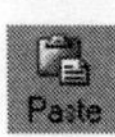

Paste - Pastes the contents of the Windows clipboard into the current message.

Undo - Undoes the last editing action.

Check Names - Checks that names match your entries in the address book, or are in correct e-mail address format.

Spelling - Checks the spelling of the current message before it is sent.

Attach File - Opens the Insert Attachment window for you to select a file to be attached to the current message.

Set Priority - Sets the message priority as high or low, to indicate its importance to the recipient.

Digitally sign message - Add a digital signature to the message to confirm to the recipient that it is from you.

Encrypt message - Encodes the message so that only the recipient can read it.

Work Offline - Closes connection to the Internet so that you can process your mail offline. The button then changes to **Work Online.**

Your Own Signature

If you have created a signature from the Main window in the **Tools**, **Options**, **Signature** tabbed box, as shown at the top of the next page, its text is automatically placed for you at the end of the message creation area.

You could also create a more fancy signature file in a text editor like Notepad, or WordPad, including the text and characters you want added to all your messages, and point to it in the **File** section of this box. We have chosen to **Add signatures to all outgoing messages**, but you could leave this option blank and use the **Insert**, **Signature** command from the New Message window menu system if you prefer.

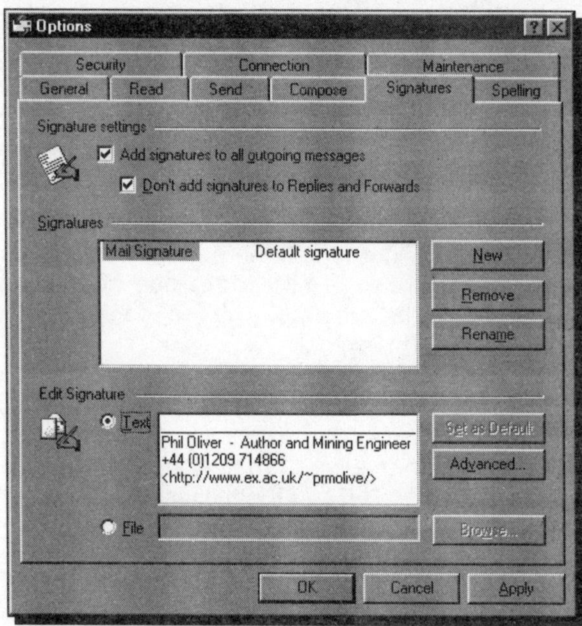

Message Formatting

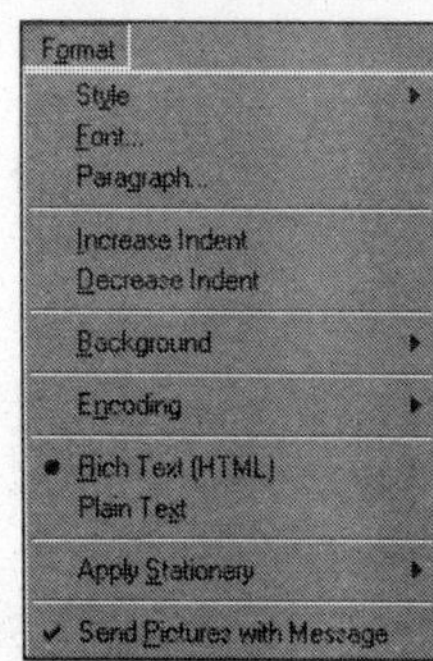

Outlook Express provides quite sophisticated formatting options for an e-mail editor from both the **Format** menu and Toolbar. These only work if you prepare the message in HTML format, as used in Web documents. In the **Tools**, **Options**, **Send** box you can set this to be your default mail sending format.

To use the format for the current message only, select **Rich Text (HTML)** from the **Format** menu, as we have done here. If **Plain Text** is selected, the black dot will be placed against this option on the menu, and the formatting features will not then be available.

The above Format Toolbar is added to the New Message window when you are in HTML mode and all the **Format** menu options are then made active.

All of the formatting features are well covered elsewhere in the book so we will not repeat them now. Most of them are quite well demonstrated in Microsoft's opening message to you. You should be able to prepare some very easily readable e-mail messages with these features, but remember that not everyone will be able to read the work in the way that you spent hours creating. Only e-mail programs that support MIME (Multipurpose Internet Mail Extensions) can read HTML formatting. When your recipient's e-mail program does not read HTML, the message appears as plain text with an HTML file attached.

At the risk of being called boring we think it is usually better to stick to plain text, not only can everyone read it, but it is much quicker to transmit and use.

Adding Attachments

If you want to send a Web page, or other type of file as an attachment to your main e-mail message you simply click the Insert File Toolbar button and select the file to attach. This opens the Insert Attachment dialogue box, for you to select the file, or files, you want to go with your message.

The attached files are shown in a special 'Attach:' section in the message header, as shown below.

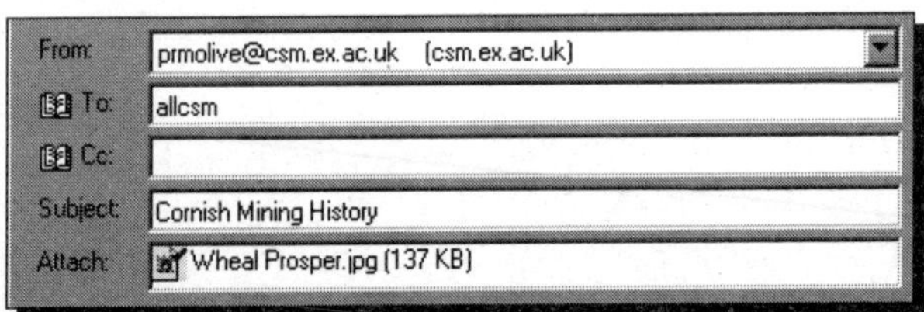

Sending E-mail Messages

When you have filled in the address fields, typed and formatted the body of your message, added any attachments, and maybe placed a signature, you simply click the Send Toolbar icon, shown here, to start the transmission process. What happens to the message next depends on your settings.

If you have a dial up connection (using a modem) you may want to keep the message and transmit it later, maybe with several others to save on your telephone bill. In that case make sure the **Send messages immediately** option is not selected in the **Tools**, **Options**, **Send** settings box. Clicking the above Send Toolbar icon will then place the message in the Outbox folder.

When you are ready to send your held messages you click the Send/Recv Toolbar icon on the Main window. If you forget to do this, Outlook Express will prompt you with a message box when you attempt to exit the program.

When the **Send messages immediately** option is selected, your messages will be sent on their way as soon as you click the Send Toolbar button. This option is best used if you have a permanent connection to the Internet, or your e-mail is being sent over an internal network, or Intranet.

Replying to a Message

When you receive an e-mail message that you want to reply to, Outlook Express makes it very easy to do. The reply address and the new message subject fields are both added automatically for you. Also, by default, the original message is quoted in the reply window for you to edit as required.

With the message you want to reply to open, either click the Reply to Sender Toolbar icon, use the **Message**, **Reply to Sender** menu command, or use the <Ctrl+R> keyboard shortcut. All these actions open the New Message window and the message you are replying to will, by default, be placed under the insertion point.

With long messages, you should not leave all of the original text in your reply. This can be bad practice, which rapidly makes new messages very large and time consuming to download. You should usually edit the quoted text, so that it is obvious what you are referring to. One or two lines may even be enough.

Removing Deleted Messages

Whenever you delete a message it is actually moved to the Deleted Items folder. If ignored, this folder gets bigger and bigger over time, so you need to check it every few days and manually re-delete messages you are sure you will not need again, in which case you are given a last warning message.

If you are confident that you will not need this safety net, you can opt to **Empty messages from the 'Deleted Items' folder on exit** in the **Tools**, **Options**, **Maintenance** settings box, opened from the Main window. You will then have a short time to change your mind before they are finally deleted.

The Address Book

E-mail addresses are often quite complicated and not easy to remember at all. Outlook Express has a very useful Address Book built in which we introduced in Chapter 12.

From Outlook Express this can be opened from the Main window with the **Tools**, **Address Book** menu command, or by clicking the Address Book Toolbar icon.

To send a new message to anyone listed in your Address Book, open a New Message window and use the **Tools**, **Select Recipients** command, or click on any of the 'Address Book' icons at the left of the Header area, as shown above.

In the Select Recipients box which is opened, you can select a person's name and click either the **To:->** button to place it in the **To:** field of your message, the **Cc->** button to place it in the **Cc:** field, or the **Bcc->**button to place it in the **Bcc:** field.

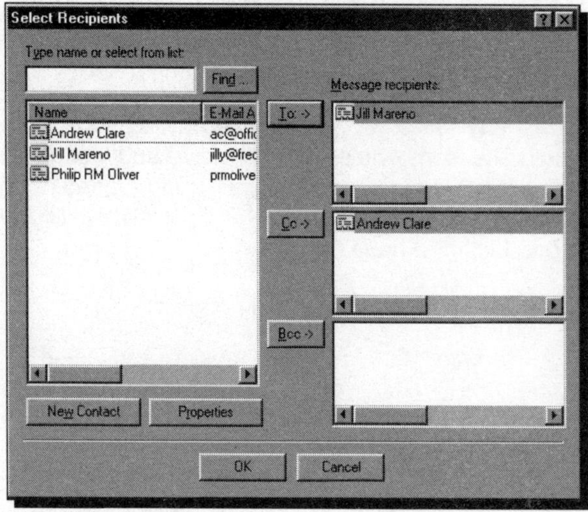

The **New Contact** button lets you add details for a new person to the Address Book, and the **Properties** button lets you edit an existing entry.

For more details of using the other features in the Address Book we suggest you have a look at Chapter 12.

****

Well that should get you started with handling all your e-mails, but there is more to Outlook Express yet. It can be used to access Discussion Groups (Newsgroups) which are another major feature of the Internet.

We will leave it to you to find out how to go about this. If you would like some help, then may we suggest you try the revised book *E-mail and News with Outlook Express* (BP464), also published by BERNARD BABANI (publishing) Ltd. Good luck and have fun.

****

15

Other Works 2000 Features

There are two more features included in the Works 2000 package that need some coverage. These are Tasks and Templates, both of which are designed to make the program more useful and easier to use.

Works Tasks

With Tasks, re-named with this version of Works, you get step-by-step assistance in creating particular types of documents. There are 10 groups of Tasks as shown below.

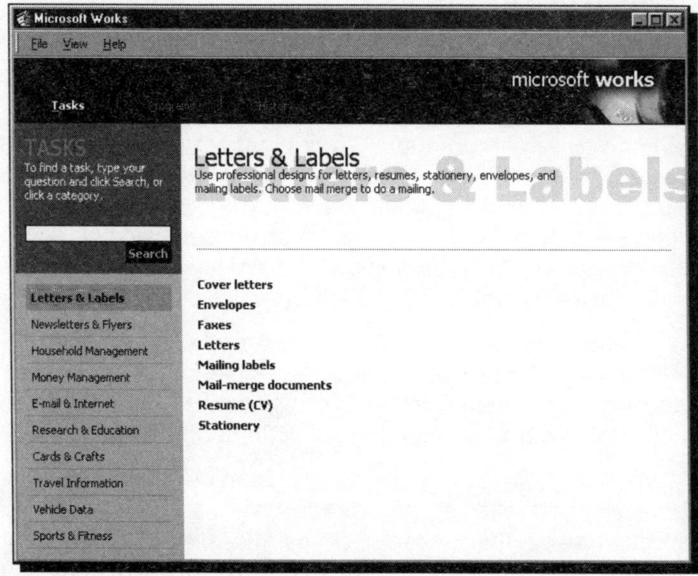

Microsoft Works

The Task Launcher is opened when Works 2000 is started, either by double-clicking the Microsoft Works Desktop shortcut icon shown on the left, or by selecting Microsoft Works from the Windows **Start** cascade menu, as shown on the right.

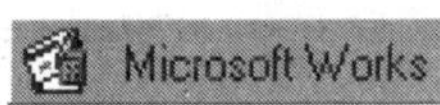

The Task Launcher has its own window and once opened will stay in the background. It can easily be reactivated, or brought to the front of your screen, by clicking its button on the Windows TaskBar, at the bottom of the screen.

If you are new to Works, or to computing in general for that matter, you can use the Works Tasks to quickly get started on a particular job, or task. Most people write letters at some time so we will see what is on offer here.

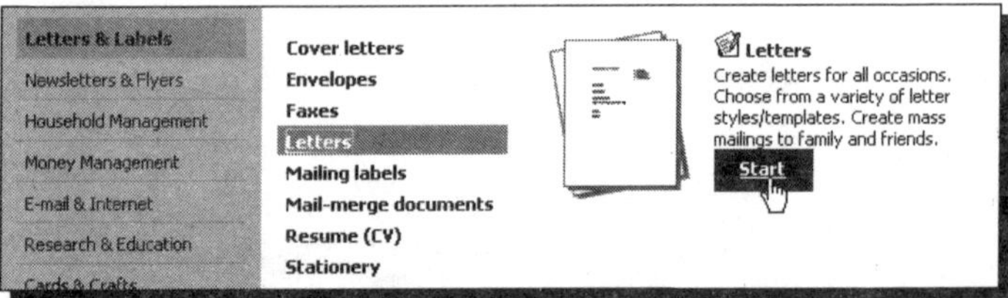

When you select a group of Tasks in the Task bar to the left of the Task Launcher window, a list of the tasks available opens up, as shown above. Selecting one of these opens a relevant picture and a few lines of descriptive text, with a **Start** link. Clicking this link will start the task procedure, which usually involves one of the in-built Wizards.

In our case the Works 2000 word processor was opened with a very elegant letter template visible in the background and with the Letter Wizard box, shown on the next page, activated. With WorksSuite Word 2000 opens instead.

In this first box you select from one of the five pre-formatted letter styles. To see what each one looks like you can select it and then click the **Minimize Wizard** button to see the resulting letter in the word processor window behind and then click **Maximize Wizard**.

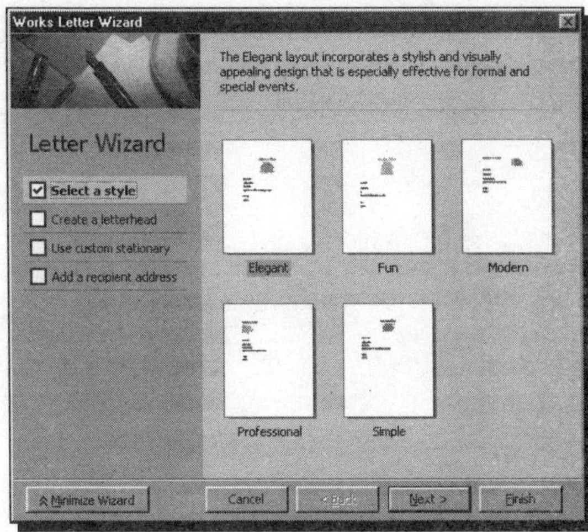

When you have chosen your letter style, leave it selected and click the **Next** button to open the second box in which you enter your own name and address details.

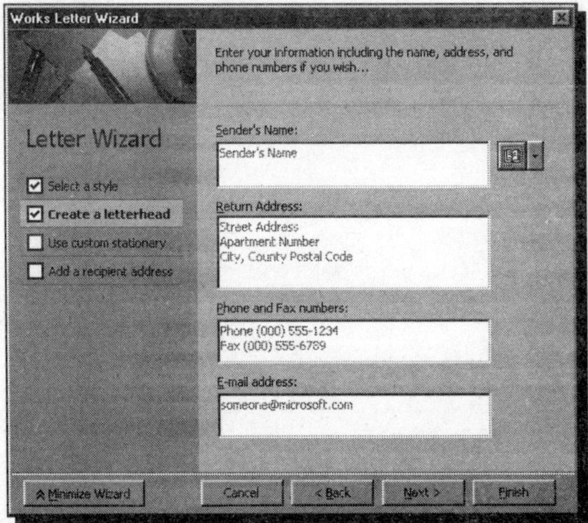

Press **Next**, and in the third box opened give the details of any pre-printed stationery you plan to use. Otherwise just press **Next** again and go straight to the last box shown next.

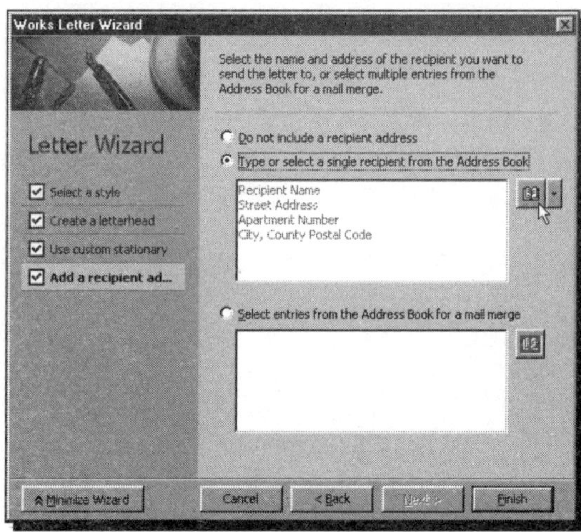

This lets you add details of the letter's recipient. When this is done clicking **Finish** opens the final product as shown below.

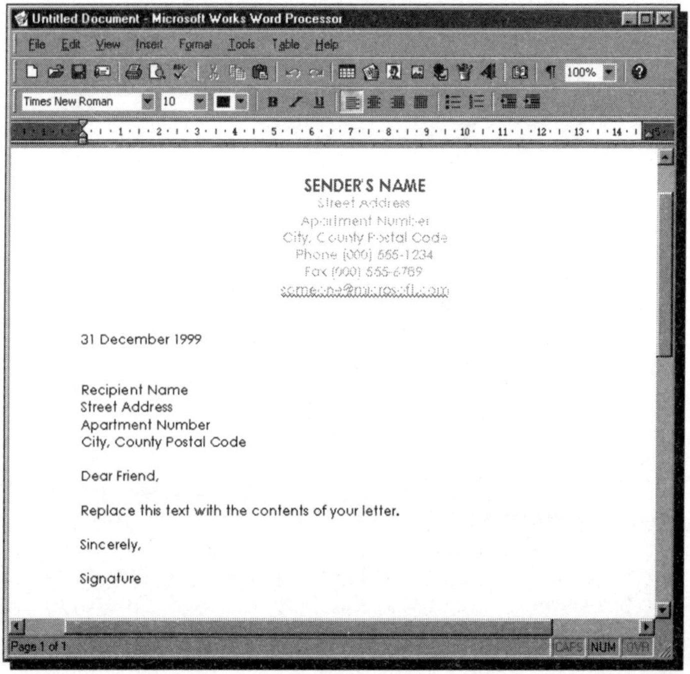

We did not bother to fill in our personal details but you obviously would need to! You must agree that this is a fine way to generate well formatted letters.

We suggest you work your way through the available Tasks, each one of which opens the Works application necessary to complete the task. Remember that pressing the **Next** button moves you to the next screen, and pressing **Cancel** will close the Task Wizard you are using.

We have not spent much time explaining Task Wizards, or covered them earlier in the book, for two very good reasons:

1. They are very user friendly and almost anyone should be able to work through them without too many problems.
2. We feel strongly that you will become more proficient with the Works 2000 program, as a whole, if you build your own applications.

Templates

A Template is a document 'blank' which can contain titles, text, formatting and other features, which do not change between documents of the same type. Once it has been created, you can open a Template, and adapt the resulting open file in any way you want, without affecting the original template file.

With Works 2000 many of the Tasks actually open templates for you, but you can also create your own. These can be either from scratch, or based on a document created from one of the Tasks.

Creating a Template

A useful Template for almost everyone, would be a blank letter heading with your address, date, etc., all laid out and ready to enter the letter contents. You could use one of the Tasks to set up such a letter for the first time. Then to save time in the future, save the letter format as a Template before adding its text.

We suggest you prepare a letter blank that you would be proud to send to anybody. It could be fairly simple, or be more sophisticated and include 'fancy fonts' and a graphic logo, etc.

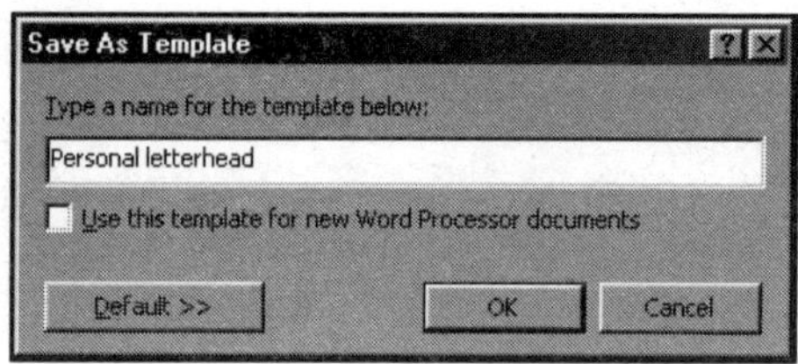

When you are happy with its layout and contents, choose the **File**, **Save As** menu command, click the **Template** button, type a suitable name, maybe 'Personal letterhead' in the Save a Template dialogue box shown here, and press **OK**.

In the future, whenever you want to send a letter, use your new Template instead of starting from scratch. To do this, go to the Tasks section of the Task Launcher, click on **Works Word Processor** and you will find the new option 'Personal letterhead' has been added to the list of available tasks, as shown below.

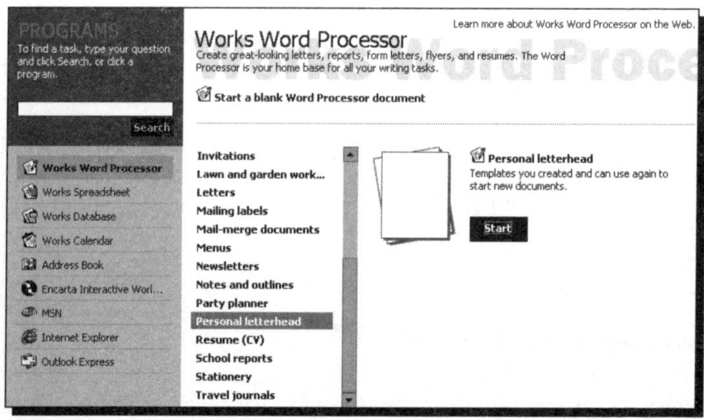

Selecting this option and pressing **Start** will open a new document with all the text and formatting already included. All you have to do then is complete the body of your letter.

Many of the Tasks in Works 2000 will produce output you could very usefully incorporate into your own Templates. We will leave it up to you to experiment with this.

Changing the Default Template

Each time you create a new document, Works bases it on the default template Normal.wpt. You can change the default template so that each new document you open uses the styles, text, or other settings you prefer.

To do this, first create and save the template, as described above, that you would like for the default. Then open it with the **File**, **Open** menu command, but in the **Look in** box, select the Template folder (with us this is in the 'Program Files/Microsoft Works' folder on the C: drive). In the **Files of type** box, select **Document Templates (*.wpt)** and in the folder list, double-click the template you want to use as the default. You must then save it again using **File**, **Save As** and click **Template** again. This time in the Save As Template dialogue box select the **Use this template for new Word Processor documents** check box.

Works will now use this template whenever you start a new document. You can revert to the original default at any time with the **File**, **Save As**, **Template** menu sequence, and then click **Default** to again use the default template Normal.wpt.

This may all sound a little complicated, but it really isn't. You must try it, we are confident you will not regret it!

* * *

Works 2000 has more commands and functions which can be used to build and run your applications and to link with other applications in special ways. What this book has tried to do is to introduce you to the overall subject and give you a solid foundation on which to build your future knowledge.

* * *

16

Glossary of Terms

ActiveX	A set of technologies that enables software components to interact with one another in a networked environment, regardless of the language in which the components were created.
Add-in	A mini-program which runs in conjunction with another and enhances its functionality.
Address	A unique number or name that identifies a specific computer or user on a network.
Anonymous FTP	Anonymous FTP allows you to connect to a remote computer and transfer public files back to your local computer without the need to have a user ID and password.
Application	Software (program) designed to carry out certain activity, such as word processing, or data management.
Applet	A program that can be downloaded over a network and launched on the user's computer.
Archie	Archie is an Internet service that allows you to locate files that can be downloaded via FTP.

ASP	Active Server Page. File format used for dynamic Web pages that get their data from a server based database.
Association	An identification of a filename extension to a program. This lets Windows open the program when its files are selected.
ASCII	A binary code representation of a character set. The name stands for 'American Standard Code for Information Interchange'.
Authoring	The process of creating web documents or software.
AVI	Audio Video Interleaved. A Windows multimedia file format for sound and moving pictures.
Backbone	The main transmission lines of the Internet, running at over 45Mbps.
Backup	To make a back-up copy of a file or a disc for safekeeping.
Bandwidth	The range of transmission frequencies a network can use. The greater the bandwidth the more information that can be transferred over a network.
Banner	An advertising graphic shown on a Web page.
BASIC	Beginner's All-purpose Symbolic Instruction Code - a high-level programming language.
BBS	Bulletin Board System, a computer equipped with software and telecoms links that allow it to act as an information host for remote computer systems.

Beta test	A test of software that is still under development, by people actually using the software.
BinHex	A file conversion format that converts binary files to ASCII text files.
Bitmap	A technique for managing the image displayed on a computer screen.
Bookmark	A marker inserted at a specific point in a document to which the user may wish to return for later reference.
Bound control	A control on a database form, report or data access page that is tied to a field in an underlying table or query.
Browse	A button in some Windows dialogue boxes that lets you view a list of files and folders before you make a selection.
Browser	A program, like the Internet Explorer, that lets you view Web pages.
Bug	An error in coding or logic that causes a program to malfunction.
Button	A graphic element in a dialogue box or toolbar that performs a specified function.
Cache	An area of memory, or disc space, reserved for data, which speeds up downloading.
Card	A removable printed-circuit board that is plugged into a computer expansion slot.
CD-ROM	Compact Disc - Read Only Memory; an optical disc which information may be read from but not written to.

CGI	Common Gateway Interface - a convention for servers to communicate with local applications and allow users to provide information to scripts attached to web pages, usually through forms.
Cgi-bin	The most common name of a directory on a web server in which CGI programs are stored.
Chart	A graphical view of data that is used to visually display trends, patterns, and comparisons.
Click	To press and release a mouse button once without moving the mouse.
Client	A computer that has access to services over a computer network. The computer providing the services is a server.
Client application	A Windows application that can accept linked, or embedded, objects.
Clipboard	A temporary storage area of memory, where text and graphics are stored with the Windows cut and copy actions.
Command	An instruction given to a computer to carry out a particular action.
Compressed file	One that is compacted to save server space and reduce transfer times. Typical file extensions for compressed files include .zip (DOS/Windows) and .tar (UNIX).
Configuration	A general purpose term referring to the way you have your computer set up.

Controls	Objects on a form, report, or data access page that display data, perform actions, or are used for decoration.
Cookies	Files stored on your hard drive by your Web browser that hold information for it to use.
CPU	The Central Processing Unit; the main chip that executes all instructions entered into a computer.
Cyberspace	Originated by William Gibson in his novel 'Neuromancer', now used to describe the Internet and the other computer networks.
Data access page	A Web page, created by Access, that has a connection to a database; you can view, add, edit, and manipulate the data in this page.
Database	A collection of data related to a particular topic or purpose.
DBMS	Database management system - A software interface between the database and the user.
Dial-up Connection	A popular form of Net connection for the home user, over standard telephone lines.
Direct Connection	A permanent connection between your computer system and the Internet.
Default	The command, device or option automatically chosen.
Desktop	The Windows screen working background, on which you place icons, folders, etc.

Device driver	A special file that must be loaded into memory for Windows to be able to address a specific procedure or hardware device.
Device name	A logical name used by DOS to identify a device, such as LPT1 or COM1 for the parallel or serial printer.
Dialogue box	A window displayed on the screen to allow the user to enter information.
Directory	An area on disc where information relating to a group of files is kept. Also known as a folder.
Disc	A device on which you can store programs and data.
Disconnect	To detach a drive, port or computer from a shared device, or to break an Internet connection.
Document	A file produced by an application program. When used in reference to the Web, a document is any file containing text, media or hyperlinks that can be transferred from an HTTP server to a browser.
Domain	A group of devices, servers and computers on a network.
Domain Name	The name of an Internet site, for example www.michaelstrang.com, which allows you to reference Internet sites without knowing their true numerical address.
DOS	Disc Operating System. A collection of small specialised programs that allow interaction between user and computer.

Double-click	To quickly press and release a mouse button twice.
Download	To transfer to your computer a file, or data, from another computer.
DPI	Dots Per Inch - a resolution standard for laser printers.
Drag	To move an object on the screen by pressing and holding down the left mouse button while moving the mouse.
Drive name	The letter followed by a colon which identifies a floppy or hard disc drive.
EISA	Extended Industry Standard Architecture, for construction of PCs with the Intel 32-bit micro-processor.
Embedded object	Information in a document that is 'copied' from its source application. Selecting the object opens the creating application from within the document.
Engine	Software used by search services.
E-mail	Electronic Mail - A system that allows computer users to send and receive messages electronically.
Ethernet	A very common method of networking computers in a LAN.
FAQ	Frequently Asked Questions - A common feature on the Internet, FAQs are files of answers to commonly asked questions.
FAT	The File Allocation Table. An area on disc where information is kept on which part of the disc a file is located.

File extension	The suffix following the period in a filename. Windows uses this to identify the source application program. For example .mdb indicates an Access file.
Filename	The name given to a file. In Windows 95 and above this can be up to 256 characters long.
Filter	A set of criteria that is applied to data to show a subset of the data.
Firewall	Security measures designed to protect a networked system from unauthorised access.
Floppy disc	A removable disc on which information can be stored magnetically.
Folder	An area used to store a group of files, usually with a common link.
Font	A graphic design representing a set of characters, numbers and symbols.
Freeware	Software that is available for downloading and unlimited use without charge.
FTP	File Transfer Protocol. The procedure for connecting to a remote computer and transferring files.
Function key	One of the series of 10 or 12 keys marked with the letter F and a numeral, used for specific operations.
Gateway	A computer system that allows otherwise incompatible networks to communicate with each other.

GIF	Graphics Interchange Format, a common standard for images on the Web.
Graphic	A picture or illustration, also called an image. Formats include GIF, JPEG, BMP, PCX, and TIFF.
Graphics card	A device that controls the display on the monitor and other allied functions.
GUI	A Graphic User Interface, such as Windows 98, the software front-end meant to provide an attractive and easy to use interface.
Hard copy	Output on paper.
Hard disc	A device built into the computer for holding programs and data.
Hardware	The equipment that makes up a computer system, excluding the programs or software.
Help	A Windows system that gives you instructions and additional information on using a program.
Helper application	A program allowing you to view multimedia files that your web browser cannot handle internally.
Hit	A single request from a web browser for a single item from a web server.
Home page	The document displayed when you first open your Web browser, or the first document you come to at a Web site.
Host	Computer connected directly to the Internet that provides services to other local and/or remote computers.

Hotlist	A list of frequently used Web locations and URL addresses.
Host	A computer acting as an information or communications server.
HTML	HyperText Markup Language, the format used in documents on the Web.
HTML editor	Authoring tool which assists with the creation of HTML pages.
HTTP	HyperText Transport Protocol, the system used to link and transfer hypertext documents on the Web.
Hyperlink	A segment of text, or an image, that refers to another document on the Web, an Intranet or your PC.
Hypermedia	Hypertext extended to include linked multimedia.
Hypertext	A system that allows documents to be cross-linked so that the reader can explore related links, or documents, by clicking on a highlighted symbol.
Icon	A small graphic image that represents a function or object. Clicking on an icon produces an action.
Image	See graphic.
Insertion point	A flashing bar that shows where typed text will be entered into a document.
Interface	A device that allows you to connect a computer to its peripherals.
Internet	The global system of computer networks.

Intranet	A private network inside an organisation using the same kind of software as the Internet.
ISA	Industry Standard Architecture; a standard for internal connections in PCs.
ISDN	Integrated Services Digital Network, a telecom standard using digital transmission technology to support voice, video and data communications applications over regular telephone lines.
IP	Internet Protocol - The rules that provide basic Internet functions.
IP Address	Internet Protocol Address - every computer on the Internet has a unique identifying number.
ISP	Internet Service Provider - A company that offers access to the Internet.
Java	An object-oriented programming language created by Sun Microsystems for developing applications and applets that are capable of running on any computer, regardless of the operating system.
JPEG /JPG	Joint Photographic Experts Group, a popular cross-platform format for image files. JPEG is best suited for true colour original images.
Kilobyte	(KB); 1024 bytes of information or storage space.
LAN	Local Area Network - High-speed, privately-owned network covering a

	limited geographical area, such as an office or a building.
Laptop	A portable computer small enough to sit on your lap.
LCD	Liquid Crystal Display.
Links	The hypertext connections between Web pages.
Local	A resource that is located on your computer, not linked to it over a network.
Location	An Internet address.
Log on	To gain access to a network.
MCI	Media Control Interface - a standard for files and multimedia devices.
Megabyte	(MB); 1024 kilobytes of information or storage space.
Megahertz	(MHz); Speed of processor in millions of cycles per second.
Memory	Part of computer consisting of storage elements organised into addressable locations that can hold data and instructions.
Menu	A list of available options in an application.
Menu bar	The horizontal bar that lists the names of menus.
MIDI	Musical Instrument Digital Interface - enables devices to transmit and receive sound and music messages.
MIME	Multipurpose Internet Mail Extensions, a messaging standard that allows Internet users to exchange

	e-mail messages enhanced with graphics, video and voice.
MIPS	Million Instructions Per Second; measures speed of a system.
Modem	Short for Modulator-demodulator devices. An electronic device that lets computers communicate electronically.
Monitor	The display device connected to your PC, also called a screen.
Mouse	A device used to manipulate a pointer around your display and activate processes by pressing buttons.
MPEG	Motion Picture Experts Group - a video file format offering excellent quality in a relatively small file.
MS-DOS	Microsoft's implementation of the Disc Operating System for PCs.
Multimedia	The use of photographs, music and sound and movie images in a presentation.
Multi-tasking	Performing more than one operation at the same time.
Network	Two or more computers connected together to share resources.
Network server	Central computer which stores files for several linked computers.
Node	Any single computer connected to a network.
ODBC	Open DataBase Connectivity - A standard protocol for accessing information in a SQL database server.

OLE	Object Linking and Embedding - A technology for transferring and sharing information among software applications.
Online	Having access to the Internet.
On-line Service	Services such as America On-line and CompuServe that provide content to subscribers and usually connections to the Internet.
Operating system	Software that runs a computer.
Page	An HTML document, or Web site.
Password	A unique character string used to gain access to a network, program, or mailbox.
PATH	The location of a file in the directory tree.
Peripheral	Any device attached to a PC.
Perl	A popular language for programming CGI applications.
PIF file	Program information file - gives information to Windows about an MS-DOS application.
Pixel	A picture element on screen; the smallest element that can be independently assigned colour and intensity.
Plug-and-play	Hardware which can be plugged into a PC and be used immediately without configuration.
POP	Post Office Protocol - a method of storing and returning e-mail.
Port	The place where information goes into or out of a computer, e.g. a

	modem might be connected to the serial port.
PPP	Point-to-Point Protocol - One of two methods (see SLIP) for using special software to establish a temporary direct connection to the Internet over regular phone lines.
Print queue	A list of print jobs waiting to be sent to a printer.
Program	A set of instructions which cause a computer to perform tasks.
Protocol	A set of rules or standards that define how computers communicate with each other.
Query	The set of keywords and operators sent by a user to a search engine, or a database search request.
Queue	A list of e-mail messages waiting to be sent over the Internet.
RAM	Random Access Memory. The computer's volatile memory. Data held in it is lost when power is switched off.
Real mode	MS-DOS mode, typically used to run programs, such as MS-DOS games, that will not run under Windows.
Resource	A directory, or printer, that can be shared over a network.
Robot	A Web agent that visits sites, by requesting documents from them, for the purposes of indexing for search engines. Also known as Wanderers, Crawlers, or Spiders.
ROM	Read Only Memory. A PC's non-volatile memory. Data is written

	into this memory at manufacture and is not affected by power loss.
Scroll bar	A bar that appears at the right side or bottom edge of a window.
Search	Submit a query to a search engine.
Search engine	A program that helps users find information across the Internet.
Serial interface	An interface that transfers data as individual bits.
Server	A computer system that manages and delivers information for client computers.
Shared resource	Any device, program or file that is available to network users.
Shareware	Software that is available on public networks and bulletin boards. Users are expected to pay a nominal amount to the software developer.
Signature file	An ASCII text file, maintained within e-mail programs, that contains text for your signature.
Site	A place on the Internet. Every Web page has a location where it resides which is called its site.
SLIP	Serial Line Internet Protocol, a method of Internet connection that enables computers to use phone lines and a modem to connect to the Internet without having to connect to a host.
SMTP	Simple Mail Transfer Protocol - a protocol dictating how e-mail messages are exchanged over the Internet.

Socket	An endpoint for sending and receiving data between computers.
Software	The programs and instructions that control your PC.
Spamming	Sending the same message to a large number of mailing lists or newsgroups. Also to overload a Web page with excessive keywords in an attempt to get a better search ranking.
Spider	See robot.
Spooler	Software which handles transfer of information to a store to be used by a peripheral device.
SQL	Structured Query Language, used with relational databases.
SSL	Secure Sockets Layer, the standard transmission security protocol developed by Netscape, which has been put into the public domain.
Subscribe	To become a member of.
Surfing	The process of looking around the Internet.
SVGA	Super Video Graphics Array; it has all the VGA modes but with 256, or more, colours.
Swap file	An area of your hard disc used to store temporary operating files, also known as virtual memory.
Sysop	System Operator - A person responsible for the physical operations of a computer system or network resource.

System disc	A disc containing files to enable a PC to start up.
T1	An Internet leased line that carries up to 1.536 million bits per second (1.536Mbps).
T3	An Internet leased line that carries up to 45 million bits per second (45Mbps).
TCP/IP	Transmission Control Protocol/ Internet Protocol, combined protocols that perform the transfer of data between two computers. TCP monitors and ensures the correct transfer of data. IP receives the data, breaks it up into packets, and sends it to a network within the Internet.
Telnet	A program which allows people to remotely use computers across networks.
Text file	An unformatted file of text characters saved in ASCII format.
Thread	An ongoing message-based conversation on a single subject.
TIFF	Tag Image File Format - a popular graphic image file format.
Tool	Software program used to support Web site creation and management.
Toolbar	A bar containing icons giving quick access to commands.
Toggle	To turn an action on and off with the same switch.
TrueType fonts	Fonts that can be scaled to any size and print as they show on the screen.

UNC	Universal Naming Convention - A convention for files that provides a machine independent means of locating the file that is particularly useful in Web based applications.
UNIX	Multitasking, multi-user computer operating system that is run by many computers that are connected to the Internet.
Upload/Download	The process of transferring files between computers. Files are uploaded from your computer to another and downloaded from another computer to your own.
URL	Uniform Resource Locator, the addressing system used on the Web, containing information about the method of access, the server to be accessed and the path of the file to be accessed.
Usenet	Informal network of computers that allow the posting and reading of messages in newsgroups that focus on specific topics.
User ID	The unique identifier, usually used in conjunction with a password, which identifies you on a computer.
Virtual Reality	Simulations of real or imaginary worlds, rendered on a flat two-dimensional screen but appearing three-dimensional.
Virus	A malicious program, downloaded from a web site or disc, designed to wipe out information on your computer.

W3C	The World Wide Web Consortium that is steering standards development for the Web.
WAIS	Wide Area Information Server, a Net-wide system for looking up specific information in Internet databases.
WAV	Waveform Audio (.wav) - a common audio file format for DOS/Windows computers.
Web	A network of hypertext-based multimedia information servers. Browsers are used to view any information on the Web.
Web Page	An HTML document that is accessible on the Web.
Webmaster	One whose job it is to manage a web site.
WINSOCK	A Microsoft Windows file that provides the interface to TCP/IP services.
Wizard	A Microsoft tool that asks you questions and then creates an object depending on your answers.

Appendix

Works Functions

Microsoft Work's functions are built-in formulae that perform specialised calculations in both the spreadsheet and database applications. Their general format is:

=name(arg1,arg2,...)

where 'name' is the function name, and 'arg1', 'arg2', etc., are the arguments required for the evaluation of the function. Arguments must appear in a parenthesised list as shown above and their exact number depends on the function being used. However, there are seven functions that do not require arguments and are used with empty parentheses. These are: =ERR( ), =FALSE( ), =NA( ), =NOW( ), =PI( ), =RAND( ) and =TRUE( ).

There are three types of arguments used with =functions: numeric values, range values and text strings, the type used being dependent on the type of function. Numeric value arguments can be entered either directly as numbers, as a cell address, a cell range name or as a formula. Range value arguments can be entered either as a range address or a range name.

Types of Functions

There are several types of functions, such as mathematical, logical, financial, statistical, date and time, text, reference and informational. Each type requires its own number and type of arguments. These are listed in the following pages under the various function categories.

Mathematical Functions

Mathematical functions evaluate a result using numeric arguments.

Function	*Description*
=ABS(X)	Returns the absolute value of X
=ACOS(X)	Returns the angle in radians, whose cosine is X (arc cos of X)
=ASIN(X)	Returns the angle in radians, whose sine is X (arc sin of X)
=ATAN(X)	Returns the angle (radians), between p/2 and -p/2, whose tangent is X (arc tan of X - 2 quadrant)
=ATAN2(X,Y)	Returns the angle (radians), between p and -p whose tangent is Y/X (arc tan of Y/X - 4 quadrant)
=COS(X)	Returns the cosine of angle X, (X must be in radians)
=EXP(X)	Raises e to the power of X
=INT(X)	Returns the integer part of X
=LN(X)	Returns the natural logarithm (base e) of X
=LOG(X)	Returns the logarithm (base 10) of X
=MOD(X,Y)	Returns the remainder of X/Y
=PI( )	Returns the value of pi (3.141593)
=RAND( )	Returns a random number between 0 and 1, excluding 1
=ROUND(X,N)	Returns the value of X rounded to N places
=SIN(X)	Returns the sine of angle X (X must be in radians)
=SQRT(X)	Returns the square root of X
=TAN(X)	Returns the tangent of angle X (X must be in radians).

Logical Functions

Logical functions produce a value based on the result of a conditional statement, using numeric arguments.

Function	*Description*
=AND(Ag0,Ag1...)	Returns 1 (TRUE) if all of the arguments are true, else returns 0 (FALSE)
=FALSE( )	Returns the logical value 0
=IF(Cr,X,Y)	Returns the value X if Cr is TRUE and Y if Cr is FALSE
=NOT(Ag)	Returns the opposite of logical value Ag
=OR(Ag0,Ag1...)	Returns 1 (TRUE) if any of the arguments are true, else returns 0 (FALSE)
=TRUE( )	Returns the logical value 1.

Financial Functions

Financial functions evaluate loans, annuities, and cash flows over a period of time, using numeric arguments.

Function	*Description*
=CTERM(Rt,Fv,Pv)	Returns the number of compounding periods for an investment of present value Pv, to grow to a future value Fv, at a fixed interest rate Rt
=DDB(Ct,Sg,Lf,Pd)	Returns the double-declining depreciation allowance of an asset, given the original cost Ct, predicted salvage value Sg, the life Lf of the asset, and the period Pd
=FV(Pt,Rt,Tm)	Returns the future value of a series of equal payments, each of equal amount Pt, earning a periodic interest rate Rt, over a

	number of payment periods in term Tm
=IRR(Gs,Rg)	Returns the internal rate of return of the series of cash flows in a range Rg, based on the approximate percentage guess Gs of the IRR
=NPV(Rt,Rg)	Returns the present value of the series of future cash flows in range Rg, discounted at a periodic interest rate Rt
=PMT(Pl,Rt,Tm)	Returns the amount of the periodic payment needed to pay off the principal Pl, at a periodic interest rate Rt, over the number of payment periods in term Tm
=PV(Pt,Rt,Tm)	Returns the present value of a series of equal payments, each of equal amount Pt, discounted at a periodic interest rate Rt, over a number of payment periods in term Tm
=RATE(Fv,Pv,Tm)	Returns the periodic interest rate necessary for a present value Pv to grow to a future value Fv, over the number of compounding periods in term Tm
=SLN(Ct,Sg,Lf)	Returns the straight-line depreciation allowance of an asset for one period, given the original cost Ct, predicted salvage value Sg, and the life Lf of the asset
=SYD(Ct,Sg,Lf,Pd)	Returns the sum-of-the-years' digits depreciation allowance of an asset, given the original cost Ct, predicted salvage value Sg, the life Lf of the asset, and the period Pd

=TERM(Pt,Rt,Fv)	Returns the number of payment periods of an investment, given the amount of each payment Pt, the periodic interest rate Rt, and the future value of the investment Fv.

Statistical Functions

Statistical functions evaluate lists of values using numeric arguments or cell ranges.

Function	*Description*
=AVG(Rg0,Rg1,...)	Returns the average of values in range(s) Rg0, Rg1, ...
=COUNT(Rg0,Rg1,...)	Returns the number of non-blank entries in range(s) Rg0, Rg1, ...
=MAX(Rg0,Rg1,...)	Returns the maximum value in range(s) Rg0, Rg1, ...
=MIN(Rg0,Rg1,...)	Returns the minimum value in range(s) Rg0, Rg1, ...
=STD(Rg0,Rg1,...)	Returns the standard deviation of values in range(s) Rg0, Rg1, ...
=SUM(Rg0,Rg1,...)	Returns the sum of values in range(s) Rg0, Rg1, ...
=VAR(Rg0,Rg1,...)	Returns the variance of values in range(s) Rg0, Rg1, ...

Text Functions

Text functions operate on strings and produce numeric or string values dependent on the function.

Function	*Description*
=EXACT(Sg1,Sg2)	Returns 1 (TRUE) if strings Sg1 and Sg2 are exactly alike, otherwise 0 (FALSE)
=FIND(Ss,Sg,Sn)	Returns position at which the first occurrence of search string Ss begins in string Sg, starting

	the search from search number Sn
=LEFT(Sg,N)	Returns the first (leftmost) N characters in string Sg
=LENGTH(Sg)	Returns the number of characters in string Sg
=LOWER(Sg)	Converts all the letters in string Sg to lowercase
=MID(Sg,Sn,N)	Returns N characters from string Sg beginning with the character at Sn
=N(Rg)	Returns the numeric value in the upper left corner cell in range Rg
=PROPER(Sg)	Converts all words in string Sg to first letter in uppercase and the rest in lowercase
=REPEAT(Sg,N)	Returns string Sg N times. Unlike the repeating character (\), the output is not limited by the column width
=REPLACE(O,S,N,Ns)	Removes N characters from original string O, starting at character S and then inserts new string Ns in the vacated place
=RIGHT(Sg,N)	Returns the last (rightmost) N characters in string Sg
=S(Rg)	Returns the string value in the upper left corner cell in range Rg
=STRING(X,N)	Returns the numeric value X as a string, with N decimal places
=TRIM(Sg)	Returns string Sg with no leading, trailing or consecutive spaces
=UPPER(Sg)	Converts all letters in string Sg to uppercase
=VALUE(Sg)	Returns the numeric value of string Sg.

Date and Time Functions

Date and time functions generate and use serial numbers to represent dates and times. Each date between 1 January, 1900 and 31 December 2079 has an integer serial number starting with 1 and ending with 65534. Each moment during a day has a decimal serial number starting with 0.000 at midnight and ending with 0.99999 just before the following midnight.

Function	*Description*
=DATE(Yr,Mh,Dy)	Returns the date number of Yr,Mh,Dy
=DAY(Dn)	Returns the day number of date number Dn
=HOUR(Tn)	Returns the hour number of time number Tn
=MINUTE(Tn)	Returns the minute number of time number Tn
=MONTH(Dn)	Returns the month number of date number Dn
=NOW( )	Returns the serial number for the current date and time
=SECOND(Tn)	Returns the second number of time number Tn
=TIME(Hr,Ms,Ss)	Returns the time number of Hr,Ms,Ss
=YEAR(Dn)	Returns the year number of date number Dn.

Special Functions

Special functions perform a variety of advanced tasks, such as looking up a value in a table.

Function	*Description*
=CHOOSE(X,V0,...,Vn)	Returns the Xth value in the list V0,...,Vn
=COLS(Rg)	Returns the number of columns in the range Rg
=ERR( )	Returns the value of ERR

=HLOOKUP(X,Rg,Rn)	Performs a horizontal table look-up by comparing the value X to each cell in the top row, or index row, in range Rg, then moves down the column in which a match is found by the specified row number Rn
=INDEX(Rg,Cn,Rw)	Returns the value of the cell in range at the intersection of column Cn and row Rw
=ISERR(X)	Returns 1 (TRUE) if X contains ERR, else returns 0 (FALSE)
=ISNA(X)	Returns 1 (TRUE) if X contains N/A, else returns 0 (FALSE)
=NA( )	Returns the numeric value of N/A
=ROWS(Rg)	Returns the number of rows in range Rg
=VLOOKUP(X,Rg,Cn)	Performs a vertical table look-up by comparing the value X to each cell in the first column, or index column, in range Rg, then moves across the row in which a match is found by the specified column number Cn.

Index

Companion Discs

COMPANION DISCS are available for most computer books written by the same author(s) and published by BERNARD BABANI (publishing) LTD, as listed at the front of this book (except for those marked with an asterisk). These books contain many pages of file/program listings. There is no reason why you should spend hours typing them into your computer, unless you wish to do so, or need the practice.

ORDERING INSTRUCTIONS

To obtain companion discs, fill in the order form below, or a copy of it, enclose a cheque (payable to **P.R.M. Oliver**) or a postal order, and send it to the address given below. **Make sure you fill in your name and address** and specify the book number and title in your order.

Book No.	Book Name	Unit Price	Total Price
BP		£3.50	
BP		£3.50	
BP		£3.50	
Name		Sub-total	£............
Address		P & P (@ 45p/disc)	£............
		Total Due	£............
Send to: P.R.M. Oliver, CSM, Pool, Redruth, Cornwall, TR15 3SE			

PLEASE NOTE

The author(s) are fully responsible for providing this Companion Disc service. The publishers of this book accept no responsibility for the supply, quality, or magnetic contents of the disc, or in respect of any damage, or injury that might be suffered or caused by its use.